Training from the BACK of the Room!

65

Ways to Step Aside and Let Them Learn

About This Book

Why is this topic important?

We talk too much. As trainers and teachers, we bore our learners to death. We don't mean to. We truly think that we are doing the opposite. But the fact remains: As long as learners are passively sitting and listening to us talk, they are not learning much. It gets worse. Those of us who train trainers, or who teach people how to teach, are often modeling the exact strategies we rail against. We lecture about not lecturing. We read straight from our PowerPoint® slides. We ignore current brain research and use outdated instructional strategies that never worked well to begin with. To compound the problem, as more people realize that they can get a wealth of knowledge from the Internet—*what* they need *when* they need it—there is absolutely *no* reason for them to sit in a classroom and waste their time while someone drones on and on. They know this. The resistance to this type of learning grows stronger with each generation.

So as trainers and teachers, the single most challenging thing for us to do is to step aside and allow learners to learn. Real learning takes place when we stop talking and our learners start talking. Real learning takes place when learners participate in the instructional process, from beginning to end. And real learning takes place when learners become active creators of their own learning experiences. Brain research on how humans learn supports this. For the sake of our learners, our companies and educational institutions, and our own satisfaction as facilitators of learning, we need to learn other ways of training, ways that engage learners from the moment they walk into the room until the moment they leave.

What can you achieve with this book?

Training from the BACK of the Room! gives you sixty-five ways to step aside and let your learners take center-stage as they discuss, question, reflect, experiment, participate, present, practice, teach, and learn from each other. You'll change the traditional and ineffective "trainers talk; learners listen" paradigm to a more powerful and brain-friendly approach: "When learners talk and teach, they learn." You'll be immersed in a simple, four-step instructional design and delivery process that involves learners every step of the way. You'll explore useful brain research and put to rest some outdated assumptions about how humans learn. In the end, you'll combine all of this to create learning experiences that are profoundly different from traditional instruction.

How is this book organized?

Training from the BACK of the Room! begins with an introduction to the need-to-know information: what's in it for you, current brain research that supports the book's concepts, and the 4

Cs—a brain-friendly instructional design and delivery process. Each of the following four parts of the book gives you definitions, descriptions, and practical training strategies for each step of the 4 Cs:

- Part One: Connections—Fifteen opening activities that connect learners to the topic, to each other, and to what they want and need to learn.
- Part Two: Concepts—Twenty strategies that engage and involve learners during the lecture or "direct instruction" training segment.
- Part Three: Concrete Practice—Fifteen strategies in which learners actively review content and practice new skills.
- Part Four: Conclusions—Fifteen learner-led summaries, evaluations, and celebration activities.

In addition, you, the reader, will be encouraged to participate in short, quick learning activities that you can use with your own training topics. Finally, this book offers a section of nice-to-know information that will add to what you have learned: the secret about adult learning theory, a fresh way approach to learning outcomes, more collaborative learning strategies, tips for interactive e-learning, and great resources to expand your own learning adventure. Welcome to *Training from the BACK of the Room!*

About Pfeiffer

Pfeiffer serves the professional development and hands-on resource needs of training and human resource practitioners and gives them products to do their jobs better. We deliver proven ideas and solutions from experts in HR development and HR management, and we offer effective and customizable tools to improve workplace performance. From novice to seasoned professional, Pfeiffer is the source you can trust to make yourself and your organization more successful.

Essential Knowledge   Pfeiffer produces insightful, practical, and comprehensive materials on topics that matter the most to training and HR professionals. Our Essential Knowledge resources translate the expertise of seasoned professionals into practical, how-to guidance on critical workplace issues and problems. These resources are supported by case studies, worksheets, and job aids and are frequently supplemented with CD-ROMs, websites, and other means of making the content easier to read, understand, and use.

Essential Tools   Pfeiffer's Essential Tools resources save time and expense by offering proven, ready-to-use materials—including exercises, activities, games, instruments, and assessments—for use during a training or team-learning event. These resources are frequently offered in looseleaf or CD-ROM format to facilitate copying and customization of the material.

Pfeiffer also recognizes the remarkable power of new technologies in expanding the reach and effectiveness of training. While e-hype has often created whizbang solutions in search of a problem, we are dedicated to bringing convenience and enhancements to proven training solutions. All our e-tools comply with rigorous functionality standards. The most appropriate technology wrapped around essential content yields the perfect solution for today's on-the-go trainers and human resource professionals.

www.pfeiffer.com

Essential resources for training and HR professionals

Training from the BACK of the Room!

65

Ways to Step Aside and Let Them Learn

Sharon L. Bowman

Foreword by Jay Cross

Pfeiffer
A Wiley Imprint
www.pfeiffer.com

An Imprint of Wiley
989 Market Street, San Francisco, CA 94103-1741
www.pfeiffer.com

For additional copies/bulk purchases of this book in the U.S. please contact 800-274-4434.

Pfeiffer books and products are available through most bookstores. To contact Pfeiffer directly call our Customer Care Department within the U.S. at 800-274-4434, outside the U.S. at 317-572-3985, fax 317-572-4002, or visit www.pfeiffer.com.

Pfeiffer also publishes its books in a variety of electronic formats. Some content that appears in print may not be available in electronic books.

Library of Congress Cataloging-in-Publication Data

Bowman, Sharon L.
     Training from the back of the room!: 65 ways to step aside and let them learn/Sharon L. Bowman; foreword by Jay Cross.
          p.   cm.
     Includes bibliographical references.
     ISBN 978-0-7879-9662-8 (pbk.)
          1. Employees—Training of.   2. Self-managed learning.   3. Employee training personnel—Training of.
     4. Organizational learning.   I. Title.
     HF5549.5.T7B6192   2009
     658.3'124—dc22
                                                                                          2008038207

Acquiring Editor: Marisa Kelley   Editor: Rebecca Taff
Director of Development: Kathleen Dolan Davies   Editorial Assistant: Michael Gilbart
Developmental Editor: Janis Chan   Manufacturing Supervisor: Becky Morgan
Production Editor: Dawn Kilgore

Printing   10   9   8   7   6   5   4   3

To my Aunt Marnet,
Margaret Cote,
who did the loving "Mom" things
and persistently pushed me
to write this book.

And to Ross Barnett,
my life mate, helper, encourager, partner,
for everything he is and does,
which makes this work possible.

Contents

Foreword

Sharon Bowman writes about how trainers need to think about learning, plan learning experiences, and deliver the goods in a class or training. Her suggestions are clear, simple, and commonsense. She doesn't get hung up with behaviorism, flow charts, human performance models, levels of evaluation, or complex learning objectives. Her writing is not sufficiently obscure to appeal to doctrinaire instructional designers and academic design gurus. So, if you consider yourself an expert instructional designer, with all the associated jargon, this book is not for you.

Roger Schank has a four-word explanation of what's wrong with training: "It's just like school." School clings to vestiges of a bygone era: Students get the summer off to help bring in the crops. Schools are literally an alternate reality, walled off from the real world to protect their "customers" (aka students), thereby guaranteeing that schools remain "out of it." Teachers coerce pupils to learn rather than motivate them to learn. New graduates find out about the unspoken hoax: Outside of schools, grades are meaningless. Teachers are the font of all the right answers—hardly a stance for developing critical thinking. In the workplace, teamwork is esteemed; in school, learning with others is called cheating.

Training has adopted most of this bad baggage from school. After all, every trainer was brainwashed for a dozen or more years that this is how you learn. An example: Most executives don't realize that there's more to leading learning than gut feel. Trainers can fall into the same trap. A training director told his sales trainers that henceforth their bonuses would be calculated as a percentage of their former trainees' sales. "But we're not responsible for that," they complained. Hello?

Suspend judgment, and go with Sharon and me for a moment. How do people learn? What comes naturally? They discover things. They experiment to see what works. They watch others and mimic them. They converse with their colleagues. They find out what they need to know to get things done. They follow their hearts.

It's time to break the schooling myth and begin doing what it takes to foster learning. It's time to

- *Encourage* discovery and coloring outside the lines.
- *Provide* opportunities to experiment, and don't punish "failures."
- *Enable* people to learn from one another.
- *Provide* challenges to groups, not individuals.
- *Make* time and room for conversation with peers.
- *Provide* resources for people to learn things for themselves.
- *Give* workers the freedom to learn.

This book offers a four-step model for engaging learners, and backs it up with sixty-five specific interventions. It's like a good cookbook. But a good cookbook does not make a good cook. The recipes are here, but they are just the starting point. Every cook tweaks the instructions to get the best from local ingredients. Every trainer will put his or her spin on things; that's what a professional does.

Here's an oversimplification of Sharon's meta-recipe:

- Create engagements that capture the learners' attention.
- Get out of the way; don't try to think for them.
- Encourage people to learn from one another.

Hans Monderman is a Dutch traffic engineer who is gaining fame for what he doesn't do. He's also famous for what he doesn't like: traffic signs. Remove the center line from a country lane, and people drive more safely. Clutter a road with signs and barriers, and people feel sufficiently protected to drive as fast as they like. If you treat people like fools, they act like fools. Take off the training wheels, and they drive like grown-ups. When Monderman's changes sink in, traffic accidents drop 30 percent.

Follow Sharon's advice. Take off the training wheels and entrust people with their own learning. Keep them engaged. You won't lower the traffic accident rate, but I guarantee you'll improve the quality of their learning.

Jay Cross
Internet Time Group
Berkeley, California
www.jaycross.com

Need-to-Know Information from the *Front* of the Book

Warm-Ups for *Training from the BACK of the Room!*

Welcome to a very different kind of learning experience! Before you begin to read this book, consider doing one or more of the following Warm-Ups, which will give your brain a head start (pun intended) as you explore the concepts and activities in *Training from the BACK of the Room!* Warm-Up activities are explained in detail in Part One. Enjoy the learning!

1. Do a short Internet search for anything related to cognitive neuroscience or how the human brain learns. Write a few notes about your findings and compare the Internet information with what you read in this book. Also make note of the URLs of a few other websites you discover that might be worth exploring.

2. Interview a person who, in your opinion, is an "expert" on any aspect of learning, teaching, or training. Find out what this person thinks is important for you to know about effective training. Compare/contrast what the expert says is important with the concepts in this book. Discuss this comparison with a training colleague.

3. Choose one training book you have already read, and compare the main ideas in that book with the main ideas in this one. Write a summary of your comparison. Share it with a colleague, and discuss whether you agree or disagree with either book's ideas, and why.

4. Write a quick list of everything you know, or think you know, about the best ways to teach and train. Come back to your list after you've read this book, and decide whether or not to change anything you've written. You may want to add, delete, or edit items on your list.

The 4 Cs Reference Guide

This is a quick reference guide for the instructional design and delivery model that is the foundation of this book. While reading this book, you will experience this model, even as you learn how to use it in your own training.

Connections

Learners make connections with what they already know or think they know about the training topic, with what they will learn, with what they want to learn, and with each other.

Concepts

Learners take in new information in multisensory ways: hearing, seeing, discussing, writing, reflecting, imagining, participating, and teaching it to others.

Concrete Practice

Learners actively practice the new skills, or they participate in an active review of the new knowledge they have learned.

Conclusions

Learners summarize what they have learned, evaluate it, celebrate it, and create action plans for how they plan to use the new knowledge or skills after the training is over.

What's In It For You?

An Introduction to *Training from the BACK of the Room!*

Put the learner to work.

Michael Allen
Michael Allen's Guide to e-Learning, 2003, p. 161

● ●

CONNECTIONS

One-Minute Connection: Fast Pass

Here is the million-dollar training question. Circle your most honest answer, then read what your answer reveals:

What do learners spend most of their time doing during your training programs?

A. Reading the text, handouts, slides, or manuals
B. Listening to you
C. Watching visuals on slides, televisions, or computers screens
D. Discussing concepts or practicing skills
E. Teaching each other and learning from each other

- *For Answer A: Reading the text, handouts, slides, or manuals.* Easy for you, maybe, but too bad for your learners. If you define "learning" as being able to remember and use information in some way, then reading is one of the least effective ways of learning for most people.

- *For Answer B: Listening to you.* As interesting as you think your lectures are, most folks remember very little of what they hear, especially if they don't immediately apply the information. Yes, strong auditory learners may be content to simply sit and listen, and sprinkling your lecture with stories, metaphors, analogies and humor definitely makes your message more memorable. But listening doesn't mean learning, even if you entertain while you talk.

- *For Answer C: Watching visuals on slides, televisions, or computers screens.* This is a step up from reading or listening, especially if the media used is saturated with images, such as video-clips, graphics, photos, cartoons, icons, and the like. In this case, information becomes more image-rich, and consequently easier to remember.

- *For Answer D: Discussing concepts or practicing skills.* Now you're heading in the right direction. Any time training participants discuss concepts and practice skills, they dramatically increase learning. Furthermore, they will be able to remember and use the new information for longer periods of time.

- *For Answer E: Teaching each other and learning from each other.* You are light years ahead of most trainers because you know that teaching another person is one of the most powerful ways to learn. When you allow learners to teach each other, and learn from each other, they increase their own confidence, competence, and ability to use—and master—what they have learned.

Allowing learners to be active participants in their own learning is what this book is about. If you already involve learners from the moment they walk into the room until the moment they leave, you will use this book as a resource to enhance what you are doing well. If you aren't engaging learners throughout the entire training process, you will use this book to learn how to train from the *back* of the room, as you step aside and allow learners to take charge of their own learning.

Imagine That . . .

You just completed a three-day train-the-trainer program in which you learned how to design and deliver effective training. But you didn't learn sitting down. Nor did you learn by passively listening to a lecture while watching a series of

PowerPoint® slides. Instead, you participated in short, quick learning activities from the moment you walked into the room until the end of the training. Most of what you learned was a result of participating in collaborative activities with other learners. Occasionally, the instructor, Marcia, spoke for about ten minutes while you wrote main ideas on note-taking pages that included cartoons, photos, and other topic-related images. A quick review activity followed each ten-minute lecture segment.

You noticed a number of unusual things. For example, Marcia often stood in back of the room while you and the other training participants took "center stage." At various time during the training, different table groups stood in the front of the room and led a presentation, discussion, or an activity that introduced new concepts. You focused most of your attention on the other participants as you learned from, and taught, each other the train-the-trainer content.

You also noticed that Marcia practiced what she preached. She never told you something was important and then didn't give you time to practice it. Nor did she bore you with dozens of slides, while telling you not to bore your training participants.

The most important thing you observed was that Marcia didn't act as if she were the only one who knew the content and all you had to do was show up and listen. Instead, she gave you and the other participants plenty of opportunities to talk about what you already knew about effective training, and to network and share best practices with each other. You worked hard and learned an immense amount of new information because you were actively involved every step of the way.

● ●

CONCEPTS

Do You Want Them to *Hear* It or *Learn* It?

This is the second million-dollar question, and probably the most important one you will ever ask yourself as a trainer: *"Do I want them to HEAR it, or do I want them to LEARN it?"* Your answer to this question is crucial, as it will impact the effectiveness of every training program you design and deliver.

If covering content is your goal, then lecturing is the quickest, easiest, and most time-efficient way of doing that. After all, learning isn't the main objective; presenting the content to your learners is.

But if *learning* is your goal, that is, enabling learners to remember and use the information you give them, then listening to you won't get them there. What *will* get them there is involvement and engagement during the entire training—high interest, content-related, physically active involvement—where they are teaching and learning from each other. That's exactly what this book will help you accomplish.

Who's Doing the Talking?

If you truly want your training participants to be able to remember and use the concepts from your training, you will ask yourself one final million-dollar question: *"In my training programs, who is doing most of the talking?"*

It takes a strong dose of honesty to answer this question, because most trainers think they spend little time lecturing when the statistics show the opposite. According to research from a variety of Internet articles on the topic, most trainers spend about two-thirds of a training program lecturing, even when they don't think they are doing all the talking. "Indeed, almost everyone seems to have the tendency to launch into content presentation as the natural, appropriate, and most essential thing to do" (Allen, 2003, p. 189).

Try This   **Time It.** The next time you attend any kind of adult learning function—a presentation, conference session, class, workshop, or training—make a note of the total amount of time the presenter or trainer talks, versus the amount of time you and the other participants talk. How close to the two-thirds figure does the trainer come? However well-intentioned or interesting the trainer is, he is *not* focused on learning if he is doing most, or all, of the talking. There is no judgment in saying this. Not all adult learning functions are really about learning; many are about content delivery only. You need to know the difference, and then make sure that your training programs are learning experiences instead of content-delivery experiences.

So, in order to increase the learning, you give learners time to discuss, question, move, act, participate, teach and learn from each other. It's that simple—and that complicated. It's simple because it seems obvious and makes sense. It's complicated because, in order to significantly change any behaviors (the usual ways you train, for example), you have to first change your beliefs about those behaviors. Otherwise, the behavior changes won't last.

The Power of the Paradigm

Changes in beliefs are commonly called "paradigm shifts," and a trainer's behavior—how a trainer most often designs and delivers instruction, for example—only changes when there is a change to the underlying paradigm that causes the behavior.

One of the most powerful paradigms held by the majority of training professionals still is "Trainers talk; learners listen." I am repeating this fact because it is this belief that creates the day-to-day reality of most training programs. With all the books and research now available about the importance of involving learners in the learning, the majority of adult instructors (corporate trainers and educators alike) are still doing most of the talking while learners do most of the listening—even if those very same trainers and teachers give lip service to the need for active learning. Why? Here are a few possible reasons:

- *Learners expect it.* It has been done that way since they were children.

- *Companies and educational institutions expect it.* It has been the traditional method of instruction for decades.

- *Trainers have been deliberately taught to do it.* They have been taught to deliver training by talking, lecturing, presenting, or telling.

- *Trainers have more control over the entire training process.* Let's face it—it's easier for trainers to stick to specific content, delivery, and timelines when learners are passive listeners rather than active learners. In addition, there are fewer group management issues when the only person talking is the trainer.

- *Trainers consider themselves to be the subject matter experts.* This implies two things: first, that trainers know all there is to know about the subject; and second, that learners know very little about the subject—otherwise they would be experts as well.

There is only one thing wrong with this "trainers talk; learners listen" paradigm: It has nothing to do with how human beings learn. Instead, it's about the ease and economics of information-delivery. The paradigm serves three non-learning related purposes:

1. *It makes information easy to deliver.* There is only one way to do it (talking) with only one person doing most/all of the talking (the trainer).

2. *It makes information-delivery easy to evaluate.* For example, when a company wants a quick way to evaluate its training investment, it's simple enough to ask, "Did you tell our employees about the safety regulations?" When the trainer answers, "Yes," the company concludes, "Good, then they all know the safety codes."

One-Minute CONCEPT review

Check It Off

Read the list below and check off the training paradigms that have been around the longest, and that may no longer be useful at all:

1. Listening is the first step to learning.
2. Learners often already know a lot about what it is they are learning.
3. The trainer's explanation of the material is better than the learner's.
4. Learners can often teach the material in ways that work better for the other learners.
5. What learners hear, they will remember.
6. When learners are actively engaged throughout the entire learning process, they retain the information longer.
7. If the teacher taught it, the students should have learned it.

Yes, numbers 1, 3, 5, and 7 are old paradigms that, even now, many trainers seldom question. Although most trainers understand the importance of numbers 2, 4, and 6, translating such beliefs into action can be difficult because these beliefs have not been demonstrated nor modeled in most train-the-trainer or teacher education programs.

3. *It makes information-delivery easy to afford.* It takes less training time to deliver a lecture than it does to engage learners in the learning, and less time means less money spent on training programs. It takes fewer resources to deliver a lecture than it does to create training activities. Finally, it takes less space: One-hundred people can sit in a room designed for fifty, if chairs are arranged theatre-style and the learners are not expected to move around.

This Book Will Get You There

Training from the BACK of the Room! will help you make the paradigm shift from instructor- and content-focused training to learner-focused training. You won't just be giving lip service to learner involvement; you will actually be engaging learners in dozens of innovative and content-related ways, even when the content is dry, technical, or complex.

Here are ten benefits that *Training from the BACK of the Room!* offers you. By applying this book's concepts and strategies, you will

1. *Engage learners in the learning process* from the moment they walk into the training room until the moment they leave, and every step along the way.
2. *Decrease the time you spend talking* and increase the time learners spend learning.
3. *Hand over much of the direct instruction to the learners* with simple, structured, collaborative learning activities.
4. *Use current brain research about human learning,* which supports allowing learners to teach and learn from each other.
5. *Shift the training focus from you to your learners* as you make them the center of the learning during the entire training process.
6. *Observe increased learner-retention* of important information through learner demonstrations and a variety of easy evaluation strategies.
7. *Design training more quickly and effectively,* using the 4 Cs—a simple four-step instructional design process that will save you considerable time and effort.
8. *Deliver training in a variety of ways* that will increase learner involvement, interest, and motivation.

9. *Increase your own energy and enthusiasm* before, during, and after training, so that it becomes an exciting process for you as well as your learners.

10. *Teach others what you have learned* about training from the BACK of the room.

One-Minute
CONCEPT review

Fab Four

Reread the list of the ten benefits, and circle the four that, for you, are the most important. Then write these four benefits on the lines below. This will help you remember them and connect what you are learning throughout this book with what you consider most important.

First important benefit:

_____

Second important benefit:

_____

Third important benefit:

_____

Fourth important benefit:

_____

How This Book Is Organized

Training from the BACK of the Room! begins with three chapters of need-to-know information, which are the foundation pieces on which the book is based. Then it gives you four major parts that include sixty-five practical training activities. These four parts apply the foundation pieces of the first three chapters. You can use the activities in your own training, regardless of the topics you teach or the ages or experience levels of your learners. Finally, the book gives you six chapters of nice-to-know information and useful resources to add to what you've already learned.

Here is an outline of what you will discover:

Need-to-Know Information from the FRONT of the Book

- *What's In It For You? An Introduction to Training from the BACK of the Room!* You are reading this chapter now. In it, you are learning what the book is about, why it is important to you, and how you can use the concepts and strategies.

- *Brain-Friendly Training: Learning About Learning.* This chapter is a summation of some of the current brain research on how the human brain learns, and how to apply that research to training.

- *The 4 Cs: A Quick and Remarkably Effective Instructional Design Process.* This chapter gives you an overview of the Accelerated Learning instructional design and delivery model on which this book is based. In addition, the seven major chapters of the book (including this one) have been formatted using the 4 Cs model. As you read the book, you will experience the process, even as you're learning about it.

Part One: Connections

- *What You Need to Know About Connections.* This is the first step of the 4 Cs instructional design process, and the one upon which all the other steps are based. The remaining sections in this part of the book contain fifteen activities that help learners make connections to the topic, the learning outcomes, and each other in relevant, content-related ways.

Part Two: Concepts

- *What You Need to Know About Concepts.* This is the second step of the 4 Cs instructional design process. The activity sections in this part of the book will give you twenty ways to engage learners during the direct instruction, including strategies that allow learners to teach and learn from each other.

Part Three: Concrete Practice

- *What You Need to Know About Concrete Practice.* This is the third step in the 4 Cs instructional design process and includes actual, skills-based or knowledge-based practice activities. The fifteen strategies in this section are time efficient ways of doing concrete practice during training.

Part Four: Conclusions

- *What You Need to Know About Conclusions.* The fourth step of the 4 Cs ensures that learners summarize what has been learned, evaluate their own learning, make a commitment to apply the learning in real-life, and celebrate the entire learning experience. The fifteen activities in this section are learner-led conclusions.

Nice-to-Know Information from the BACK of the Book

- *The Secret of Adult Learning Theory: It's NOT About Age!* Much of the traditional research about adult learning is based on false assumptions about the differences between children and adults. Find out what the most current research says about adult learning theory.

- *Begin with the End: A Fresh Approach to Learning Outcomes.* Discover an easier way to write learning outcomes than the traditional methods taught in train-the-trainer and teacher education programs.

- *The World Cafe: An Innovative Process with Conversations That Matter.* This collaborative, conversation-based learning tool is an innovative way to engage learners in creative thinking and collective knowledge-sharing, while strengthening the learning community.

- *Wake 'Em Up! Ten Tips for Interactive e-Learning.* Not sure how to apply the concepts in this book to computer-based training? This chapter will get you started.

- *The Author's Epilogue.* A personal note from the author, with a final reminder that we, as trainers, need to let the learners do the talking if they are to do the learning.

- *Great Resources.* The resources in this book serve two purposes. First, you will find relevant and useful brain science books, articles, and websites on how the human brain learns. Second, the resources give you practical ways of applying the brain research. As such, they combine the best of human learning theory and application.

Using the Thing to Teach the Thing

In this book, I use the thing to teach the thing, that is, I use effective design and delivery strategies to teach you about effective instructional design and delivery. This book includes a variety of brain-friendly activities for you, the reader, to do—activities that teach you how to use the concepts, even as you're learning about them. Furthermore, you can use these same activities with the topics you teach. Because many readers learn more through active participation while reading, this book provides you with opportunities to participate as you learn. Whether you choose to do the activities or not is up to you. In effect, these quick, active learning strategies will deepen your own understanding of the book's concepts while also giving you concrete examples of how to do the same in your training programs. They include:

- *One-Minute Connections.* These are the chapters' opening activities that connect you to what you already know or what you are about to learn.

- *One-Minute Concept Reviews.* These quick review activities reinforce what you are learning, and help you understand it better and remember it longer.

- *One-Minute Concrete Practice.* These are active review strategies in which you apply what you have learned.

- *One-Minute Conclusions.* These closing activities give you practice in summarizing and evaluating what you have learned from the chapter.

In addition to the quick, one-minute activities sprinkled throughout this book, you'll also notice that seven chapters, including the one you are reading now, demonstrate the 4 Cs instructional design process. You get to see the process in action, in written format, as you read and actively participate. In other words, you experience this effective design and delivery method even as you learn about it. Here is an overview of the 4 Cs, as they relate to you, the reader:

- *Connections.* During this section of a chapter, you'll make your own personal connections to the chapter's concepts and to what you already know (or don't yet know) about the concepts. This section will also let you know what you will get out of the chapter.

- *Concepts.* This chapter segment contains the need-to-know information about the concepts being introduced and discussed. Occasionally, it may contain some nice-to-know information as well—material that is not essential to your learning, but that may help deepen your understanding of the concepts.

- *Concrete Practice.* This chapter section gives you ideas and suggestions for practical ways of applying the concepts. For Parts One, Two, Three, and Four, this section also lists the activities you'll find in those parts of the book.

- *Conclusions.* This segment contains a summary of what was covered in the chapter, a short self-assessment of what you learned and ways to remember and apply the learning to your own training. It may also offer some resources to explore and a celebration of your learning journey so far.

Finally, in using the thing to teach the thing, this book includes four other tools that you can use in your own training:

- *Concept Maps.* At the beginning of the major chapter for each of the four book parts (Parts One, Two, Three, and Four), you'll find a visual outline of the chapter's main ideas. This is a Concept Map, an example of a visual-spatial, note-taking tool. I encourage you to fill this page out as you read these chapters. You'll remember the information longer if you do. In Part Two, you will find the definition, rationale, and instructions for five learner-created Concept Maps.

- *Try It.* These are activity suggestions that you can try later, either in your spare time or during training, in order to further your understanding of the concepts you're learning about.

- *Learning Logs.* At the end of each major chapter is a section in which you can write your responses to questions posted there, write your own summary statements, or write your reactions to the chapter's concepts. In effect, this is your summary and evaluation of your own learning.

- *Trainer's Toolboxes.* Each major chapter ends with a box in which you can write all the tools you've collected along the way - ideas, strategies, and activities from the chapter - that are important to you and that you might want to use in your own training. By listing these tools in a specific place in the book, you will remember them longer and be able to find them more easily.

● ●

CONCRETE PRACTICE

There are many ways of approaching *Training from the BACK of the Room!* You can choose from the ideas below, or create your own:

- *Begin at the beginning.* If you are a novice trainer, or if you want the "whys" first, begin with the part of the book you are reading now, titled: "Need to Know Information from the FRONT of the Book." These three chapters will give you the foundation on which the rest of the book is based. You will also find many helpful suggestions for gradually changing your own training strategies to be more activity-based and learner-centered.

- *Begin in the middle.* If you are an experienced trainer, or if you want the "hows" first, skim Parts One, Two, Three, and Four. From the activity sections in these parts, you can choose many strategies that will help you polish what you already do well. The information in these parts will also help you pull in any pieces that are missing from your current training programs.

- *Begin at the end.* If you want a fresh way of looking at some traditional training material—adult learning theory and writing learning outcomes, to name two—then flip to the book section titled "Nice-to-Know Information from the BACK of the Book." Because most trainers are already familiar with some of this material, and because most trainers need quick, "grab-and-go" ideas for engaging learners, the focus of this book is on interactive instructional strategies and the brain research that supports this approach to training.

- *Identify your strengths and stretches.* Which segments of a training program are you really good at leading and including: the opening, direct instruction or lecture, learner discussions, review activities, or the closing? Identify these segments—they are your strengths. Which training segments are more difficult or challenging for you to lead or include? These are your stretches. With your stretches in mind, review the "How This Book Is Organized" section in this chapter, and flip to the part of the book that will help you strengthen your stretches, meaning the part that will give you ways to turn your training challenges into strengths. For example, if your opening activities don't have much to do with the training topic, turn to "Part One: Connections." This part will give you the rationale, suggestions, and activity instructions for effective openings. Or if you always run out of time at the end of a training, turn to "Part Four: Conclusions." You'll find short, quick closing activities to choose from.

- *Skim, stop, read, and apply.* You may be one of many readers who do this. You quickly skim a book, looking for bold-print headings, graphics, or any details that catch your attention. Then you stop and read those paragraphs or sections. This book lends itself to that process. Find a paragraph or section that interests you, grab a gem or two from it, and apply the idea or suggestion to your next training.

- *Mark it up.* As you read, highlight the phrases, sentences, or sections that are important to you. Circle or box suggestions you can use. Use sticky notes

Data Hunt

Skim this chapter once more. How many of the following items can you find? Go on a Data Hunt to find the items, and fill in the answers below.

1. Find one connection activity at the beginning of the chapter and write the title here:

   _____

   _____

2. Find the three "million-dollar questions" in the chapter and write them here:

   _____

   _____

   _____

3. On what page does each of the 4 Cs process steps begin? Jot down the page numbers:
   Connections—Page
   Concepts—Page
   Concrete Practice—Page
   Conclusions—Page

4. What are the titles of the two one-minute Concept Review activities?

   _____

   _____

5. What is the title of the Concrete Practice review activity you are doing right now?

   _____

   _____

Turn to the end of this chapter to check your answers. How did you do? Is there a way you can use a Data Hunt like this with your own training material? Think about it.

to flag pages you want to come back to. Add your own comments in the margins. Do the activities. Write in the blank spaces. When you do this, the book becomes a record of your learning journey, as well as a personalized resource of material that is meaningful and useful to you. Marking up a book in this fashion means that you'll remember the information longer than if you read it without any time for reflection.

- *Take what you can use and let the rest go by.* What you find useful in this book will be different from what another reader finds useful. And what you think isn't applicable to your training programs may be exactly what someone else needs to make his or her training more effective. Use what makes sense to you, or what you think will work best with your learners. Don't waste time trying to fit everything into what you do. Pick and choose, and let go of the rest.

• •

CONCLUSIONS

Training from the BACK of the Room! is advanced experiential training at its best. It isn't for the faint of heart. Its concepts and strategies are challenges to the traditional training paradigms still held dear by many trainers and educators. When you make the paradigm-shift from "trainers talk; learners listen," to "when learners talk and teach, they learn," you open up a whole new world of exciting learning possibilities for yourself, as well as your training participants. Instead of a traditional approach to training that is instructor-led and content-centered, you'll experiment with new paradigms, new research, and new instructional strategies - all designed to put learners center-stage, as you move to the back of the room, get out of the way, and let them learn!

Break the rules!
Instead of beginning with the tedious task of explaining
flush, royal flush, pairs, and so on to teach poker,
deal the cards and play the game.

Michael Allen
Michael Allen's Guide to e-Learning, 2003, p. 202

One-Minute Conclusion: Learning Log

A Learning Log is a written record of your own learning journey: what you know that you didn't know before, what you feel are the important concepts, and how you might use these concepts in your own training. Usually a Learning Log is in written format, but you can also draw, doodle, or make a Concept Map of your thoughts as well (see Part Two for Concept Map instructions).

In the space below, jot down a few sentences summarizing what you consider important from this chapter. What do you think will make this book different from the other training books you have read? How do you think what you learn will improve the way you train?

Bonus One-Minute Conclusion: Mark-Ups

Listed below are the ten benefits stated earlier in this chapter, along with five outcomes that, hopefully, *won't* happen as a result of your reading this book. Draw a star beside each statement that describes one of the book's benefits, and cross out the statements that do not apply. Then check your answers.

After reading this book and applying its ideas and strategies, I'll be able to

1. Engage learners in the learning process from the moment they walk into the training room until the moment they leave, and every step along the way.
2. Show learners how to listen better so that they get more from my lectures.
3. Decrease the time I spend talking and increase the time learners spend learning.
4. Hand over much of the direct instruction to the learners with simple, structured, collaborative learning activities.
5. Apply the most up-to-date brain research about human learning, which supports allowing learners to teach each other and learn from each other.
6. Polish my presentation techniques so that I can hold learners' interest with entertaining stories and case studies.
7. Shift the training focus from me to my learners, making them the center of the learning during the entire training process.
8. Use the traditional ADDIE instructional design model: analysis, design, development, implementation, and evaluation.
9. Design training more quickly and effectively, using the 4 Cs, a simple four-step instructional design process that will save me considerable time and effort.
10. Deliver training in a variety of ways that will increase learner involvement, interest, and motivation.
11. Talk more, even if some training participants learn less.
12. Observe increased learner retention of important information through learner demonstrations and a variety of easy evaluation strategies.

(continued)

13. Increase my own energy and enthusiasm before, during, and after a training program, so that it becomes an exciting process for myself and my learners.

14. Look at job options other than training because I get so exhausted at having to present the same information to training participants day after day.

By starring numbers 1, 3, 4, 5, 7, 9, 10, 12, 13, and 15, you reviewed the book's benefits again, which will help you remember them longer. Of course, you crossed out numbers 2, 6, 8, 11, and 14.

Trainer's Toolbox

Each of the seven major chapters of this book ends with a Trainer's Toolbox, in which you can write all the training ideas and strategies you've collected from the chapter that you might be able to use. Below is the toolbox space for this chapter. To get started, look back through the chapter for all the activities you just participated in, and write those titles in this box. Anything you might be able to use in your own training becomes part of your Trainer's Toolbox. You will decide later whether or not to use them - right now, you are playing with possibilities and listing ideas in one place to find them more easily. Then flag this page with a sticky note so you don't have to hunt for it later.

Answers to the One-Minute Concrete Practice: Data Hunt

1. Find one connection activity at the beginning of the chapter and write the title here:

    Fast Pass

2. Find the three "million dollar questions" in the chapter and write them here:

    What do learners spend most of their time doing during your training programs?

    Do I want them to HEAR it, or do I want them to LEARN it?

    In my training programs, who is doing most of the talking?

3. On what page does each of the 4 Cs process steps begin? Jot down the page numbers:

    Connections—Page 7

    Concepts—Page 9

    Concrete Practice—Page 18

    Conclusions—Page 21

4. What are the titles of the two one-minute Concept Review activities?

    Check it Off; Fab Four

5. What is the title of the Concrete Practice review activity you are doing right now?

    Data Hunt

Brain-Friendly Training

Learning About Learning

Can a profession [that] is defined by the development
of an effective and efficient human brain
continue to remain uninformed about that brain?

Robert Sylwester
A Celebration of Neurons, 1995, p. 6

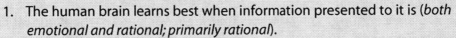

CONNECTIONS

One-Minute Connection: Fast Pass

How much do you know about how the human brain learns?
Underline the phrases that correctly complete the sentences.

1. The human brain learns best when information presented to it is (*both emotional and rational; primarily rational*).
2. For the human brain, paying attention is most often (*a conscious choice; an unconscious choice*).
3. Attention increases when the learning environment (*changes; doesn't change*), and decreases when the environment (*changes; doesn't change*).
4. (*Longer; shorter*) segments of instruction are better than (*longer; shorter*) ones.

(continued)

5. Humans remember more (*when they figure things out for themselves; when someone else shows them how to figure things out*).

6. For optimal learning, the physical body needs to be (*motionless; active*) while the brain/mind is engaged.

To check your answers, turn to the end of this chapter.

In this chapter you will discover relevant research about how the human brain *really* learns, which may not be the same as what you were taught about learning. This research may surprise you as it lays to rest some outdated assumptions about learning and training. This chapter also gives you practical ways to apply this research.

Imagine That . . .

As the senior trainer on a training team, you've been given the job of evaluating the other less-experienced trainers. Since two of them are training in side-by-side classrooms this morning, you sit in the back of one room and then the other and watch what is going on during both training programs.

In the first room, the trainer is standing in front of the class. He is reading aloud from a set of slides displayed on a screen. He pauses occasionally to interject some extra facts that aren't on the slides and to ask whether there are any questions. His presentation manner is pleasant enough as he lectures. Sometimes he even stops and asks, "Did you all understand that?" Since no one responds negatively, he goes on. The training participants are all sitting quietly while the trainer talks. You look around the room and observe that the participants have paper copies of the trainer's slides. Very few are taking notes; one or two are doodling. The tables are in long rows, with participants all facing the trainer. The walls are blank. The tables hold the slide handouts, pens, and a water glass for each participant. By most standards, it's an ordinary training room with a traditionally delivered training. Since the break time isn't scheduled for another sixty minutes, chances are the trainer will be talking for that length of time. You watch for a while, then quietly leave to go to the next room.

Here things are very different. The walls jump out at you when you walk in the room because charts hang everywhere, some with colorful printing on them and some blank. In fact, participants are just returning to their seats after clustering around a few wall charts and writing some facts on them with colorful markers. The tables are round, with participants seated in circles so that they face each other and can talk to each other. In the middle of the tables are a variety of writing materials: markers, colored pens, index cards, sticky notes, interesting note-taking pages, and more. As the trainer talks, she walks around the room, pausing often to engage participants in a number of short, quick activities. During the entire hour, she encourages participants to talk, ask, answer, write, and participate. There is a lot going on in this room, and the room reflects the activity with a quiet buzz of conversation, energy, participation, and enthusiasm. With so much to hold your interest, you could comfortably spend an hour in this training without becoming bored.

Your evaluations will describe your impressions of both training sessions. What will you say? Think about it.

● ●

CONCEPTS

Brain-friendly learning is about how the brain naturally thrives and grows as it learns. It is born from a new branch of study called "cognitive neuroscience" that studies how the brain takes in, stores, retrieves, and uses information. This field is unique in that it is interdisciplinary—not only scientists and physicians study the human brain, but also biologists, chemists, psychologists, educators, philosophers, anthropologists, linguists, trainers, and anyone whose job depends on knowing more about how the human brain learns.

Brain-friendly training is a direct result of brain-friendly learning. In *Brain Matters* (2001), author Patricia Wolfe explains: "The more we understand the brain, the better we'll be able to design instruction to match how the brain learns best" (p. 2). Given that statement, you would think that all training is brain-friendly. However, when it comes to traditional methods of instruction (meaning trainer-led, content-centered, and lecture-saturated), the human brain was never an important part of the equation. At best, traditional instruction is brain-neutral. At worst, it is brain-antagonistic.

"Brain-neutral" refers to training that doesn't have much impact on whether or not anyone learns anything. Most of the real learning will be done on the job after the training is over. An example of brain-neutral training is the typical new-hire orientation: Employees watch a slide show about the company's history, listen to welcoming speeches from various department managers, sign the required paperwork, and receive their company name badges on the way out the door. What they really need to know about their new jobs will take place later, within their departments.

"Brain-antagonistic" refers to training that actually interferes with the learning process, decreases learning, and may even cause emotional distress. Examples of brain-antagonistic training abound. There are the usual stories of trainers who resort to sarcasm or ridicule, who are egocentric, defensive, ill-informed, or indifferent to their learners' needs. Less obvious but even worse are the mind-numbing training programs that are taught in sterile environments, lecture-heavy, with little sensory stimulation to engage the brain. In effect, boring training is brain-antagonistic.

From Boring to Beneficial

Let's explore what brain research has to say about boring versus brain-friendly instruction. First, the research stresses the following fact: Regardless of a person's age, culture, race, or gender, the human brain *loves* to learn. It's a mean, lean, thinking machine, if you will, always on the prowl for new things to explore, think about, make sense of, experience, and use. Its reason for existing is to learn, and it's genetically programmed to learn. "There is no such thing as not paying attention; the brain is *always* paying attention to something" (Wolfe, 2001, p. 81).

Furthermore, the human brain cannot *not* learn. If deprived of enough stimulation, the brain turns inward and begins to create its own rich internal world. In other words, it daydreams. People become bored and begin to daydream when they are doing tasks that are routine or repetitive, when they are reading or listening to uninteresting information, when they stay in one physical position for too long, and when environments never change.

Put another way, the human brain loves newness and thrives on sensory stimulation. The brain actually grows new connections, called dendrites, between neurons, or brain cells, when it is actively engaged in learning. Learning takes place when attention is guided by "interest, novelty, emotion, and meaning" (Caine, Cain, McClintic, & Klimek, 2005, p. 199).

On the other hand, "habituation", that is anything repetitive or routine, causes the brain to pay less and less attention to what is going on around it. If an experience occurs over and over in the same fashion (same sights, sounds, movement, environment, and so on), "the brain normally becomes so accustomed to the stimulus that it ignores it" (Wolfe, 2001, p. 82).

Unfortunately, most traditional classrooms are boring places to be. In these environments, people find it difficult to pay attention and to learn. The teacher does most/all of the talking, students do most/all of the listening, the delivery never changes, the physical environment never changes, and the information, albeit important to the teacher or the institution, is not yet important to the students. Over time, learning decreases drastically in these environments because students are literally bored to tears (Whittle, 2005, p. 148).

The same can be said for traditional training programs. Author Michael Allen puts it this way: "Boring and effective are mutually exclusive attributes in learning. You can't be effective if your training is boring" (2003, p. 6). In fact, Allen is so passionate about the ill effects of boredom that he elaborates: "Minds wander, attention wanes. . . . When learners are through, they're through—relieved that it's over, and ready to escape to something else as quickly as possible. Little is retained. . . . It's bad. It's a waste" (p. 5).

But training doesn't have to be boring, even if it is highly technical or content-heavy. When trainers shift from brain-antagonistic to brain-friendly instructional strategies, the entire learning experience becomes more beneficial to the learners—and to the trainer and the institution or company, as well.

The benefits to learners are numerous: They become enthusiastic, motivated, receptive to new learning, and eager to apply what they've learned to their jobs and future performance. The trainer's benefits are obvious: He/she stays on top of the game, passionate, and challenged to create the best possible learning experiences—and is far more likely to have increased energy at the end of the day. The benefits to the institution or company are profound: Employee competence and motivation to succeed increases, remediation time and number of mistakes decrease, and customer service and employee efficiency improve (Allen, 2003, pp. 13–14).

Brain-Friendly Learning and Training

You have experienced brain-friendly learning thousands of times in your own life, so you are already familiar with what it means. Any time you did the following, you were immersed in brain-friendly learning:

- You learned something for the sheer *joy* of learning it.

- You learned it when you *wanted* to learn it.

- You felt a great sense of *accomplishment* after learning it.

- You learned what you *needed*, when you needed it, and at your own pace.

- You chose *how* you were going to learn.

- You learned by *doing* it instead of watching someone else do it.

- You learned by *teaching* it to someone else.

- You learned in an *informal environment* where collaboration was encouraged, competition was de-emphasized, and mistakes were viewed as a necessary part of the learning process.

Brain-friendly training, then, is about designing and delivering instruction in ways that the human brain learns best. It will include many of the points listed above: joy, accomplishment, desire, need, choice, active participation, and informal surroundings. "Research now indicates that people learn through their whole bodies and their whole minds: verbally, nonverbally, rationally, emotionally, physically, intuitively—all at the same time" (Meier, 2000, p. xxiv). We can summarize this by saying that brain-friendly training uses the following five general elements to enhance learning:

1. Positive emotional experiences

2. Multi-sensory stimulation and novelty

3. Instructional variety and choices

4. Active participation and collaboration

5. Informal learning environments

Try This

Choose and Use. Look over the list of five brain-friendly elements. Choose one that you know you can include in your next training. Think about how you will specifically apply it. For example, if you choose active participation/collaboration, you might allow a few minutes for table group discussions after each concept you present. If you choose multisensory stimulation/novelty, you might bring in some props as visual aids for what you are teaching. If you choose informal learning environments, you might have a lot of colorful writing materials available, as well as music and wall charts. You get the idea. Jot a few notes describing how you plan to apply the brain-friendly element in your next training.

Let's explore each of these five brain-friendly elements in more detail.

Positive Emotional Experiences: From Emotions to Attention to Learning

Brain-friendly training breaks many of the old training paradigms held so dear by so many, not the least of which is the long-held belief that learning is a rational activity.

No matter how hard we try, we can't bypass emotions. We can't pretend that what we teach or learn is only about information; all thoughts pass through an emotional field first. It's as if we have a detective inside our heads that constantly searches data for its emotional counterpart: "I like this, I don't like that; I agree with this, I disagree with that; this makes me fearful, that makes me comfortable; I want more of that, I don't want more of this," and so on. Every fact that enters our head has to pass through our emotional filters first. No exceptions.

This connection between facts and feelings is hardwired in the human brain because it is crucial to our physical survival. Let's look at one graphic example: If you live in the woods, you probably know that black bears instinctively avoid humans. But if one suddenly lumbers onto your deck, your first reaction will most likely be: "I'm outa here!" Your emotions will take precedence over the information you have in your head. The fact that the bear is more afraid of you than you are of it is of little consequence at that moment.

Let's take another example: You're attending a travel agency presentation about a possible visit to the state of Hawaii. While the travel agent lists facts about the islands, a video plays on a background screen. The video includes panoramic shots of the islands in all their colorful splendor, complete with volcanoes, beaches, palm trees, and tropical birds and flowers. Which holds most of your attention: the agent or the video? Chances are that it's the video.

Both examples demonstrate that anything that is strongly tied to emotion, either negative or positive, will grab—and keep—our attention longer than anything that isn't. And what we attend to, we learn. Author Robert Sylwester describes this phenomenon in *A Celebration of Neurons* (1995): "Emotion and attention are the principle processes that our body/brain uses in its efforts to survive [and thrive]" (p. 71). The brain constantly uses emotions and attention to determine what is, and isn't, important. Both provide the neural mechanisms (meaning brain power) that cause us to "focus on the things that seem important, while monitoring *or ignoring* the unimportant" (Sylwester, 1995, p. 71).

Emotions also become our survival guideposts. We will avoid anything that causes us pain—psychological distress as well as physical discomfort—and seek out anything that gives us pleasure. More specifically, as learners, we psychologically resist training that makes us feel uncomfortable (as in

One-Minute CONCEPT review

The Choice Is Yours

Listed below are some statements made by two trainers. As you read them, compare and contrast the emotional climate created by each. Decide for yourself which you would rather attend, Trainer A's class or Trainer B's class:

- Trainer A: "Welcome. Please take a few moments to introduce yourself to the people at your table and let them know why you are here today, and what you want to learn from this class."

- Trainer B: "Welcome. Let me tell you about myself so you know my background, credentials, and why I am an expert in this field."

- Trainer A: "Let's begin by brainstorming at least a half-dozen facts you already know about this topic."

- Trainer B: "I'm going to begin by telling you what you are going to learn about this topic."

- Trainer A: "That's an interesting answer to the question. In addition, you might consider this answer as well. . . ."

- Trainer B: "That's incorrect. Here's the correct answer to the question."

- Trainer A: "Together, before the training ends, let's make a list of all the new facts you now know about this topic."

- Trainer B: "In summation, here is what you learned about this topic."

As you can tell, Trainer A's class is collaborative, participatory, and inclusive—in other words, brain-friendly. Not so with Trainer B's class.

"I feel bored, humiliated, or stupid"). We are willing to participate in training that creates pleasant feelings (as in "I feel competent, respected, or smart"). The information or skills to be learned can be very challenging, but if we *feel* confident that we can learn, we will learn more quickly than if we learn because we are told we have to learn, or run the risk of failure if we don't.

The same holds true for the learners in our training programs. They will seek out, and return to, learning experiences in which they feel confident and successful. They will avoid learning experiences in which they feel stupid or humiliated.

Multi-Sensory Stimulation and Novelty: Timing and Movement

How long can you sit and listen to someone talk? Let's rephrase that: How long can you sit and listen to a fact-based lecture, devoid of stories, emotion, or anything that connects you personally to the content? Your tolerance for such a learning experience is probably minimal, and the actual time you can remain sitting without getting fidgety is probably a matter of minutes, not hours.

In *The Ten-Minute Trainer* (2005), I point out that television has conditioned us to receive information in small segments of about ten minutes in length, which is the average duration of a program segment between commercial breaks. Of course we *can* pay attention longer than that, but the amount of information we remember may decrease. And, because the body is simply sitting, less oxygen flows to the brain, meaning that our thinking gets fuzzy. Commercial breaks give us the excuse we need to stand and move, even for just a few minutes.

The same timing applies to training. Information-delivery that lasts longer than ten minutes (close enough is okay—twenty minutes will still work; anything longer probably won't) will see a diminishing return in terms of how much information learners will remember. The brain doesn't absorb information well when the body is totally passive and the only sensory stimulation is auditory.

However, add physical movement (learners' movement, not yours) to the mix, and both the body *and* mind become stimulated. Toss in timing—physical movement that learners participate in about every ten to twenty minutes—and learners themselves see a dramatic change in their own energy and interest, as well as recall and retention.

The reason physical movement is important while learning is elementary. The simple act of standing after sitting awhile increases blood flow, and therefore oxygen, to the brain by about 15 to 20 percent (Sousa, 2006, p. 34). So when learners move from sitting to standing, their capacity to learn also increases by about 20 percent. Put another way, a simple change in posture can lead to a profound change in learning.

> **Try This**
>
> **Stretch Breaks.** In an hour of lecture, build in at least four short, one-minute stretch breaks for the learners to do. Tell them *what* to do and *why* it's important for them to do it. Ask learners to stand, then say to them: *"By changing your position from sitting to standing, you have just now increased the oxygen to your brain by about 20 percent, which means your brain is suddenly working better. Now stretch your body, and then turn to the person standing next to you and give him/her a short verbal summary of what you've just learned from the lecture so far. Sit when you have finished."*
>
> To vary the stretch break, change your instructions slightly each time you include this type of activity: Learners can stretch with different partners, stretch large muscles (arms, legs, torso), then small muscles (fingers, toes, face), or turn in a circle before discussing with a partner what they have learned. Making it humorous also adds a release of endorphins––the pleasure chemicals of the brain.

In *Brain-Based Learning* (2000), author Eric Jensen explains: "Any stimuli introduced into our immediate environment, which is either new (novel) or of sufficiently strong emotional intensity (high contrast), will immediately gain our attention" (p. 122). Movement and timing are two ways of including multisensory stimulation and novelty in training. Here are more ideas:

- *Auditory stimulation.* Use music, rhythm, rhyme, unexpected noises or silence, verbal discussions, reading aloud, changes in voice tones or volume, and the like.

- *Visual stimulation.* Use colors, shapes, charts, slides, graphics, images, stories and analogies, metaphors, analogies, props, photos, and anything else that helps create strong mental pictures of important concepts.

- *Kinesthetic stimulation.* Include learners' movement (as was discussed in this section), using different writing materials to take notes, participatory activities, manipulating written material (highlighting, underlining, circling important points, turning pages, etc.), signals (thumbs up for "yes" and down for "no," claps or stomps, hands raised or lowered), and anything that engages the body while learning.

One caveat about timing: The ten-minute rule may not apply to storytelling. Authors Chip and Dan Heath, in their book *Made to Stick* (2007), make the point that messages that stick longest in the minds of learners are simple, concrete, emotional, and taught in story form. A good story transports the listener into a mentally stimulating world, in which the mental images are so real, and the emotional connections so strong, that the length of time spent sitting and listening can become inconsequential. Listeners can tolerate storytellers far longer than they can tolerate trainers who simply recite facts.

Instructional Variety and Choices: Reaching Most of the Learners Most of the Time

Adding a variety of instructional strategies to the mix is another way to increase learners' attention to and retention of important content. Using more than one or two information-accessing exercises "stimulates learners to think, make connections, build new neural networks, and create actionable meaning and value for themselves" (Meier, 2000, p. 40). Such instructional strategies can include brief lectures, question-and-answer time, whole and small group discussions, multi-media segments, pre- and post-assessments, reading, writing, listening, talking, watching, quiet reflection time, and games. In *The Owner's Manual for the Human Brain* (2000), cognitive scientist Howard Pierce maintains that learners are able to achieve at higher levels when they become personally involved with the content by handling the information in various ways (p. 519). Will all learners be happy with all the instructional strategies all of the time? Probably not. Will most learners be happy with most of the strategies, especially when they have opportunities to learn in ways that work best for them? Definitely.

In addition to instructional variety, when learners can choose how to learn some of the content, they will buy into the learning for specific, meaningful benefits because they are creating their own learning (Allen, 2003, pp. 154, 156). Give learners choices during the training program by doing one or more of the following:

- *Post a list of introductory activities.* This list will help learners become familiar with training concepts or terms. Examples: doing Internet searches, interviewing experts in the room, skimming the handouts, discussing what they already know with other learners, or writing topic-related questions they want answers for. Invite learners to choose one activity to do from the list either before or during the beginning of the training program. Allow about five minutes for the activity duration. Follow the activity with a short, whole group discussion of what they learned. Part One in this book contains more ideas.

- *Post a list of direct instruction strategies.* Learners use this list during the lecture segment of training. Invite each table group to teach a small piece of new information by using one of these strategies. Obviously, groups must have the concept information in written form to learn from before choosing the way they will present it. They will also need some time (usually about ten or fifteen minutes) to learn the material and create their presentation of it. The activities they choose may only be five minutes or less in duration. Examples: short lectures, demonstrations, whole group discussions, role plays or skits, chart explanations, or games. Turn to Part Two in this book for more activities.

- *Give learners a timeline and choices for content review.* During a ten-minute review time, learners can read, write, talk about concepts with a partner, complete a quiz, make flashcards or other memory aids, write a news article, create test questions, and the like. You can also invite learners to create conceptual posters with a variety of materials: colored markers, colored construction paper, index cards, and three-dimensional craft items such as pipe cleaners, stickers, dowels, or Play-Doh®. After the review time has ended, learners hang the posters on the walls as a visual review for the whole class. You will find more ideas in Part Three of this book.

- *Hand over a specific part of the training for them to lead.* You provide the guidelines learners need to follow and give them the time and materials they will need to create the instructional segment. You may also want to do this by table groups, instead of the whole group. For example, you invite one table group to be responsible for a five-minute conclusion activity at the closing of the training. You suggest that the activity must be an active review of what they learned, it must involve all participants, and it must include either verbal or written summaries that all learners create. Give this group time during the training or at breaks to work together. Have them describe their activity to you before they facilitate it, so that you can offer any necessary suggestions. Then step aside and let them lead the activity when the time comes. Look at Part Four in this book for more ideas.

In effect, learners are meeting their own learning needs and goals when they participate in, or direct part of, the training design and delivery (El-Shamy, 2004, p. 69).

Active Participation and Collaboration: Stepping Aside While Letting Them Learn

When you were a kid, you wanted to learn how to ride a bike *by riding a bike*. You wanted to learn how to color a picture *by coloring*, and you wanted to learn how to put a model together *by putting it together*. You didn't want to watch your mom put the model together, or watch your dad color the picture, or watch your sister ride the bike. Yes, you did, in fact, see them do these things at other times. And, yes, it was nice having them there to help you or to offer encouragement if you got stuck. But the doing belonged to you, and somehow you knew it did and you felt frustrated if you weren't allowed to do it.

As trainers, we need to give learners just enough information to start, then step aside while they learn from using the information in some fashion. They can ask for more information when they need it. Here is an example: In a customer service training, learners first brainstorm effective customer service skills. Then the trainer gives each table group a real-life written scenario involving a service problem. Learners access printed or Internet resources that help them solve the problem and report to the whole group when done. The trainer follows this with more detailed, company-specific customer service information and an active review in which learners, again, play a major role.

This type of learning leads to dramatically different results: Learners remember more for longer periods of time, need fewer reminders or remediation, and feel more competent and confident about the learning. In other words, most learners want "to participate actively, contribute to their own learning and to be treated as independent, capable people" (Stolovich, 2002, p. 51).

Here are a few more suggestions for encouraging active participation and collaboration:

- *Begin with the frame.* Let learners know the "frame," meaning structure, of the activity first: the purpose, time allowed, expectations for participation, and results they will be accountable for. Here is an example of the frame for a short, Make a List review activity:

  - You explain that learners will be reviewing concepts from the lecture with partners.

  - They will have two minutes to work together on a written list of six or more facts they remember from the lecture.

  - At the end of two minutes, they will report their lists to their table groups.

  - You may also want to post the activity instructions on a slide or chart so that learners can refer to them if necessary.

- *Move from low-risk to high-risk.* At the beginning, use collaborative strategies that make learners feel psychologically safe with each other and you. Short, simple ones like Dot-Voting or Turn and Talk (see Part One for instructions), where learners discuss concepts with one or two other people, are low-risk. No one has to speak in front of the entire group, nor worry about looking foolish if he or she doesn't understand a concept. Later, you can encourage learners to work in larger groups on collaborative projects, which are more high-risk than paired activities.

- *Choose collaboration over competition.* For many people, a game with a high degree of competition feels like a high-risk activity. Egos come to the forefront and the traditional "I win, you lose" paradigm swings into play. Some learners thrive on games and winning; others don't. No one wants to be the loser. When possible, choose games that are more collaborative in nature, or ones in which whole teams compete (with everyone taking a part), rather than individuals against individuals. Or leave the competition out of the training—most people don't miss it.

    Hand it over. As with giving learners choices in leading some of the instructional activities, you can also invite learners to create collaborative review activities. Assign one or two table groups, or ask for volunteers, to create a five- or ten-minute collaborative review activity. The activity must be short, must involve all table groups, must review the material presented, and must have clear instructions. Suggestions: card games, small group discussions, verbal or written quizzes, posted chart pages, ball toss with questions and answers, and so on. As the groups prepare their collaborative reviews, check to make sure they are following the guidelines and offer help if necessary. Allow about ten minutes for activity preparation.

    In *Engaging Learning* (2005), e-learning consultant Clark Quinn tells us that learners "must develop their own understanding . . . this has changed our notion of learning to emphasize the social nature of learning through dialogue between learners, and between learners and mentors, as the active process of learners refining their understanding" (p. 32).

    Author Jay Cross summarizes it best: "Teachers learn. Learners teach. . . . The gung-ho learners enjoy doing things their own way. They learn from teaching others" (2007, pp. 76–77).

Try This

Supplement the Slide. Choose a training slide that has three or four bulleted facts on it. Instead of posting the slide on a screen, give each table group a printed copy of the slide. Say: *"Read the slide aloud at your table group. As a group, discuss the bulleted facts and make a list of information you already know that can supplement any of the facts. You will have three minutes to do so. You will report your list later."* Then include their lists of supplementary information as part of the lecture.

    You can take this idea one step further and have each table group report out on one of the bulleted points, summarizing what they already know as well as any other written information you give them about that particular point. In effect, learners are taking part in the direct instruction, with you adding the details they may have missed or may not have known.

Informal Learning Environments: "Do Not Touch" Versus "Make Yourself at Home"

Have you ever thought about why traditional classrooms are set up with individual desks in rows, and all facing one way? It's not that it's better for learning—it's about the janitorial services! In the past, it was easier to clean a room where the desks or tables were lined up in evenly spaced rows. While this may not be the case today, because it was done that way for so many years, it may not ever occur to many teachers or trainers that there are more effective ways to set up a room than theater-style, with everyone facing the instructor and slide screen, somewhat like an audience facing performers on a stage.

The subtle message this type of formal learning environment creates is just as brain-antagonistic as the traditional instruction it houses: "Sit down, face forward, be quiet, don't move around, don't talk to anyone, look at the instructor, and listen, listen, listen." Formal learning environments have a do-not-touch feel about them.

Contrast this with the hands-on feeling of an informal, brain-friendly learning environment: round tables or desks in circled clusters, colored paper, pens, and other writing materials for each group, posters on walls, music, maybe even snack food and beverages on a side table. There is enough visual stimulation to make the room seem inviting, friendly, and interesting. The subtle message in this learning environment is very different: "Make yourself at home, move around, help yourself to what you need, talk, converse, teach and learn from each other."

Although an informal learning environment is no guarantee that training is brain-friendly, it is definitely an indication of instruction that is more compatible with how the human brain learns. Author Donald Finkel, in *Teaching with Your Mouth Shut* (2001), suggests that we "let the classroom environment do the talking . . . [trainers] who wish to stimulate active discussion do well to rearrange their [learners'] chairs into a circle, to leave the front of the class, and to occupy one of those chairs" (pp. 116–117). Learning is more effective when the environment "attracts the attention and interest of the learner, is obviously relevant, and requires action on the part of the learner…. We need to address the emotional side of learning as well as the knowledge side [so that] learners are captured, heart and mind, in learning—or to use formal terms, are cognitively and affectively connected to the learning experience" (Quinn, 2005, pp. 10, 12).

Compare and Contrast

Think about some of the assumptions you made, or were taught, about human learning before you read this chapter. Write a few brief sentences comparing and contrasting the old with the new, that is, what you were taught about learning and training versus what the brain research says. What are the similarities and differences? What, if anything, surprised you from the current research? What questions do you still have?

CONCRETE PRACTICE

Now let's put some of these concepts to work in your training programs. Remember, the goal is to create brain-friendly training that works for your learners. You can do a number of things with this concrete practice section:

- *For beginning trainers.* Read the First Steps list below and choose one strategy to experiment with in your next training. Keep a record of how it works and any changes that you try in order to make it more effective. Then choose another strategy, then another, until you feel comfortable with them all.

- *For experienced trainers.* Read the Next Steps list below and choose two or more strategies to experiment with. These strategies are more challenging than the First Steps. Keep a record of their effectiveness and any changes you make.

- *Guided by need.* First identify a training need that you should address. Then skim both the First Steps and Next Steps lists and choose one or more strategies that address the need. For example, you may decide there should be more participant discussion in your training. Choose activities that encourage learners to talk to each other.

- *Guided by interest.* Skim the two lists below. Choose any strategy that catches your interest and curiosity. Experiment with it in your next training and jot down the results.

Here is the list of First Steps as you begin to use brain-friendly elements in training:

1. *Change the room environment.* Look around. Take note of how it feels. You want it to feel friendly, informal, and inviting. Rearrange some of the furniture so that learners face each other and can easily talk to each other. Add splashes of color (wall charts, colorful paper on the tables, colored markers, and so on) to stimulate visual interest. Play upbeat background music before the program begins. Post a bright welcome sign at the entrance.

2. *Shorten your direct instruction time.* Divide your content or lecture material into smaller segments of about ten to twenty minutes of direct instruction. Time yourself if you aren't sure as to how long each segment lasts. Ask a training participant to give you a "time's up" signal so that you don't talk longer than the allotted time.

3. *Use short, quick review activities that engage all learners.* Between lecture segments, use one-minute review strategies from this book or from *The Ten-Minute Trainer.* These activities add interest, lengthen retention, and keep learners engaged. They will make all the difference between a boring lecture and a brain-friendly one.

4. *Vary the review activities.* Even if an activity is fun, habituation sets in when the activity is repeated the same way. Vary the interactive strategies so that learners review material in a slightly different way each time.

5. *Use a Concept Map.* Choose one of the note-taking tools from Part Two of this book. Instead of handing out copies of your slides, give each learner a Concept Map and remind them to take notes on it. Pause during the direct instruction to give them time to do so.

Here is a list of Next Steps for more experienced trainers:

1. *Begin and end training with the focus on the learners, not on you*. Simply put, this means you step aside as learners participate in meaningful connection and conclusion activities. Use strategies from Parts One and Four of this book.

2. *Begin and end direct instruction with learner discussion*. Engage learners with short, small group discussions before and after your lecture segments. Vary what they talk about and the length of the discussions. Here are some suggested discussion instructions to say to learners:

   - *Create a quick list of facts you already know about this concept.*

   - *What are some questions you want answers for? Write them down.*

   - *Take two minutes to summarize what you have learned so far.*

   - *In the next three minutes, create two test questions about this content.*

   - *Compare and contrast what you've just learned with your own experiences related to this topic.*

   - *Make a quick, written list of at least six new facts you've just learned about this topic.*

   - *Tell your table group what you think is important about what you just heard.*

3. *Hand over some of the content to the learners to teach*. Begin by choosing the easiest concept for participants to learn. Ask yourself, "If I lost my voice, how could I have them teach this to each other?" Then set up an activity accordingly. Use ideas from Part Two of this book to assist you. Keep a record of the most effective strategies and use them in various ways throughout the training.

4. *Ask open-ended questions*. Phrase questions so that learners have to come up with several answers, not just one right answer (if a question only has one right answer, don't ask it). Before learners verbally state their answers, have them discuss possible answers among themselves. Give them a goal: "We need six answers to this question" or "Let's see whether you can come up with at least three answers to the following question." Other variations include:

   - *With a partner, create two answers to this question.*

   - *With your table group, list five possible answers.*

   - *Let's see how many answers our whole class can create in one minute.*

- *How many answers to this question can your table group come up with in two minutes?*

- *With a partner, create a list of steps you would need to take to find answers to this question.*

5. *Pay attention to the message behind the message.* Begin to observe your own patterns of interaction to make sure they are inclusive and respectful. For example, in conversations with learners, do you allow them to be the center of attention, or do you bring the attention back to yourself as quickly as you can? Do you allow time for learners to share their own personal experiences, or do you tell your own stories and leave little time for learner interaction? Do you say, "Now we'll discuss . . ." and then do all the talking? Do you paraphrase what a learner has said so that she knows you have listened to her? Is what you say congruent with your body language and voice tone? Both your verbal and nonverbal habits of interaction will either enhance or detract from the learning experience. Learners will pick up the messages you send, even when you're not aware of sending them. Pay attention, and then change the messages that aren't consistent with brain-friendly training.

6. *Step aside and let them learn.* Leave your ego at the door. Forget that you know more than your learners do. Forget that you are the subject-matter expert. Challenge yourself to find ways to teach them without always being the center of their attention and focus. Make this your goal in choosing activities that engage and involve them throughout the entire learning experience. Put them center-stage, and create ways for them to shine as they learn.

CONCLUSIONS

In *How the Brain Learns* (2006), David Sousa sums up the crucial role educators and trainers play in creating learning experiences that are brain-friendly. "Educators [and trainers] are in the only profession whose job is to change the human brain every day" (p. 10). It is our challenge to figure out what works and what doesn't, to determine the effectiveness of new training strategies, to let go of old ones that serve learners poorly, to add to existing knowledge about how the human brain learns, and to teach others what we know.

Brain-friendly training is nothing more (or less) than delivering instruction designed around the human brain. We are the brain scientists of the classroom. We get to do the experiments, make the discoveries, and record the results so that others can use what we learn.

Knowledge depends on engagement.
Engagement is inseparable from empowerment.
Empowerment means the opportunity to contribute.
Learning is an act of participation.
We are all lifelong learners.

Jay Cross and the IRL (Institute for Research on Learning)
Informal Learning, 2007, pp. 245–246

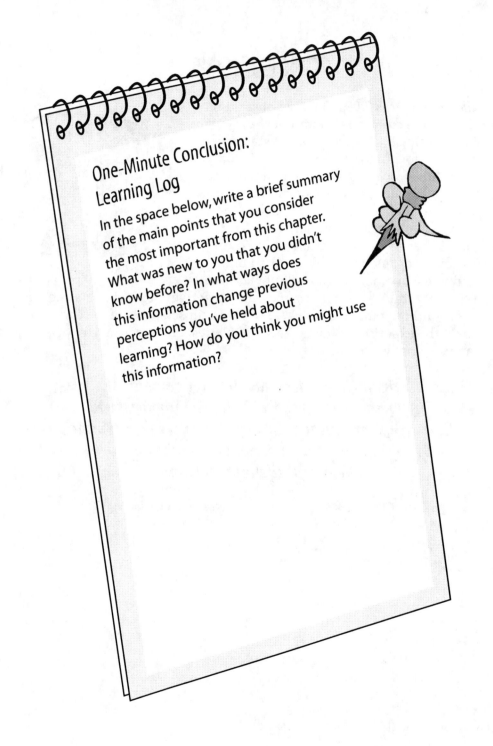

One-Minute Conclusion:
Learning Log

In the space below, write a brief summary of the main points that you consider the most important from this chapter. What was new to you that you didn't know before? In what ways does this information change previous perceptions you've held about learning? How do you think you might use this information?

Training from the BACK of the Room!

Bonus One-Minute Conclusion: Find That Phrase

BONUS

Fill in the following sentences with the phrases listed below. Each phrase will be used just once, so you can self-check your answers by reading the sentences aloud. If they make sense, your answers are correct.

1. My greatest challenge, according to this book, is to....

   _____
   _____.

2. _____ describes the brain's ability to ignore anything repetitive or routine.

3. Brain-friendly training uses _____
   _____
   _____.

4. Instructor-led, content-centered, lecture-saturated training is
   _____

5. Television has conditioned us to getting our information in
   _____

6. Brain-friendly training environments are
   _____

Phrases:
- small "chunks" or segments of time
- brain-antagonistic
- habituation
- informal, visually interesting, collaborative places to be
- positive emotions, multisensory stimulation, instructional variety, and active participation
- step aside and talk less, so that learners can talk, interact, teach and learn from each other

Trainer's Toolbox

Look back through this chapter and gather the concepts and activities that are the most useful to you. Write them in this toolbox and flag this page so you can find these tools quickly.

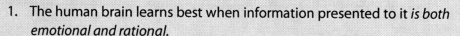

Answers to the One-Minute Connections: Fast Pass

Check your answers against the ones below. One question remains: How are you going to apply this information the next time you teach or train?

1. The human brain learns best when information presented to it *is both emotional and rational.*
2. For the human brain, paying attention is most often *an unconscious choice.*
3. Attention increases when the learning environment *changes,* and decreases when the environment *doesn't change.*
4. *Shorter* segments of instruction are better than *longer* ones.
5. Humans remember more *when they figure things out for themselves.*
6. For optimal learning, the physical body needs to be *active* while the brain/mind is engaged.

Training from the BACK of the Room!

The 4 Cs

A Quick and Remarkably Effective Instructional Design Process

We are not, cannot be, about designing content.
A fundamental perspective I want you to take away
is that we are designing experiences.

Clark Quinn
Engaging Learning, 2005, p. 10

● ●

CONNECTIONS

One-Minute Connection: Fast Pass

When you create a new learning experience, that is, a class, lesson, workshop, presentation, or training, which sentence best describes what you do? Circle one, or write in your own answer:

- *I just put it all together without any formal plan.*
- *I use an instructional design model I was taught.*
- *I make up my own instructional design plan and use it.*
- *Someone else has done the design; I just teach the material.*
- *I haven't a clue - I just do it and have never thought much about it.*
- *Another answer:* _____

(continued)

You need to be aware of how you currently design training so that, after reading this chapter, you'll know what you want to continue doing, and what you want to change. This chapter introduces you to the 4 Cs, a four-step instructional design and delivery process that is easy, takes little time to learn and apply, and is simple enough to remember. You can use this process with any training topic or audience, and whenever you plan any kind of information-delivery program.

Many trainers design training without any formal process or procedure. Or, if they learned a specific method, they may not use it because it isn't easy, time-relevant, or memorable enough. The 4 Cs is the answer to these issues.

Imagine That . . .

You are attending Don's community college night class titled "An Introduction to Financial Investment." As you walk into the room, Don greets you and hands you an index card that reads: *"New to financial investing? Please stand by the wall on your right. Have some experience at investing? Please stand by the wall on your left. Then introduce yourself to three other people and tell them what you want to learn from this class."* Two groups of students begin to form, and you join the less-experienced one. You spend a few minutes chatting with the others; then Don instructs you to find someone from the opposite group to be a learning partner for the class. You and your partner sit at a table with two other pairs of students—a pleasant mix of more-experienced and less-experienced investors.

After Don introduces himself, he asks the table groups to work together to quickly sort a pile of index cards that are on each table. Each card is printed with a statement related to financial investment, and your group has to sort the cards into two piles: a "Myth" pile and a "Fact" pile. Following this quick card-sorting activity, Don says that you will find out if your group sorted the cards correctly by listening for that information in his introductory lecture. He passes out an interesting note-taking page labeled "Concept Map" and directs you to take notes as he speaks. He pauses after short segments of information so that you can jot down some notes and so that your table group can check its Myth/Fact cards. At the end of the short lecture, your table group has changed a few of the cards from one pile to the other. In addition, you have filled in the note-taking page with the learning outcomes of the class, as well as some introductory investment information.

Then Don announces that you will spend the next fifty minutes at Concept Centers around the room. He draws your attention to a number of tables set up along the walls. Each table is marked with a number and a title: #1—Stocks; #2—Bonds; #3—Mutual Funds; #4—Annuities; #5—Money Markets. You join a Concept Centers group and spend about ten minutes at each center, learning about different investment options from the handouts, discussion questions, games, and short quizzes found on the tables. The hour passes quickly, as you rotate from center to center, participating in a quick overview of each investment option. The activity ends with a discussion of what students learned from the centers that they didn't know before.

Following the Concept Center activity, Don hands out printed case studies to each table group. He explains that your table group is a financial planning company that has to give investment advice to the person in the case study. Your group will discuss the case, agree on the best advice to give, and then present this information to the class. The class will have a chance to discuss the advice and offer any comments or suggestions. Don will give his advice too. This practice activity lasts about forty-five minutes.

Finally, before the class ends for the evening, Don instructs you to fill out a "Learning Log"—sort of a journal page—of what you learned, questions you have for the next class, and possible ways you might use this new information.

There is an excited buzz among students as you walk out the door. You realize that Don's design of the class made all the difference between a topic that could have been dull and boring and a topic that ended up being fascinating and engaging from beginning to end.

Let's step back and take a look at what Don did to keep you actively engaged for three full hours. He designed and delivered the class using a powerful, four-step instructional method called the 4 Cs:

1. First, you made meaningful *connections* to the topic and to the other students with the Where Do You Stand and Myth/Fact activities.

2. Second, you were actively involved as you learned a number of investment *concepts*, first by taking notes on a Graphic Organizer, and then by participating in Concept Centers.

3. Third, you discussed and presented the case studies with your table group, a *concrete practice* strategy that was relevant and useful.

4. Fourth, you and the other students reached your own *conclusions* about what you learned as you used a Learning Log to summarize and evaluate your own learning progress.

CONCEPTS

The 4 Cs instructional design process is easy for trainers to remember and use, and it's a training delivery process that is brain-friendly for learners as well. In fact, that is what makes it different from so many other instructional design models: Its steps are *both* design and delivery guides. They go hand-in-hand. As you design, you are creating the delivery at the same time—sort of a two-for-one approach that saves you time while integrating the two processes—design and delivery—into one seamless whole.

   Here is a short description of each of the four design and delivery steps, and what learners will be doing during each step:

1. *Connections.* This is the beginning or opening of a training. It can also include pre-training time as well. During the Connections step, learners make connections with what they already know, or think they know, about the training topic. They also make connections with what they will learn or want to learn with other learners in the training group, and with you, the trainer. Part One of this book gives you more details about this step, as well as fifteen Connection activities.

2. *Concepts.* This is the direct instruction, lecture, or presentation part of a training. During the Concepts step, learners take in new information in multi-sensory ways: hearing, seeing, discussing, writing, reflecting, imagining, participating, and teaching it to others. Part Two of this book gives you more information about Concepts, as well as twenty activities.

3. *Concrete Practice.* This is the active review that usually follows information-delivery. During the Concrete Practice step, learners actively practice a skill using the new information, participate in an active review of what they have learned, and again teach others what they know or can now do. Part Three of this book offers you detailed information and fifteen activities for this step.

4. *Conclusions.* This is the wrap-up or closing part of a training. It can also include post-training time as well. During the Conclusions step, learners summarize what they have learned, evaluate it, make a commitment to use it at work or in their lives, and end with a short celebration of their learning experience. Part Four of this book includes detailed information and fifteen activities for this step.

The 4 Cs and Accelerated Learning

The 4 Cs instructional design and delivery process has its roots in educational and psychological research, which began in the latter half of the 20th century. More recently, discoveries in the field of neuroscience, as well as availability of new information on learning styles, learning modalities, and multiple intelligences, have all contributed to an approach to teaching and training that we now call Accelerated Learning (International Alliance for Learning, *The History of Accelerated Learning,* www.ialearn.org,/ALHistory.php).

Dave Meier, the director for The Center for Accelerated Learning in Lake Geneva, Wisconsin, synthesized the best of the research from the past five decades in his book *The Accelerated Learning Handbook* (2000). According to Meier, the following are the basic tenets of Accelerated Learning:

- Learning involves the body as well as the mind.

- Learning is fundamentally an act of creation, not consumption of information.

- Learning takes place on many levels at once in the human brain, and is not a linear, one-thing-at-a-time brain activity.

- Collaboration increases learning; isolation and competition decrease it.

- Learning occurs through active doing, with time for reflection and feedback, not through passive listening.

- Positive emotions and mental imagery improve learning; the lack of both inhibits learning.

(pp. 9–10)

Accelerated Learning, therefore, is a brain-friendly approach to teaching and learning. The brain-friendly training elements from the previous chapter (listed below as a reminder) are also elements of Accelerated Learning:

1. Positive emotional experiences

2. Multi-sensory stimulation and novelty

3. Instructional variety and choices

4. Active participation and collaboration

5. Informal learning environments

From the Accelerated Learning research, as well as work done by others in the fields of education and psychology, came a four-step instructional design and delivery model based on the way most people learn best. The model has been

Try This

An AL Data Hunt. If you are interested in learning more about the 20th century research on Accelerated Learning, or more about brain research in general, browse the Great Resources section in the back of this book for an anecdotal list of some of the best. Also, do an Internet search with the following keywords, and see what you find:

- Accelerated Learning
- Brain-Based Learning and Training
- Brain-Friendly Learning and Training
- The Learning Cycle
- Neuroscience and Learning

The best Internet resource for Accelerated Learning information is www.alcenter.com, the official website for The Center for Accelerated Learning. You'll find free tips, as well as information about one of the most outstanding reference tools available: *The Accelerated Learning Coursebuilder* (1999), authored and compiled by the Center's co-director, Tom Meier. The Coursebuilder covers all aspects of Accelerated Learning, and includes hundreds of useful learning activities and dozens of examples of the four-step instructional design and delivery model.

adapted by many educators and trainers, as they adjust it to fit the needs of their own training programs and learners.

In his book, Meier titled the model "the four-phase learning cycle" (p. 53), with the following labels for each step:

- Phase One: Preparation—the arousal of interest and opening up to learning

- Phase Two: Presentation—the encounter of new knowledge or skills

- Phase Three: Practice—the integration of what has been learned

- Phase Four: Performance—the application of the new knowledge or skills in real life

In *The Ten-Minute Trainer*, I called the model "The Training Map" and gave the four steps these labels:

- Step One: Making the Connections
- Step Two: Explaining the Concepts
- Step Three: Practicing the Skills
- Step Four: Celebrating the Learning

In this book, the 4 Cs is my current adaptation of the research, with simpler labels for each of the four steps, to make them easier to remember and apply.

I point this out only to illustrate that the labels serve to help you remember the design and delivery process. It doesn't really matter what you call each step. In fact, as you familiarize yourself with the model, you will probably create your own version of it, one that fits both your expertise as a trainer and the learning needs of your training participants. Many participants in my train-the-trainer programs have already shortened the 4 Cs words (Connections, Concepts, Concrete Practice, Conclusions) to the simpler C1, C2, C3, and C4. It still works.

In *The Accelerated Learning Coursebuilder* (1999, p. 19), Tom Meier summarizes the four steps by saying, "This four-part model is universal. It applies to children . . . teenagers . . . workers . . . people of all ages. Unless all four of these phases are present in one form or another in a learning program, fast and effective learning cannot occur."

Design and Delivery Reminders

Here are a few general suggestions to keep in mind as you experiment with this design and delivery model:

- *Begin with the end in mind.* This reminder is from Stephen Covey's *The Seven Habits of Highly Effective People* (2004). The quote applies to effective training as well. What do you want your learners to be able to do with what they learn? Put another way, what are the *observable behaviors,* also called learning outcomes or objectives, that will show you (or your company/institution) that training participants "got it"? Make a list, then tie everything in the training to this list. An example of an observable learning outcome is: In an insect abatement class, technicians will *demonstrate* appropriate insecticide spraying procedures. An unobservable learning outcome is: Technicians will *know* the spraying procedures. For more detailed information about writing effective learning outcomes, see the chapter in this book titled "Begin with the End: A Fresh Approach to Learning Outcomes."

- *Teach only the need-to-knows.* One of the most challenging things for trainers to do is to sort out the concepts learners need to know from the nice-to-know but unessential information. All too often, trainers assume that all the conceptual details are equally important and must be taught. Here is an example: In using a new database program, company employees need to know how to log on, log off, and when the security codes will change—these are important facts, without which they cannot do their jobs. Unessential information might be why the company decided to change the database program, and the extra benefits of using the new program versus the old one. Regarding your own training programs, ask yourself, *"What it is the learners need to know in order to do their jobs better, or in order to improve their lives?"* A more specific question is, *"What is it that employees need to know, the lack of which could cost them their jobs?"* This is the information you design into the concepts segment of the 4 Cs. You put all the other nice-to-know information into handouts or resource materials, or save it for later in the training when there is extra time to cover it.

- *Design out of order.* It doesn't matter how you put the pieces together. Some trainers list all the concepts, then decide the practice activities, connections, and conclusions. Other trainers design in order, beginning with connections and moving through the other three steps. Still others brainstorm a dozen or so instructional activities, then choose from this list the ones to put into the design steps. You can design the pieces that are the most interesting first, or the most difficult, or the ones you already have information or activities for. Do what is easiest or works best for you.

- *Play with the pieces.* As you put the design elements together, play with a variety of options before making a final decision as to what you will include in each step. One way you can do this is to write down all the important topic-related concepts and a number of topic-related activities, each on a different piece of paper or sticky note. After that, move pieces around, and figure out what goes together and what to let go of. For example, if a game you love doesn't really fit into the time allotted or the concepts being learned, don't include the game. Save it for another training. Here is another example: In a customer service training, it makes sense to follow the lecture on effective customer service with skits (role plays) in which learners practice the service procedures. It doesn't make sense to immediately begin the next lecture segment on Point of Service (POS) procedures without reviewing the first lecture segment. It also doesn't make sense to include concepts that aren't part of the learning outcomes. Remember to align every concept and activity with the learning outcomes of the training.

- *Work out the flow.* Once you have all the pieces in place, then imagine how they would flow together, how one piece fits with the other, and how they segue from one to the other. If they seem disjointed or fragmented, change them so that each step links to the next. At this point, you can even change the order of the steps, if that seems to work better. For example, you might begin with connections, then flip back and forth between concepts and concrete practice as you cover a number of content pieces. Then you wrap the whole training up with conclusions. Here is a more specific example: In a job search training, learners first decide the kind of jobs they want to apply for (Connections). Then they learn and practice how to fill out the application, write a resume, call for an appointment, go to a job interview, and follow up afterwards (Concepts and Concrete Practice go hand in hand here). Finally, they actually experience a real job interview and assess how they did (Conclusions).

- *Deliver in order.* Once you have designed each of the four steps and have included learner activities in each step, you will actually deliver the training in the order the steps naturally flow: Connections, Concepts, Concrete Practice, Conclusions. As I mentioned above, sometimes you'll vary the order by going back and forth between two steps, or you'll combine two steps (Concepts and Concrete Practice often work better this way). This is totally acceptable. Generally, though, your delivery will be sequential. The timing of each step will depend on many variables: the length of the training, the amount of information to be taught, group size, access to resources, and specific learning outcomes, to name a few.

- *Hand over as much of it as you can.* Consider the option of letting learners teach some of the content to each other. Also allow them to lead as many of the review activities as possible. With a little preparation (and ideas from Parts One, Two, Three, and Four of this book), you will be surprised at how effective learners are at teaching and learning from each other.

- *If it doesn't work, change it.* The saying "Nothing works all the time" holds true for instructional design as well. Although the 4 Cs will work most of the time for most of your learners, sometimes even the best planned training will hit unexpected bumps. Be flexible and ready to change the plan if you need to.

- *Step aside and let them learn.* Remind yourself that, the more your learners talk (read that: discuss, write, move, create, question, participate, practice, and teach each other), the more they will learn. Make sure you have created opportunities for their active involvement during each step of the design and delivery process.

CONCRETE PRACTICE

Ten-Minute CONCEPT practice

Bringing It Home

Let's put the 4 Cs into practice with a topic *you* teach. If you decide to do this activity, allow yourself about ten minutes. Your time will be well spent because, at the end of the activity, you will

- *Have completed* an instructional design piece you can use the next time you train.
- *Have experienced* the instructional design process using material that is meaningful to you.
- *Be able to duplicate* the process more easily the next time you use it.
- *Be able to explain* the process to colleagues when they ask you how you design training.

In order to do this exercise, you'll need a dozen index cards or medium-size Post-it® Notes, five sheets of blank printer paper, and a pen or pencil. Once

Training from the BACK of the Room!

you've gathered the materials, work through the following steps (the italicized steps are those that were listed earlier in this chapter):

1. In large print, label one paper "Topic and Learning Outcomes." Label each of the four other sheets with one of each of the 4 Cs steps: Connections, Concepts, Concrete Practice, and Conclusions. Lay the sheets of paper out on the table in front of you.

2. Think of a topic you teach. For example, your topic might be customer service skills, using a company database program, new hire orientation, safety on the job, leadership, or others. Write one topic on one index card and lay it on the Topic and Learning Outcomes paper. (The topic card from Don's financial investment class, the example that began this chapter, reads: " An Introduction to Financial Investment.")

3. *Begin with the end in mind.* Think of one learning outcome, that is, one observable behavior you want your learners to be able to demonstrate by the end of the training. Although there can be many learning outcomes for one topic, just choose one outcome for now. You can go back and write the others later. A reminder: Learning outcomes must be observable, so do *not* use the words "know," "understand," or "learn." Write the learning outcome on another index card and put it below your topic card on the Topic and Learning Outcomes paper. Everything you do from this point on will be tied to this learning outcome. (Don's learning outcome card reads: "Define and explain five investment options.")

4. *Teach only the need-to-knows.* Write down a few topic-related concepts, one per card. Place these on the Concepts paper. This is the need-to-know information that you'll cover during the training. (Don's concept cards read: "Overview of financial investment; investment options: stocks, bonds, annuities, mutual funds, money markets—definitions, descriptions, examples.")

5. *Design out of order.* Think of some ways you might involve learners as you teach them the concepts. Jot these down on index cards as well and place them on the Concepts paper, along with the concepts cards. Your activities can be ones you've used before, ones you've seen other trainers use, or ones listed in Part Two of this book. (For Don, these cards read: "Concept Map note-taking page; Concept Centers." Both activities are from Part Two of this book.)

(continued)

6. Fill in one or two concrete practice cards and put them on the Concrete Practice paper. Remember, these will be the skills practice or review activities to follow the concepts step. You can use activities from Part Three of this book. (Don's practice cards read: "Small group case study discussions; small group presentations to large group; large group discussion.")

7. Now that you have the concepts and concrete practice pieces planned, in your mind return to the beginning of the training. Think about the connections to the topic and to each other that learners need to make during the opening. Again, you can choose activities you're familiar with, ones you've seen used, or ones from Part One of this book. Jot down your connection activities on index cards and place them on the Connections paper. You can choose just one activity, or more than one, if you have time for others. (Don's cards read: "Where Do You Stand" and "Myth/Fact activities." Both are from Part One of this book.)

8. Think about how you want learners to summarize, evaluate, and use what they've learned. Write out another card or two that describe the conclusion pieces, and place these on the Conclusions paper. (Don's conclusion card reads: "Learning Logs"—from Part Four of this book.)

9. *Play with the pieces and work out the flow.* Imagine how the training would flow from step to step as you orchestrate the 4 Cs' concepts and activities. Imagine how it would feel to be a learner as each step is implemented. Ask yourself the following questions; then rearrange the index cards as necessary:
   - *What can I add or change so that the training flows easily from one step to the next?*
   - *Am I teaching only the need-to-know information?*
   - *What can I hand over to the learners to teach?*
   - *Are all the steps tied to the learning outcome?*
   - *Are learners engaged during every step of the process?*

10. *Deliver in order.* Now that you have all the pieces filled in, put the entire training process in order by rearranging the papers and cards to read: Topic and Learning Outcomes, Connections, Concepts, Concrete Practice, Conclusions.

11. *Hand over as much of it as you can, then step aside and let them learn.* Enough said!

You're done with your design. All that remains is to translate the training design into a printable form that works for you. Type it into your computer and print it out, outline it on paper, arrange the index cards into a sequential stack, script it—do whatever works so that you'll have it ready to go. You'll also need to list the details later: training materials, slides, handouts, timeline, and all the training essentials. But you have the basic design and delivery process outlined from this exercise. And you've created a brain-friendly training, one that engages learners during the entire experience, in a very short period of time. Give yourself a pat on the back. Then go deliver the training and record the results.

● ●

CONCLUSIONS

This chapter has given you an overview of the 4 Cs instructional design and delivery process. Because the model is based on Accelerated Learning, it is a brain-friendly and whole-brain approach to designing and delivering effective training. This process also ensures that participants will be engaged and involved during the entire learning experience, which ultimately increases retention and application of learned material.

At the end of this chapter you will find:

● 4 Cs reference guide and job aid

● 4 Cs template for designing your own training

● 4 Cs example with a classroom lesson

● 4 Cs example with a webinar lesson

● 4 Cs example with a computer-based self-study lesson

The next four parts of the book give you detailed definitions and explanations of each of the four steps in this design and delivery model. In addition, these four parts also give you sixty-five instructional strategies to choose from as you design each step. You'll find plenty of guidance, suggestions, activities, resources, tips, and more, to help you use this easy and remarkably effective instructional design process.

What if students everywhere,
in addition to just reading books,
listening to lectures, and writing homework papers,
truly engaged (and ultimately created)
wondrous new [learning] environments?

Clark Quinn
Engaging Learning, 2005, p. 271

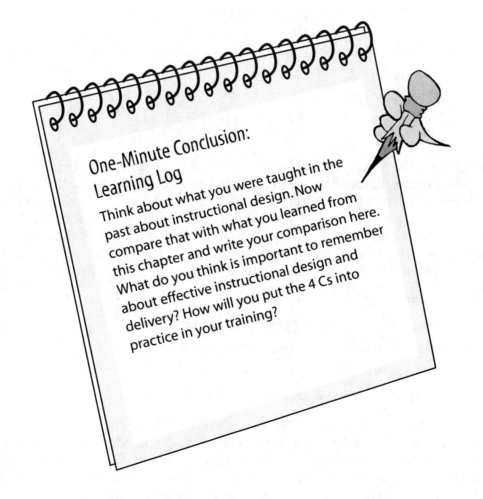

One-Minute Conclusion:
Learning Log

Think about what you were taught in the
past about instructional design. Now
compare that with what you learned from
this chapter and write your comparison here.
What do you think is important to remember
about effective instructional design and
delivery? How will you put the 4 Cs into
practice in your training?

Trainer's Toolbox

Look back through this chapter for ideas and strategies you might use in your own training. By writing them here, you increase the likelihood that you will remember and use them later. Don't forget to flag this page.

The 4 Cs Instructional Design Model

This is a reference page and a training job aid. Use it whenever you design a training, presentation, workshop, class, or lesson.

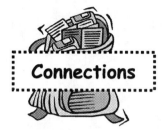

Connections

Learners make connections with what they already know or think they know about the training topic, with what they will learn, with what they want to learn, and with each other.

Concepts

Learners take in new information in multisensory ways: hearing, seeing, discussing, writing, reflecting, imagining, participating, and teaching it to others.

Concrete Practice

Learners actively practice the new skills, or they participate in an active review of the new knowledge they have learned.

Conclusions

Learners summarize what they have learned, evaluate it, celebrate it, and create action plans for how they plan to use the new knowledge or skills after the training is over.

The 4 Cs
Template for Designing Your Own Training

Topic: _____

Audience: _____ **Time:** _____

Learning Outcomes: _____

_____

_____

> **Connections**
>
>
>
>

> **Concepts**
>
>
>
>
>

> **Concrete Practice**
>
>
>
>

> **Conclusions**
>
>
>
>

Note: This is an example of a lesson using the 4 Cs. This example is from the "Imagine That ..." beginning section of this chapter: Don's class on financial investment.

The 4 Cs
Template for Designing Your Own Training

Topic: *An Introduction to Financial Investment*

Audience: *Twenty community college students*   **Time:** *Three hours*

Learning Outcomes: *Define and explain five investment options.*

Connections

1. Concepts: Investment experience; prior investment knowledge; learning outcomes.

2. Learner Activities: Where Do You Stand; Myth and Fact Game.

Concepts

1. Concepts: Overview of financial investment; overview of five investment options - stocks, bonds, annuities, mutual funds, money markets.

2. Learner Activities: Concept Maps; Myth and Fact Game (revisited); Concept Centers.

Concrete Practice

1. Concepts: Using the financial investment information in a simulation.

2. Learner Activities: Small group case study discussions; small group presentations to large group; large group discussion.

Conclusions

1. Concepts: Defining, explaining, and summarizing the information.

2. Learner Activities: Learning Logs.

Note: This is an example of a synchronous (real-time), webinar lesson, using computers and printed worksheets for the visuals components and phone lines for the auditory components.

The 4 Cs
Template for Designing Your Own Training

Topic: *An Introduction to the World of Medicare Insurance*

Audience: *Twelve new customer service representatives* **Time:** *One hour*

Learning Outcomes: *Explain Medicare's purpose and history, and state a fact about each of four parts - Parts A, B, C, and D.*

Connections

1. Concepts: Pre-knowledge - "Write five facts you know, or have heard, about the Medicare Insurance Program" - learning outcomes; learners' goals.

2. Learner Activities: Think It Then Ink It; Dot-Voting; pre-test.

Concepts

1. Concepts: Overview of Medicare's purpose, history, and the differences among the four insurance programs offered - Parts A, B, C, and D.

2. Learner Activities: Fill-in worksheets; Rapid Responses; Stand, Stretch, and Speak.

Concrete Practice

1. Concepts: Active review of the information.

2. Learner Activities: Myth and Fact Game (using computers instead of cards), quiz questions, whole group discussion.

Conclusions

1. Concepts: Explaining and summarizing what they learned and listing facts about the four programs offered - "If someone asked you to write a short newspaper article about Medicare, what would you write?"

2. Learner Activities: News article writing and reporting; post-test.

Note: This is an example of a computer-based, self-study lesson using a self-paced, computerized manual, and downloaded worksheets.

The 4 Cs
Template for Designing Your Own Training

Topic: *Native Subterranean Termites*

Audience: *self-study*   **Time:** *One hour*

Learning Outcomes: *List at least a dozen facts about termites that would be beneficial for an insect abatement specialist to know.*

Connections

1. Concepts: Prior knowledge of termites; learning outcomes.

2. Learner Activities: Web Hunt; Take a Guess.

Concepts

1. Concepts: Termite terms, biology, habits, food, caste system, life cycle, reasons for pest-control.

2. Learner Activities: Termite-shaped Concept Map and other worksheets; Beat the Clock; Think It Then Ink It; Bend, Breathe, and Write.

Concrete Practice

1. Concepts: Using the information in vignettes from real-life abatement situations.

2. Learner Activities: Written responses to Flash animation vignettes; written quiz questions with immediate feedback.

Conclusions

1. Concepts: Facts about termites.

2. Learner Activities: 4-Square Feedback (to be emailed to supervisor); post-test.

     Training from the BACK of the Room!

part ONE

Connections

What You Need to Know About Connections

Since most learning is social,
wouldn't it be more effective
to put [learners] in touch with others
so they can learn from one another?

Jay Cross
Informal Learning, 2007, p. 39

Basic Concept Map for This Chapter

As you read, write a summary for each concept.

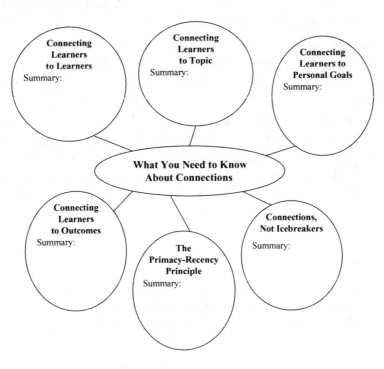

CONNECTIONS

One-Minute Connection: Fast Pass

Check off one or more of the sentences below that describe the usual ways most traditional training programs begin:

- ❑ Trainer welcomes learners and introduces himself/herself.
- ❑ Trainer announces the training title, topics, and learning objectives.
- ❑ If using slides, trainer reads aloud the training title, purpose, goals, and learning objectives displayed on the screen.
- ❑ Trainer reviews ground rules and housekeeping suggestions (breaks, exits, bathroom locations, cell phone protocol, and the like).
- ❑ Learners stand and introduce themselves.
- ❑ Learners participate in an icebreaker or social activity that may have nothing to do with the training topic.

You probably checked off most, if not all, of the sentences because they all describe components of the beginning of traditional training programs. There is nothing wrong with this list, except that these components have *nothing* to do with learning.

That is not to say that these pieces should be left out of the opening. They can be included later; they just don't belong at the very beginning of a training. Something else needs to happen first so that participants are *learning* from the moment they walk in the door. In this chapter, you will discover the importance of connections, and why and how to engage learners right from the start.

Imagine That . . .

You are attending a training about a new database program your company has purchased. This is highly technical information that is being taught in a computer lab. You are somewhat familiar with the program's general features because you read the electronic overview that the company sent to you as part of the training warm-up exercises. You walk in expecting to sit at a computer and wait for the trainer, Marie, to begin talking. Instead, you notice a slide displayed on the front screen that says: "Please form a standing group with three other employees and tell them what you learned from the overview page you read before coming here." Upbeat music plays in the background as you join a standing group and begin discussing what you already know about the database program.

After a few minutes, Marie directs everyone's attention to a wall chart on which she has listed learning outcomes for the training. She passes out sheets of colored dots and explains that you will read the chart and place dots beside two learning outcomes that, for you, are the most important. After sticking the two dots to the chart, you find a computer station and sit down. You notice that you are sitting next to another employee and that you will be working as partners on the same computer as you learn the new program.

Marie gives you another couple of minutes to tell your computer partner which learning outcomes you dotted, why you dotted them, and what you want to take away from the training.

Only now does Marie introduce herself. She summarizes what you have done so far, what you will learn, and other general suggestions for making the training a success.

What have you done during the first ten minutes of this training? Let's make a short list:

- *You made some mental connections* with what you already know and what you really want to learn.

- *You made social connections* with the other learners in content-related ways, first by forming standing groups, and then by pairing up with a computer partner. Both times you discussed information related to the training topic.

- *You reviewed the learning outcomes* three times and three different ways: by reading them silently, evaluating and prioritizing them with the dots, and explaining them to a partner.

You didn't realize it, but you actually participated in three connection activities: a Standing Fast Pass, Dot-Voting, and a Turn and Talk. Marie waited until after the connection activities were over before she gave her introduction and class overview.

CONCEPTS

Connections are short, learner-focused opening activities that include the following four important elements:

- *Connecting learners to other learners* in positive and meaningful ways that are relevant to the training topic
- *Connecting learners to the topic*, that is, to what they already know, or think they know, about the information to be learned
- *Connecting learners to their own learning goals*—what they personally want to take away from the training
- *Connecting learners to the learning outcomes*—what they will be able to do as a result of what they learn

In addition, learners also connect to the trainer and to the training environment. This means that learners begin to feel relaxed and at ease with the trainer—they see the trainer as friendly, knowledgeable, professional yet approachable. And they feel comfortable in the learning environment, which is welcoming, informal, visually pleasant, and mentally stimulating.

With opening activities that engage learners from the moment they walk into the room, learners can make all these connections in a matter of a few minutes. With connections, learners quickly become interested, engaged, intrigued, motivated, and eager to learn more.

Let's take a closer look at these four connection elements.

Connecting Learners to Learners

Most people learn better when they are with friends rather than with a group of strangers. This is because humans usually feel psychologically safer with people they know. Psychological safety means that learners can

- *Ask questions.*
- *Try things out.*
- *Make mistakes.*
- *Express opinions.*
- *Take risks while learning.*

Psychological safety, therefore, is really important to the learning process.

Often, people who attend a training together also work together. Trainers may assume that, because they work together, they are friends, or at least on friendly terms with each other. Because of this assumption, trainers may think that individuals in the group feel safe with one another. This is not always the case.

Some work environments are tense, stressful places, competitive rather than cooperative, where employees learn to hide mistakes, refrain from voicing opinions or asking questions, and play it safe rather than taking risks. So when people who work together attend a training together, they may not automatically feel safe with each other. Psychological safety must be designed and built into the learning experience, and it must be nurtured during the entire time learners spend together.

During a training program, psychological safety goes deeper than learners simply introducing themselves to each other or sharing a few facts about themselves with other learners. In training, psychological safety means that, from the moment learners enter the room, they are immersed in meaningful, topic-related activities that help them form a strong learning community, that is, a group of folks who share a common goal of learning together in positive, respectful ways. As Jay Cross puts it in *Informal Learning* (2007), "Learning is social. We learn from, by, and with other people. . . . Learning is best understood as an interaction among practitioners, rather than a process in which a producer provides knowledge to a consumer" (p. 63).

Connecting Learners to Topic

No matter what the age, culture, or gender, learners do not come to a learning experience with blank slates for brains. Learners, especially adults, come with experiences and information they have gathered along the way, some of it accurate and some of it not, but all of it in their heads nevertheless.

Most learners know something about most training topics. If they don't know a few facts about the specific content, they certainly know facts about more generalized information that can include the topic at hand.

For example, if the training topic is a specific database program and the learner is a new employee, she may not know that particular program but she may have had prior experience with another company's database program. Or she may know some facts about other database programs that are popular with the general public.

Another example: A new hire at a retail store may not have any experience waiting on customers but has a lifetime of experience being a customer. He brings his own perspective of customer service from the receiving end, if not the service end.

The point is that when learners have a chance to review, discuss, or write down what they already know (or think they know) about the topic, they learn more because now any new information they learn during the training can be connected to the old, and the learning pathways in the brain are strengthened. Put another way, the brain's network of neural connections checks out information as soon as it is perceived to see if it fits with anything familiar. "Sustained attention to something that makes no sense is not only boring, it's almost impossible" (Wolfe, 2001, pp. 83–84). Making sense means connecting new information to older, more familiar learning.

Connecting Learners to Personal Goals

We all have our own reasons for learning. They may run a continuum from "My boss told me to take this workshop" to "I'm really interested in this topic" to " I'm considering a new job and want to learn all I can about this line of work."

Every learner who walks into a training room has his personal reasons for being there, even if he hasn't consciously thought about them. By bringing these reasons to the conscious level ("I guess I really want to learn how to be a better machine operator," or "I just want to learn how to do my job better") through discussion or writing, learners do the following:

- They align their own goals with the outcomes of the training.

- They have a clearer mental picture of what they want to take away from the training.

- They let go of any resistance because now they are focusing on what *they* consider important, and not just what the trainer says is important.

- They strengthen their ability to explain what they learned when the training is over because they took some time at the beginning to explain what they wanted to learn.

As Dave Meier asks in *The Accelerated Learning Handbook* (2000): "What do learners want the course to do for them and why? What would make the learning program truly valuable for them? The more people can articulate this up front, the more likely they are to connect with the course and find their own points of relevance" (p. 30).

Connecting Learners to Outcomes

Learning outcomes (also called learning objectives or performance criteria) are the knowledge or skills learners will be able to apply once the training is over. Learning outcomes provide the benchmarks for the success or failure of the learning experience.

What often happens in traditional training programs is that the trainer quickly lectures about the outcomes, perhaps using a set of slides and reading from them, perhaps not. Often, the trainer never mentions the outcomes again. Worse, the learners haven't had a chance to think about the outcomes or to align them with their own learning goals.

When you give learners the opportunity to talk about the learning outcomes, learners not only know what they will be able to do once the training is over, but they have a better chance of ending up there. They also have a greater degree of buy-in to the training because they've had time to connect the stated outcomes to their own personal learning goals. This connection doesn't happen when learners simply listen to, or read silently, a bulleted list. They must do something with the list: talk about it, evaluate it, prioritize it, add to it, debate it, edit it, or create their own lists.

Learning outcomes can also serve as periodic benchmarks during the training itself. Besides actively going over them at the beginning of the training, learners can review them at different times throughout the training—much like looking at signposts—to see where they are on their learning journey. Making the learning outcomes an integral part of the entire training is a much more interesting, and effective, way of helping learners assess their own learning while in the middle of it. When they do this, they get a sense of what they've learned so far, what they have yet to learn, and how much of the learning they can put to use in their own work or lives.

Fill-in-the-Blanks

Finish the sentences by filling in the missing words. Then check your answers.
  During the beginning or opening of a training, learners

1. Connect to _____   _____
   in positive and meaningful ways that are relevant to the training topic.
2. Connect to the _____ that is, to what they already know, or think they know, about the information to be learned.
3. Connect to their own _____   _____
   what they personally want to take away from the training.
4. Connect to the _____   _____
   what they will be able to do as a result of what they learn.

Here are the answers. Did you get them all?

1. Connect to *other learners* in positive and meaningful ways that are relevant to the training topic.
2. Connect to the *topic*, that is, to what they already know, or think they know, about the information to be learned.
3. Connect to their own *learning goals*—what they personally want to take away from the training.
4. Connect to the *learning outcomes*—what they will be able to do as a

The Primacy-Recency Principle

Remember the last vacation you took? Which parts of the vacation do you remember best: the beginning, middle, or end? How about a story you heard or read? Again, which pieces stand out in your mind: how it began, the middle action, or how it ended? Now think about a formal learning experience you participated in—a class, workshop, conference, presentation, or training. What parts of that experience stand out in your mind?

Most people remember the beginning and ending of an experience more easily than they remember all the events that took place in the middle. In addition, if the beginning and ending events are unusual or out-of-the-ordinary, people remember them longer than routine beginnings and endings. According to author David Sousa in *How the Brain Learns* (2006), "During a learning episode, we remember best that which comes first, second best that which comes last, and least that which comes just past the middle" (p. 89).

The Primacy-Recency Principle, then, is a reminder that learners will remember how the training begins and ends more easily than all the pieces in the middle, especially if the beginning and ending are not the traditional ones that most trainers use. Whenever you add interactive and memorable opening or closing activities—ones that create interesting and relevant connections—the opening or closing becomes an important part of the entire learning process.

As you learned from the Fast Pass activity at the beginning of this chapter, most training programs begin with housekeeping details—information that needs to be covered but not necessarily during the first few minutes of the program. Spending these precious "primacy" moments on introductions, agendas, overviews, and the like, is a waste of valuable *learning* time. You can always cover these details *after* learners have participated in an engaging, meaningful, topic-related opening.

Try This

Google It. Google is both a noun (as in the name of an Internet browser) and a commonly used, "computer-speak" verb (as in "to google" something, which means to search on www.Google.com for information by using keywords or concepts related to what you want to know about).

If you are curious to learn more, google "Primacy Recency Effect" and quickly skim the titles of over 22,000 articles about this concept. What you read will reinforce the importance of beginning and ending a training program with activities that engage learners and that connect them to the training concepts.

Connections, Not Icebreakers

Connection activities are *not* icebreakers, at least not as most trainers define and use icebreakers. Icebreakers are opening activities that usually have little to do with the training topic. Yes, icebreakers help people get to know each other socially so that they feel psychologically safer learning with each other. However, because many icebreakers have nothing to do with the training topic or concepts, they waste valuable learning time. Furthermore, when many trainers have a lot of content to cover in a short amount of time, they often launch into the content without any icebreaker.

Connections, on the other hand, connect learners to each other *and* to the training topic and concepts. When the opening activity is a connection, it adds to the overall learning.

An example of a common, non-topic-related icebreaker that many trainers use is "Two Truths and a Lie." During this exercise, learners state two truths and a one lie about themselves, and the group tries to guess what the lie is. Fun? Yes. Interesting? Perhaps. Relevant to learning? No. In order to make this particular icebreaker a connection activity, learners can make statements about the training topic instead (example: "When using this database program, change your password monthly"). Or they can make statements about their relationship to the topic (example: "I have used this database program for thirteen years"). Now the exercise connects learners to the topic, as well as to each other.

Again, there is a place in training for social icebreakers. Even though they do not help people learn about the topic, they do build social connections among learners. And when folks feel socially comfortable with each other, they are more willing to ask questions, state opinions, and make mistakes. If you have the gift of time to include icebreakers, fine. But if you have a lot of training material to cover in a limited amount of time, then convert the icebreaker you plan to use into a connection activity, so that learners connect to the topic as well as to each other.

● ●

CONCRETE PRACTICE

For your own concrete practice with this part of the book, you will choose one or more of the fifteen connection activities to use in your training programs.

Experiment with these activities, vary them, and change them to fit your group's learning needs. When you know which ones work best for your learners, integrate them into what you do and make them a regular part of your training.

The activities are divided into three sections. Here are the section and activity titles, and brief summaries:

- *Five Warm-Up (Pre-Training) Activities: Interview an Expert, Web Hunt, Scavenger Hunt, People and Personal Surveys, Pop Quiz.* Use these activities to spark learners' curiosity, interest, and involvement in training concepts a week or so before the training begins.

- *Five Fast Pass Activities: Dot Voting, Think It, Then Ink It, Post It, Turn and Talk, Take a Guess.* These activities engage learners from the moment they walk into the room. They are short and quick, only lasting a minute or two.

- *Five Start-Up Activities: Standing Survey, Wall Writing, Table Talk, Where Do You Stand?, Card Carousel.* These activities involve learners for a longer time at the beginning of a training. They usually last from about five to ten minutes.

One-Minute CONCRETE practice

Label It

Can you identify elements of the connections step of the 4 Cs? Label each opening activity with its correct element. Some activities may be labeled with two or more elements. Then check your answers.

Connection Components
1. Connecting learners to learners
2. Connecting learners to topic
3. Connecting learners to personal goals
4. Connecting learners to learning outcomes

(*continued*)

Opening Activities

A. Learners fill out WIIFMs ("What's In It For Me?") sticky notes stating what they want to learn. They stick the notes to a wall chart to review at the end of the training. Number _____

B. Learners do a Standing Survey, in which they walk around and ask other participants what they already know about the topic. They report the survey results when they return to their table groups. Number

_____

C. On index cards, learners do a quick Think and Write, jotting down at least three facts they already know about the topic. They read their lists to the people seated next to them. Number _____

D. Learners read a wall chart list of the learning outcomes. They pair up, discuss, and agree on which outcome is the most important to them. Each pair then uses a brightly-colored marker to circle the outcome they chose. Number _____

E. Learners form standing groups and discuss what it is they want to learn and which of the learning outcomes listed in the handout comes closest to their own learning goals. Number _____

F. Learners fill out a survey before the training, stating what they already know about the topic, what they want to learn from the training, and questions they have that they want answers for. Number

_____

Compare your answers to the ones below and receive a standing ovation if you got them all!

A. *3 Connecting learners to personal goals*
B. *1, 2 Connecting learners to learners and to topic*
C. *1, 2 Connecting learners to learners and to topic*
D. *1, 4 Connecting learners to learners and to learning outcomes*
E. *1, 3, 4 Connecting learners to learners, to personal goals, and to learning outcomes*
F. *2, 3 Connecting learners to topic and to personal goals*

CONCLUSIONS

The opening is an important time to connect learners to each other, to the topic, to their own learning goals, and to the learning outcomes. Any opening activity that does not have one or more of these connection components in it is a waste of *learning* time. If training truly focuses on learning, then connections will come first, and standard opening activities—introductions, agenda announcements, housekeeping suggestions, and the like—will take place second.

From now on, in your training programs, you will put the introductions, goals, agendas, announcements, ground rules, and other non-learning details *after* the connection activity or activities. And, while the connection activities take place, you will be walking around the room listening to the learners' conversations. There is no need for you to be in the front of the room since the learners are focusing on each other, *and not on you*, during the opening. What a radically different way to begin a learning experience!

We learn in context, with others, as we live and work.
Recognizing this fact is the first step
to crafting effective learning experiences.

Jay Cross
Informal Learning, 2007, p. 7

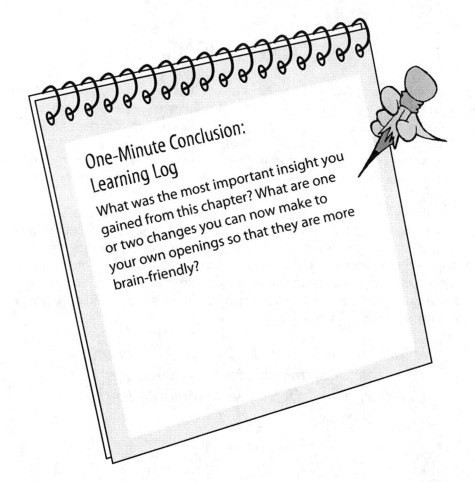

One-Minute Conclusion: Learning Log

What was the most important insight you gained from this chapter? What are one or two changes you can now make to your own openings so that they are more brain-friendly?

BONUS

Bonus One-Minute Conclusion: Card Sort

Let's do a quick activity to check your understanding of this chapter. On the facing page are two category headings: Effective Openings, Ineffective Openings. Sort the cards that are randomly listed under the headings by drawing a line from the card to its correct category. Then check your answers.

Cards

Effective Openings

1. The trainer begins by stating his background, experience, and credentials.

2. Learners listen while the trainer talks about the goals of the session.

3. In standing groups, learners discuss what they want to learn from the training.

4. Learners read the slides that state the learning outcomes of the training.

5. The trainer directs learners to gather around a chart listing the learning outcomes. They read the list together, and then each puts her initials beside the outcome she feels is most important.

6. Learners write the learning outcomes on a note-taking page, then check off the ones they consider important. Each tells another person what he checked, and then refers to the page again at the end of the training to review what was learned.

7. The trainer states the learning outcomes, agenda, and miscellaneous announcements.

Ineffective Openings

8. Learners form small collaborative groups and discuss what they already know about the topic and any questions they have that are related to the topic.

9. With partners, learners make lists of topic-related facts they already know. Then they share their lists with other pairs.

Turn the page for the answers.

Answer to Card Sort: Numbers 3, 5, 6, 8, and 9 are Effective Openings. Numbers 1, 2, 4, and 7 are Ineffective Openings. You are a master at connections!

Trainer's Toolbox

As you did with other chapters, look back through this chapter for anything you can use in your own training. Write these ideas here and then flag this page for later reference.

Connections:
Warm-Up Activities

What Is a Warm-Up?

A Warm-Up is a pre-training activity that learners do a week or so before the actual training program begins. Also called pre-exposure, a Warm-Up is a way of exposing learners to, and creating interest in, the topic and concepts they will be learning about. A Warm-Up creates a common language of topic-related words and phrases that learners will use when attending the training. A Warm-Up can also be a pre- and post-assessment tool, in that learners compare what they know before the training with what they know after the training is over. In effect, a Warm-Up is a wake up call to the brain, that is, a way of alerting the brain to get ready to learn.

What Does a Warm-Up Do?

By doing one or more Warm-Up activities, learners will

- *Begin* to gather information relevant to the training topic.
- *Add* to what they already know about the topic.
- *Correct* any beginning misconceptions they have about the topic.
- *List* their own experiences and learning goals related to the topic.
- *Familiarize* themselves with terms, language, and concepts of the training.
- *Become* curious about the topic and motivated to learn more.
- *Teach* others in the training what they have learned from the Warm-Up.
- *Assess and compare* what they know before and after the training.

Here are the important components of a successful Warm-Up activity:

- *Choices.* Warm-Ups work best when learners are able to choose from a list of pre-training activities. With choices, learners have a say in the kinds of activities they will do and will usually choose ones that are most interesting to *them*. Being able to choose motivates learners to do more than they might have done if they had only one required Warm-Up to do.

- *Individual accountability*. Learners need to know they will be expected to complete at least one Warm-Up activity. In order to build in this accountability, you must alert learners to how they will report what they have learned from the Warm-Up. Here are three examples:

  - Before the training, each learner sends an email to the trainer, or to all participants, with a short summary of what he has learned from the Warm-Up.

  - During training, learners present short Warm-Up summaries to partners.

  - After training, learners write short reports, comparing the Warm-Up information with facts learned during the training.

- *Timing*. Learners usually do Warm-Ups about one or two weeks prior to the training. If too long a time passes between the Warm-Ups and the actual training, the connections may be forgotten. If the Warm-Ups are too close to the training date, learners may not have the time to do them. In order for training participants to receive the Warm-Up choices in a timely fashion, send the activity instructions to them via email, blog, or intranet site.

Getting Ready

- **Materials:** No extra materials are necessary.
- **Setup:** No setup is necessary.
- **Group Size:** These activities can be done with one-on-one training as well as large groups.
- **Time**: Whatever time it takes for you to create the Warm-Up and for learners to do it.

Five Warm-Up Activities

1. Interview an Expert

Send out a Warm-Up that reads: *"During the two weeks prior to the training, find a person who knows a lot about this topic. Conduct a short interview in which you ask this person what he/she knows, what is important to learn, and some questions that you need to ask during the training. Write a short summary of your interview and be ready to present your summary during the training."*

2. Web Hunt

The printed instructions read: *"Before the training, look over the topic-related list of concepts, phrases, and words below. Choose two or three phrases from the list and do a Web Hunt (Internet search) with these key words. Jot down what you learn from the Web Hunt and be ready to share this information with other training participants."* Include a list of topic-related words, phrases, or concepts after the printed instructions.

3. Scavenger Hunt

Do the following:

- Create a list of from five to ten unusual, topic-related items, such as facts, objects, concepts, questions, books, articles, and so forth.

- Send out printed instructions that read: *"How many Scavenger Hunt items can you find? Find as many you can before the training. Record the date you find the item or the results asked for. There will be prizes at the training for those who find them all."*

- Learners write the information discovered or the date of completion. During the training, have small prizes available for the learners who found all the items.

Scavenger Hunt examples:

- *Find a topic-related article and write the title, source, and article date here.*

- *Find another employee who has taken this training and write his/her name here.*

- *Find out what you will be able to do once you have taken this training and write it here.*

- *Look up one the following authors* [include the names of some authors] *and write the titles of their topic-related books here.*

- *Find an object that can be a metaphor (a representation) of the training topic. Bring the object to the training, and be ready to explain how the training topic is like this object. Write down the name of the object you are bringing.* (Examples: For a team-building training, a branch with leaves can represent the company and its many employees. For a customer service class, a spoon can represent ladling out dollops of positive service, one "bite"—customer—at a time.

For a new-hire orientation, a light bulb can represent each employee who will bring new light and energy to the company.)

◎ *Find a worksheet, handout, newspaper article, or other printed material that is topic-related and bring it to the training. Write the title of what you are bringing.*

◎ *Ask another employee a topic-related question he has. Write down his name and question.*

◎ *Look up the training topic and write down the URLs of three topic-related websites.*

◎ *Write a topic-related question you want an answer for during the training.*

◎ *Find an object related to the topic and bring it to the training. Write what it is here.* (Examples: A real estate training participant brings a new flyer layout. A call center employee brings a job aid that lists the questions he wants to ask. A management training attendee brings a positive note card she sends to outstanding employees.)

◎ *Find out what your supervisor, manager, or administrator thinks is important to know about this topic. Record his/her name and responses here.*

4. People and Personal Surveys

A People Survey is a list of questions that participants will ask others and then bring the results to the training for discussion. The printed instructions read: *"Create a short list of topic-related survey questions and another list of colleagues who may know something about the topic. Ask these people the survey questions and record their names and responses. Be ready to repot to the training group the results of your survey."*

People Survey examples:

◎ *What is the most important fact you know about the topic?*

◎ *What is something topic-related that you were taught but that you didn't really need to know?*

◎ *What is your next step in learning more about this topic?*

◎ *What do you wish you had known in the beginning that you know now?*

◎ *What is some advice you can give me that is related to this training topic?*

A Personal Survey is one that participants will fill in and email back to you. For the Personal Survey, the printed instructions read: *"So that we can better customize the upcoming training to meet your learning needs, please write your responses to some or all of the following questions. Then email or fax your completed responses to the trainer. Thank you."*

Personal Survey examples:

- *What are three facts you already know about this topic?*

- *What is a topic-related area that you wish to explore in more depth?*

- *What do you want to take away from this training experience?*

- *What is one question pertaining to this topic that you want an answer for during the training?*

- *What do you plan to do with what you learn?*

- *What do you want the trainer to know about you?*

5. Pop Quiz

Create a list of topic-related quiz questions to send to learners. The questions should be challenging enough that learners won't know the answers to all of them until they attend the training (the more curious learners will probably do an Internet search for some of the concepts).

The printed instructions read: *"Write your answers to the quiz questions below. Once you have attended the training, come back to this quiz and change any answers you feel are incorrect. Or add details to your pre-training answers. Compare what you know now with what you will learn. Be ready to talk about this comparison at the end of the training."*

Below are train-the-trainer examples:

- *What is one opening activity that is both topic-related and learner-focused?*

- *What is the longest length of time most learners can simply sit and listen, without their learning diminishing?*

- *List the five important elements of brain-friendly training.*

- *Explain the difference between a connection and an icebreaker.*

- *List the 4 Cs of effective instructional design and delivery.*

Your Turn

In the space below, make a Concept Map of your own Warm-Up activities. On the next page I've done a Concept Map example of the activities in this section for you.

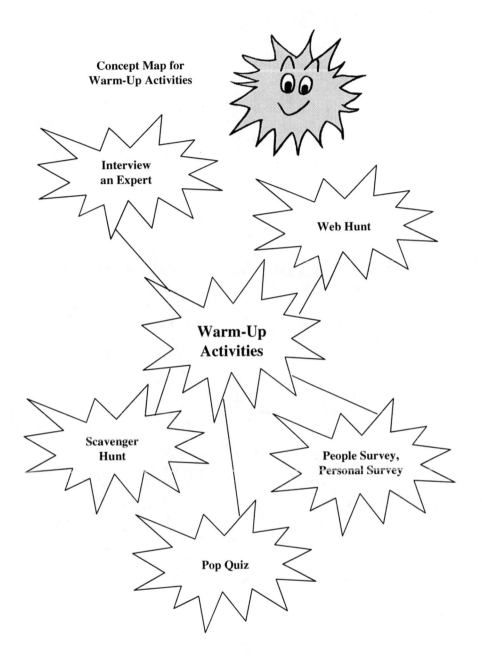

Concept Map for Warm-Up Activities

Interview an Expert

Web Hunt

Warm-Up Activities

Scavenger Hunt

People Survey, Personal Survey

Pop Quiz

Connections:
Fast Pass Activities

What Is a Fast Pass?

A Fast Pass is a quick, one- or two-minute, topic-related activity that engages learners from the moment they walk into the room. It is an immediate way to create a sense of curiosity about the topic. Like a Quick Start in *The Ten-Minute Trainer*, a Fast Pass is also a time sponge, that is, it soaks up non-training time—minutes that learners would normally spend doing things that aren't topic-related. For example, at the beginning of a traditional training, participants often spend time getting settled, chatting, making cell phone calls, or checking email. With a Fast Pass, learners can choose to participate in a quick activity instead—one that connects them to each other and to the topic in active, interesting ways.

What Does a Fast Pass Do?

A Fast Pass is a quick way to

- *Engage* learners from the moment they walk into the room.
- *Encourage* learners to become actively involved.
- *Create* interest in, and curiosity about, the topic.
- *Involve* learners immediately, in topic-related ways.
- *Connect* learners to what they already know or think they know about the topic, to what others know, or to what they will learn.

Getting Ready

- **Materials:** Before the training begins, print and post the Fast Pass instructions on a slide, entrance chart, wall chart, group table tent, or on worksheets placed at each participant's chair. The Fast Pass must be visible to everyone. You may need standard training materials (colored markers, chart paper, blank printing paper, index cards, and pens/pencils, to name a few), as well as specific materials for certain activities.

- **Setup:** No special setup is necessary, other than posting the Fast Pass instructions. Depending on the activity requirements, participants may need enough space in the room to stand, move, or walk around.

- **Group Size:** Any size group is fine.

- **Time:** Most Fast Pass activities will last about a minute or two, unless you wish to allow more time.

Five Fast Pass Activities

1. Dot Voting

For this activity, you will need chart paper, colored markers, and tape to hang the charts. Learners will need large, colored sticky dots (available at office supply stores). Do the following:

- Before the training begins, print and post the learning outcomes on large wall charts that are accessible by all. Have sheets of colored dots available at each table.

- Post these instructions on a slide or other chart: *"After reading this, please take two colored dots from the tables, read the learning outcomes on the wall charts, and put the dots beside the two outcomes that are the most important to you. Be ready to explain your choices."*

- If you don't have enough wall space for the charts, print the learning outcomes on a worksheet, one per table, or include them on a page in the handout materials. Revise the posted instructions accordingly.

- Instead of using colored dots, learners can draw dots, circle, underline, or check off the important learning outcomes.

- If time allows, ask learners to tell their table groups what they dotted and why.

2. Think It Then Ink It

For this activity, learners will need index cards and pens. Do the following:

- The posted instructions read: *"Think about what you already know about the topic. Write three of these facts on an index card, and be ready to state them when asked."*

- Give learners time to write and share their facts with partners, their table groups, or the whole class.

- Learners can also write one question they want answered, or one thing they want to be able to do as a result of the training.

3. Post It

For this activity, learners will need sticky notes to write on. You will need chart paper and colored markers. Do the following:

- Before the training, create a wall chart titled "What's In It For Me?" and hang it on a wall that is accessible to all.

- The posted instructions read: *"After reading this, take a sticky note and write what you want to learn from today's training. Post your note on the WIIFM ("What's In It For Me") chart on the wall. You will revisit this chart at the end of the training to assess what you learned."*

- Learners write and post their WIIFMs.

- At the end of the training, have learners retrieve their WIIFMs from the wall chart, read them to partners or to their table group, and discuss what they learned.

4. Turn and Talk

The posted instructions read: *"After reading this, introduce yourself to a person seated next to you. Tell this person why you are here and what you want to learn from this training."* If time allows, ask for a few volunteers to state what their partners said.
Turn and Talk variations:

- *Introduce yourself to someone at another table.*

- *Introduce yourself to someone you don't yet know well.*

- *Introduce yourself to someone from another department (job, agency, building).*

- *Introduce yourself to someone with more or less job experience than you.*

5. Take a Guess

Do the following:

- Before the training, create a worksheet with a list of statements—some topic-related and others not topic-related.

- Put one worksheet on each participant chair. When participants enter the room, they have to pick up and read their worksheets before sitting down.

- The printed instructions on the worksheets read:*"Skim the list of statements below. Circle the statements that are related to the topic and cross out those that are unrelated. Compare your answers to those of your neighbors."*

- Learners read and do what the worksheet states. If time allows, follow the activity with a quick group discussion about the worksheet items.

Examples of worksheet statements for a safety training:

- *First aid kits are located at each workstation.*

- *Employee timesheets need to be filled out daily.*

- *Pull the canister pin before using a fire extinguisher.*

- *The HR department tracks employee bonuses.*

- *The Heimlich maneuver is used with choking victims.*

Other Take-a-Guess variations:

- *Read the list of statements on the worksheet in front of you. Mark T for True and F for False. Compare your answers with those of a person seated near you.*

- *Read the procedural steps that are listed out of order on the worksheet. Take one minute to put them in order by labeling them 1, 2, 3, and so on.*

- *Skim the worksheet at your desk. Fill in any of the missing words you think you know. Be ready to compare your answers with the instructor's.*

Your Turn

Now create a Concept Map of your own Fast Pass activities.

Connections:
Start-Up Activities

What Is a Start-Up?

A Start-Up is a longer Fast Pass activity in which learners make more in-depth connections to each other and to the topic. A Start-Up usually lasts from five to ten minutes and includes a discussion in which participants talk about what they learned from the activity.

Both the Fast Pass and the Start-Up activities engage participants in the learning from the moment they walk into the room. You may choose to use a Fast Pass or a Start-Up, or a combination of both.

What Does a Start-Up Do?

Like a Fast Pass, a Start-Up will

- *Involve* learners immediately, in topic-related ways.
- *Encourage* learners to be actively involved.
- *Create* interest in, and curiosity about, the topic.
- *Connect* learners to what they already know or think they know about the topic, to what others know, or to what they will learn.

By participating in a Start-Up, learners also

- *Teach* each other what they know about the topic.
- *Create* a learning community within the training group.
- *Become* more familiar with topic-related terms, phrases, and concepts.
- *Discuss* what they have learned from the activity.

Getting Ready

- **Materials:** For certain activities, you will need standard training materials, as well as any extra materials mentioned in the activity instructions.

- **Setup:** There needs to be enough space in the room for participants to stand and move around.

- **Group Size:** Any size group is fine.

- **Time:** Usually a Start-Up lasts from five to ten minutes. A few can last as long as twenty minutes, depending on the amount of time you allow for a whole-group discussion afterward.

Five Start-Up Activities

1. Standing Survey

Print a list of topic-related questions on a wall chart. The posted instructions read: *"Skim the questions on the wall chart, and choose one to ask three or more people in the room who are <u>not</u> seated near you. Record their answers on an index card and be ready to report the results of the survey to your table group."*
   Examples of Standing Survey questions:

- *What is the most important fact you already know about this topic?*

- *What is something you want to learn about this topic?*

- *How will this topic affect the work you do?*

- *What is a question you already have about this topic?*

- *What do you think is NOT important about this topic?*

- *Where can you find more information about this topic after the training is over?*

2. Wall Writing

You will need a number of wall charts, colored markers, and tape to hang the charts. Learners will need broad-tip, colored markers at each table. Do the following:

- In large, readable print, title each of a number of wall charts with concepts from the training. Hang the charts at various accessible places on all walls of the room. Concept examples from a customer service training might be phone service, face-to-face service, greetings, problem solving, follow-up, reporting procedures, and so forth.

- The posted activity instructions read: *"After reading this, pair up with another learner, take a marker, and go to a wall chart. Discuss and agree on what you already know about that concept and print it on the chart. Do the same with the other charts."*

- After about three minutes, stop the chart writing and direct learners to walk around and read the charts before sitting down.

- Facilitate a whole-group discussion by asking:

  - *What new facts did you learn from the charts?*

  - *What facts were repeated on a number of charts?*

  - *What facts did you think might not be accurate?*

  - *What concepts do you want to learn more about?*

  - *What else did you learn from the Wall Writing?*

- At different times during the training, ask learners to revisit the charts and add new facts, correct any misconceptions, or take notes from the information.

- At the end of the training, learners read the charts once more and comment on what they have written and learned.

3. Table Talk

Do the following:

- Post a topic-related question on a slide or wall chart, where everyone can read it. The question should have more than one right answer, and require more than a yes/no response. Some examples:

  - (Communication training) *What are the most important communication facts to keep in mind when dealing with employee conflicts in the workplace?*

  - (Forklift operations training) *What are three important safety procedures you need to do before operating the forklift?*

  - (Real estate training) *What are some of the best ways to advertise a new listing?*

  - (Call center training) *What are four important questions to ask a customer before initiating the help desk procedure?*

- Ask learners to discuss the question with a person seated near them or with their table group. Allow about three minutes for this discussion.

- After the short discussion, learners prepare a one- or two-sentence summary of their discussions.

- Each pair of learners, or each table group, reports its summary to the class. If time is short, or if there are a dozen or more table groups, ask for a few volunteers instead.

4. Where Do You Stand?

Do the following:

- State a topic-related issue with a specific course of action as one solution to the issue.

- Say to participants:

  - *Stand to one side of the room (point to one side) if you strongly agree with this course of action.*

  - *Stand to the other side (point to other side) if you strongly disagree with this course of action.*

  - *Stand in the center of the room if you are undecided about this course of action or if you need more information about the situation.*

- Learners then form standing pairs/triads with others standing near them, and discuss why they made the choice they did.

- Follow this with a whole-group discussion in which you ask questions like:

  - *What did you learn from your partners about the choices they made?*

  - *What would make you stand in a different place?*

  - *What did you learn about the issue from this activity?*

  - *What other information might you need to make a more-informed choice?*

  - *What questions do you need to have answered in order to make another choice?*

- As a variation, ask learners to pair up with others who are standing on the opposite sides or in the middle of the room. Then have them discuss their different positions on the issue.

5. Card Carousel

The learners will need index cards and writing materials. Do the following:

● Before the training, create a set of index cards for each table group—about four to seven cards per group, depending on the table group's size. On each card print one concept that will be covered during the training.

● Table groups pass out the cards, one card to each group member. Individuals read their respective cards, then turn the cards over and write a related concept, phrase, fact, idea, or question on the back.

● Participants pass their cards to the right. On the new cards, each person repeats the same process. They pass the cards again until each person has written on at least three cards.

● When the time ends, learners keep the cards they have. When you cover that concept during the training, stop and ask for a few volunteers to read aloud some of the responses that learners wrote on the concept cards.

Your Turn

Make a Concept Map of other Start-Up activities in the space below.

part TWO

Concepts

What You Need to Know About Concepts

The best way to learn something is to teach it.
In other words, whoever explains learns.

David Sousa
How the Brain Learns, 2006, p. 95

Flow Chart Concept Map for This Chapter

As you read the chapter, write the important details that you want to remember about each concept.

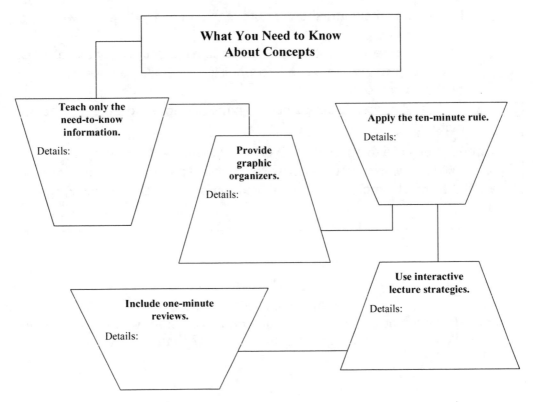

CONNECTIONS

One-Minute Connection: Fast Pass

Score yourself. Give each of the sentence completions below a number using the following scoring system: 1 = Seldom, if ever; 2 = Sometimes; 3 = Almost always.

When I am presenting the content-heavy parts of my training program, I

_____ Only present the need-to-know concepts; I put the nice-to-know concepts in a resource handout for later reference.

_____ Give learners an interesting note-taking page, and remind them to take notes (a copy of the PowerPoint® slides does *not* count as an interesting page).

_____ Divide my content into short, lecture segments of about ten to twenty minutes in length.

_____ Use interactive lecture strategies so that I am not doing all of the talking.

_____ Involve learners in a variety of short, quick review activities every ten to twenty minutes.

_____ Do less talking while the learners do more talking—and still cover the material.

Obviously, you are aiming for all 3s. If you aren't there yet, don't worry. This part of the book will get you there. Use the concepts and strategies in this part of the book to improve your scores and increase learner retention in your training.

Imagine That . . .

You are a new employee attending a new-hire orientation. All the information to be covered during the orientation is in an employee binder which you received as you walked in the door. When the time comes to go through the material in the binder, you expect the trainer, Marianne, to lecture, section by section. She doesn't.

Instead, Marianne announces that each table group will be responsible for presenting the major concepts from different sections of the binder. You and your table group members will have about thirty minutes to read, discuss, and prepare a ten-minute verbal summary of your assigned section. Marianne suggests that you choose a group facilitator, highlight the important concepts as you discuss them, and write out your summary before presenting it. She also encourages you to use chart paper and colorful markers to create a visual representation of the important points. As the table groups get to work, Marianne moves from group to group, making sure all groups understand the important concepts from their sections of the manual.

Before the presentations begin, Marianne reminds everyone to take notes when group presents its information. All groups receive a round of applause when they finish.

The new-hire orientation ends with a high-energy game in which you review what you have learned. You also fill out a quick, written assessment of important points. Finally, you bid farewell to your table group—now all new friends you will see daily in your new job.

* *

CONCEPTS

Concepts (also called direct instruction) are the important facts that learners need to know in order to demonstrate competency or do their jobs more effectively. Nowhere in any of the research books on human learning does it say that the concepts *must* come out of the trainer's mouth, that is, be spoken by the trainer in order to be remembered by the learner. As you know by now, the opposite is the case. The more learners are involved in the direct instruction, the more they remember what they are learning.

This is not to say that a trainer can hand all of the direct instruction over to learners to teach, but often a surprising amount of content *can* be presented by the learners instead of the trainer. Bob Pike, author of *The Creative Training Techniques Handbook* (2003), maintains that learners probably know about 70 percent of what trainers plan to teach them; they just may not realize that they already know it. Or they may not yet know it, but they could learn it fairly quickly on their own, if given the opportunity to do so. According to Maryellen Weimer in *Learner-Centered Teaching* (2002), "[Learners] need not wait until they have developed expertise before they interact with content. [They can] explore it, handle it, relate it to their own experience, and challenge it, whatever their level of expertise" (p. 13).

There are five important elements to keep in mind during the concepts segments of training:

- *Need-to-know information.* As I explained, this is the content that is necessary for learners' success.

- *Graphic organizers.* These are note-taking pages that are visually interesting, as well as important to learners' long-term memory.

- *The ten-minute rule.* This is a reminder to divide concepts into smaller segments of direct instruction time.

- *Interactive lecture strategies.* These are ways to involve learners during the direct-instruction segments.

- *One-minute reviews.* These are short, quick learning activities sprinkled throughout the direct instruction.

Let's take a more detailed look at each element.

Teach Only the Need-to-Know Information

As I mentioned in the previous chapter that gave you an overview of the 4 Cs, in order to separate need-to-know from nice-to-know information, ask yourself these questions:

- *"If I only had time to present half the content of this training, what would I leave out?"*

- *"What are the concepts that the learner needs in order to be successful at her job?"*

- *"If I only had ten minutes to summarize this information, what would I include and what would I put in a resource packet for learners to read later?"*

The main concepts are the need-to-know pieces to be taught and reinforced during the training. The nice-to-know information is reference material; you can cover it if you have extra time, or assign it as an "evening opportunity" (aka "homework").

Provide Graphic Organizers

These are note-taking pages that include topic-related graphics (cartoons, icons, photos, graphs, pictures) to capture learners' interest, and plenty of white space for learners to write and doodle on. There are five graphic organizer examples in the Concept Maps section of this part of the book. There are also other examples in this book: one each at the beginning of Parts One, Two, Three, and Four.

Graphic organizers help learners remember important information because

- *Learners remember what <u>they</u> write.* Writing is a kinesthetic way of remembering, meaning that it's the movement of pen over paper that helps the brain remember the written facts. Therefore, *learners* need to write down the need-to-know information themselves, instead of you writing it down for them.

- *Learners remember <u>where</u> they write.* Visual-spatial memory is a powerful way to remember facts. Learners write information in different places on the page. Later, when they need to recall the information, *where* they wrote will help them remember *what* they wrote.

Graphic organizers can be trainer-created or learner-created. You can provide one or more note-taking pages for learners to use, or they can create their own during the training. Either way, you need to remind training participants to write on them. This may sound elementary, but learners aren't used to taking notes; they've been conditioned to just sit and listen, so frequent reminders are useful. You can do that humorously by saying, "This is profound, so write it down."

A warning about handing out copies of the slides or using the handout templates that comes with the PowerPoint® program: They are visually and cognitively *boring*. Furthermore, many learners think, "If I have all the slides here in the handout, and if the trainer is going to stand and read these slides to me, why do I need to be here? I could take this handout home and read it myself over a cup of coffee."

If you have to hand out copies of slides, or if learners ask for them, wait until the end of the training to do so, and hand them out as reference material only. Copies of slides are *not* graphic organizers.

Try This

Variations on a Theme. Two of the best books on the subject of graphic organizers are *Mapping Inner Space* (Margulies, 2002) and *Visual Thinking* (Margulies, 2005). These books give you dozens of tips and ideas for using graphic organizers as an important part of every training program. You can find both books on www.amazon.com.

Additionally, if you do an Internet search for "Graphic Organizers," you'll find over 200,000 websites, many with free, downloadable note-taking tools. Don't be put off by the age levels for some of them. Graphic organizers work equally well with both adults and children. These sites will give you many ideas for note-taking tools that are specific to your topics and audiences.

Cornell Notes

Date: _____ Topic: _____

Main Ideas	Facts and Details

Summary:

Another phrase to explore is "Cornell Notes," which will yield a particular graphic organizer that many colleges are now using. Also read the Concept Map activities that are included in this part of the book.

Apply the Ten-Minute Rule

As I've said before, learning begins to diminish when lectures last longer than ten to twenty minutes. This is not to say that you should simplify your content. It's just a matter of timing. All you have to do to make the concepts easier for learners to remember is to divide your direct instruction into shorter segments of about ten minutes in length, and follow each segment with a short, one- or two-minute review that engages all learners. This ensures increased learner attention, motivation, and retention of important information.

Use Interactive Lecture Strategies

For the purposes of this book, the word "lecture" means an instructional monologue, when only the trainer is speaking, and the learners do nothing except listen. Lecture is also synonymous with "presentation, talk, direct instruction, or speech." Even when a trainer says, "Now let's discuss . . ." or "Now we'll talk about . . .", if the trainer is doing most or all of the talking, it's still a lecture. One of the greatest challenges trainers have is to make a realistic appraisal of how much of the training time they spend talking while learners passively sit and listen.

Interactive lecture strategies involve *most or all* of the learners. Eliciting one answer to one question is *not* an interactive lecture. Eliciting a dozen answers from a dozen different learners is. Encouraging all learners to use a graphic organizer is an interactive lecture strategy. So are one-minute review activities between lecture segments. Of course, allowing learners to present some of the content is one of the most powerful interactive lecture strategies around.

> **Try This**
>
> **Three Before Me.** Not sure how to get started engaging learners as you lecture? Use the "Three Before Me" rule. When a learner asks a question during the lecture, stop and say, *"Before I answer this question, let's take three answers from the group."* Accept all answers. Then add your own to the mix. Obviously, if the question has only one right answer, you won't use this strategy. And you won't use it every time a question is asked. However, it is a powerful way to
>
> *(continued)*

acknowledge the expertise in the room, to keep learners engaged, and to demonstrate that there are often many right answers. Vary the strategy by asking learners a question and stating that they need to come up with three answers.

When you have time, do an Internet search for "Interactive Lecture." This will elicit over 300,000 articles, many with excellent, free ideas and suggestions for involving learners during the direct instruction. Although a number of these articles are related to college courses, most can be applied to corporate training as well.

Include One-Minute Reviews

Between lecture segments, stop the content delivery and have learners do short, one-minute reviews (similar to the ones you have been doing in this book) of the content you just covered. These quick activities deepen the learners' understanding of the material, clarify any misconceptions or confusion, and help learners link the new information to information they already know. They also function as "brain breaks," which give learners a chance to figuratively step away  from the material for a moment and assess what they have learned so far. This part of the book gives you a number of quick reviews, and you can find over one hundred, sixty-second activities in *The Ten-Minute Trainer*.

● ●

CONCRETE PRACTICE

For your own concrete practice with this part of the book, plan to use one or more of the twenty concepts strategies in your next training. When you know which ones work best, make them a regular part of your training. Be sure to vary the strategies, so neither you, nor your training participants, become bored.

The activities are divided into four sections. Here are the section and activity titles, and brief summaries:

- *Five Concept Maps: Basic Map, Flow Chart Map, Burger Map, Free Flow Map, Timeline Map.* These are learner-created graphic organizers. Because they are visual-spatial memory tools, they help learners remember important material.

- *Five Interactive Lecture Strategies: Rapid Response; Pass That Card; Stand, Stretch and Speak; Beat the Clock; Bend, Breathe, and Write.* These activities help you insert one- and two-minute reviews into your direct instruction without sacrificing time or content.

- *Five Jigsaw Activities: One-Person Experts, Table Group Experts, Concept Card Experts, Concept Clinic, Jigsaw Choices.* Allow learners to do parts of the direct instruction using one or more of these collaborative activities.

- *Five Concept Center Activities: Table Centers. Wall Centers. Discussion Centers, Computer Centers, Learner-Created Centers.* When you design the delivery of concepts using centers like the ones in this section, you truly do step aside and allow learners learn, in their own way and at their own pace.

One-Minute CONCRETE practice

Cross It Out

Find out how much you have learned about the concepts step of the 4 Cs. Read each sentence below and cross out the phrase that is incorrect. Then check your answers.

1. The concepts part of training is the *(direct instruction; opening)*.
2. Only the *(need-to-know; nice-to-know)* information should be covered during the direct instruction, unless there is extra training time available.
3. During the concept segments, learners should be taking notes on *(handout copies of slides; graphic organizers)*.

(continued)

4. When learners *(actually teach some of the concepts; listen while the trainer teaches the concepts)*, they will remember the information longer.
5. Interactive lecture formats also include *(one person answering a trainer's question; one-minute review activities that involve everyone)*.

Once you've crossed out the incorrect phrases, the sentences should read:

1. The concepts part of training is the *direct instruction*.
2. Only the *need-to-know* information should be covered during the direct instruction, unless there is extra training time available.
3. During the concept segments, learners should be taking notes on *graphic organizers*.
4. When learners *actually teach some of the concepts*, they will remember the information longer.
5. Interactive lecture formats also include *one-minute review activities that involve everyone*.

• •

CONCLUSIONS

There is so much more to training than simply standing and talking about a topic. And there is much more to the concepts part of a training program than lecturing from a series of PowerPoint® slides. From now on, you will teach only the need-to-know information, provide graphic organizers, apply the ten-minute rule, use interactive lecture strategies, and include one-minute reviews.

In addition, you'll begin to experiment with strategies that allow learners to do some of the teaching. This is learning at its best—when learners are involved in every step of the learning process, even the direct instruction.

If you build it, they will sleep.
If they build it, they will learn.

Dave Meier
The Accelerated Learning Handbook, 2000, p. 86

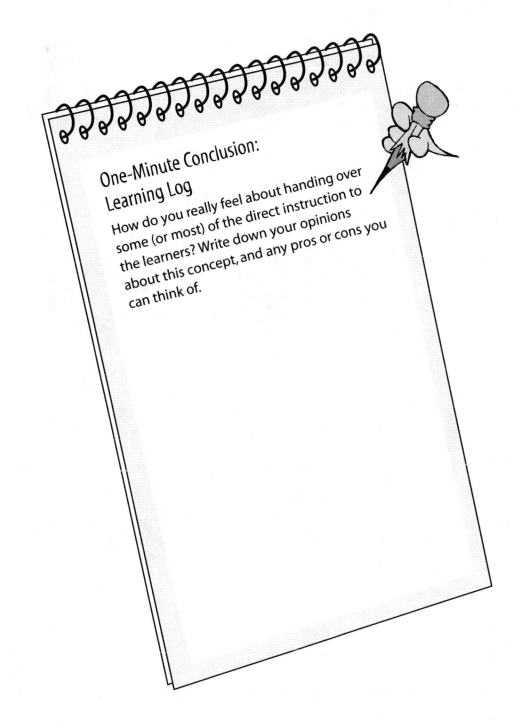

One-Minute Conclusion:
Learning Log

How do you really feel about handing over some (or most) of the direct instruction to the learners? Write down your opinions about this concept, and any pros or cons you can think of.

Trainer's Toolbox

Collect as many ideas as you can for this toolbox—from the chapter and from Internet searches—and write them here. Flag this page as you did the other toolbox pages.

Concepts: Concept Maps

What Is a Concept Map?

A Concept Map is a note-taking tool that gives learners a visual outline of verbal information. It is a picture of words: the important concepts, facts, and data, and their relationship to one another. The position of words on paper, with accompanying shapes, lines, and spaces, creates a mental image of what the topic is all about. A Concept Map is such an important part of learning that no training should be conducted without one.

According to Patricia Wolfe in *Brain Matters* (2001), "Humans are intensely visual animals. The eyes contain 70 percent of the body's sensory receptors. . . . It's not surprising that the visual components of memory are so robust" (p. 152). Put another way, the human brain is hardwired to think in pictures first, and words second. In fact, words are really only representations of mental images (which, in turn, are representations of people, objects, experiences, and ideas). Furthermore, the human brain usually remembers visual images better than printed data. Wolfe elaborates: "The capacity for long-term memory of pictures seems almost unlimited" (2001, p. 153). So Concept Maps are *not* about art; they *are* about retention and recall of important information.

Concept Maps are also called graphic organizers, mind maps, mindscapes, cluster or bubble maps, information maps, and the like. But all Concept Maps are based on the same principle: The visual layout of information is vitally important to the learner's retention of important data. You use Concept Maps every day. The road map you use to find your way around a new area is a Concept Map. So is the diagram of a shopping mall that is located near the mall's entrance. Your home's electrical fuse box, with its labeled diagram of switches, is a Concept Map.

In training, examples of Concept Maps are flow charts, Venn diagrams, pie charts, bar graphs, and just about any note-taking method that uses images, lines, and symbols as well as words. On the other hand, most topic outlines and training agendas, written in a linear, bulleted fashion without any images, are not Concept Maps. Neither are the PowerPoint® handout templates that many trainers use.

A Concept Map taps into many different ways of knowing and remembering: visual/spatial (images and symbols), linguistic (words and phrases), logical/mathematical (patterns and relationships between concepts), and kinesthetic (muscle movement—drawing and writing). Mapping also engages both hemispheres of the neocortex or thinking brain: the left hemisphere, which primarily processes words, and the right hemisphere, which primarily processes images.

Here are the important elements to keep in mind when using Concept Maps in your own training:

- *Word and images.* Learners use both the written words and visual representations of the words, or use shapes and lines signifying the relationships among ideas, to create Concept Maps. In addition, when learners add color to the images (with colored pens, pencils, crayons, or markers), the maps becomes even more visually interesting and memorable.

- *Learner-created.* Because each person organizes and remembers information differently, it's important for learners to create their own Concept Maps. You can help them start by giving them a basic map to use, but essentially learners remember what *they* draw and write better than what *you* draw and write for them.

- *Timing.* Since Concept Maps are note-taking tools, learners should be using them *during* the lecture or presentation, not afterward. You need to build mapping time into your direct instruction. You should also remind and encourage learners to map what they hear. Don't expect them to do this without reminders, as this type of note-taking will be new to most training participants.

- *Why and how.* Along with encouraging learners to take notes in ways that differ from what they are used to, give them the brain-based reasons for using this note-taking method. By your doing this, learners will realize that a Concept Map isn't about art or being back in grade school; rather, it truly is a tool to aid long-term retention of important data. When you give them an example or two or hand out a basic map to help them start, you ease their way into using this powerful retention tool.

What Does a Concept Map Do?

With a Concept Map, learners will

- *Create* visual images of important concepts.
- *Use* a variety of ways of learning: visual/spatial, linguistic, logical/mathematical, and kinesthetic.
- *Engage* both hemispheres of their neocortex or thinking brain.

- *Lengthen* long-term retention of important information.
- *Remain* involved and engaged throughout the entire direct instruction.
- *Leave* the training with a visually interesting reminder of what they learned, one that they can use as an information resource later.

Getting Ready

- **Materials:** For most Concept Maps, you will need standard training materials, as well as extra drawing materials—a variety of colored pens, pencils, markers, and colored paper—on each table. You may also want to include colored stickers, dots, stamps, or craft items, if you want the final maps to have a more creative, three-dimensional appearance.
- **Setup:** The mapping materials have to be on the tables and accessible to all participants.
- **Group Size:** Any size group is fine.
- **Time:** Because Concept Maps are an integral part of the direct instruction, learners should use them during all lecture segments.

Five Concept Maps

1. Basic Map

The Basic Map is also called a Cluster or Bubble Map. With it, learners write the topic, main ideas, and details on paper and then put colored circles, boxes, or other geometric shapes around the words and phrases. Learners use colored lines to link the main ideas to the topic and the details to the main ideas.

Before you begin your presentation or lecture, say to learners:

- *Choose a piece of colored paper and share the colored pens or markers.*
- *In the center of your paper, write the topic title and draw a colored box around it.*
- *As I lecture, you will write the main ideas (concepts) around the topic, Put a colored circle around each main idea and attach it to the topic box with a colored line.*
- *Around each main idea circle, draw spokes and write the concept details on the spokes.*
- *Add images to your Basic Map (icons, geometric shapes, squiggles, cartoons, stick figures, and so forth) to help you remember these facts.*

Concept Map Example: Basic Map (Cluster Map)

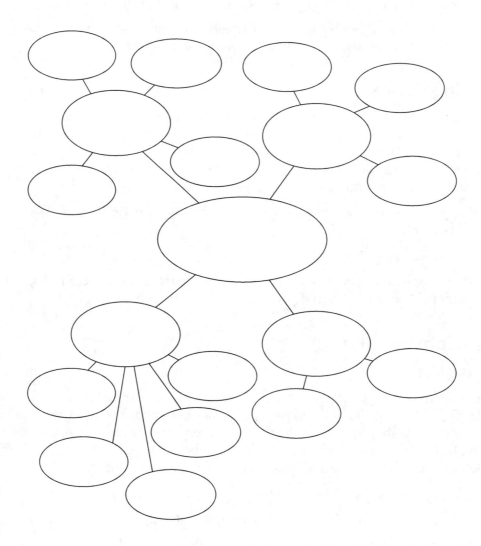

⦿ *You can make your Basic Map as colorful as you wish. The colors and geometric shapes will help you remember the information you write on it.*

Be sure to pause periodically during your lecture to give learners time to draw their maps and write the main ideas and details.

Training from the BACK of the Room!

2. Flow Chart Map

Concept Map Example: Flow Chart Map

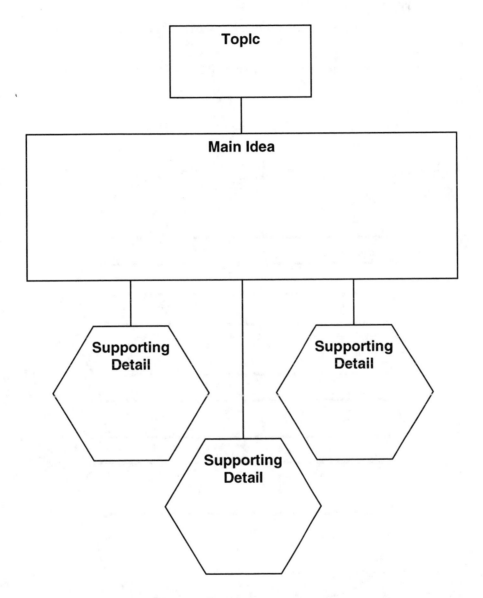

Most learners are familiar with standard flow charts and find it relatively easy to recreate one. With the Flow Chart Map, learners take notes in a more structured, linear form than with the Basic Map. Instructions to learners:

* Write the topic title at the top of the page. Draw a colorful box around it.

* As I lecture, write each main idea under the topic title, and draw a box around it. Link it to the topic with a line.

* Under each main idea, write the details, put boxes around them, and link them to the main ideas.

* Add colorful images, lines, or shapes that will help you remember the material.

3. Burger Map

Concept Map Example: Burger Map

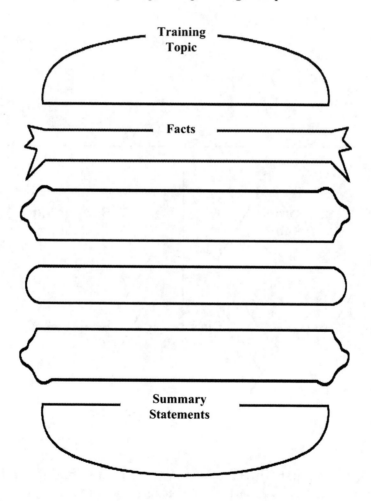

Training from the BACK of the Room!

The whimsical Burger Map has a topic bun and summary bun, with main ideas and details as the "burger" parts in the middle. Learners can create their own Burger Maps or use one you have printed for them. They can spice up (pun intended) their burgers with colorful, doodled additions: pickles, cheese, chips, sodas, and the like. The Burger Map adds a bit of humor to the note-taking process.

Actually, any object's shape can be used as a note-taking map. Think of household objects (chairs, spoons, phones, dishes), office objects (tablets, pencils, calculators), objects related to the training topic (examples: a computer shape for technical training, a tee-shirt outline for customer service, a ladder outline for procedural steps, and so on), nature shapes (trees, fish, leaves, water drops), body parts (head, hands, feet), and, of course, food. Using a shape that is either metaphorical (the ladder above) or topic-related (the tee-shirt above) will make the map even more memorable.

Your instructions to learners will be similar to the instructions listed for the two previous maps.

4. Free Flow Map

A lot more fun and creative, the Free Flow Map allows for unlimited, artistic variations, while still enhancing long-term memory. With the Free Flow Map, learners begin and end the map anywhere on the page, The information they write meanders along lines that look like a curvy road or river. Learners use an abundance of lines, shapes, images, and color. When finished, the note-taking pages look somewhat like pieces of artwork that are interesting and visually appealing. Learners can post the art-like pages at work and use them as job aids. Examples of Free Flow Maps are collages with both words and images, fireworks-like shapes with lots of flowing lines and spaces, and three-dimensional notes, where learners use craft materials to represent concepts, main ideas, and details.

For three-dimensional Free Flow Maps, have a small bag or box of craft items available at each table: pipe cleaners, small sticks, glitter, stickers, foam shapes, Play-Doh®, tape, glue, and the like. Your instructions to learners will be similar to the instructions for previous maps. In addition, you will remind learners to use the craft materials. Give them time to do this during the lecture segments.

Concept Map Example: Free Flow Map

Topic: _____

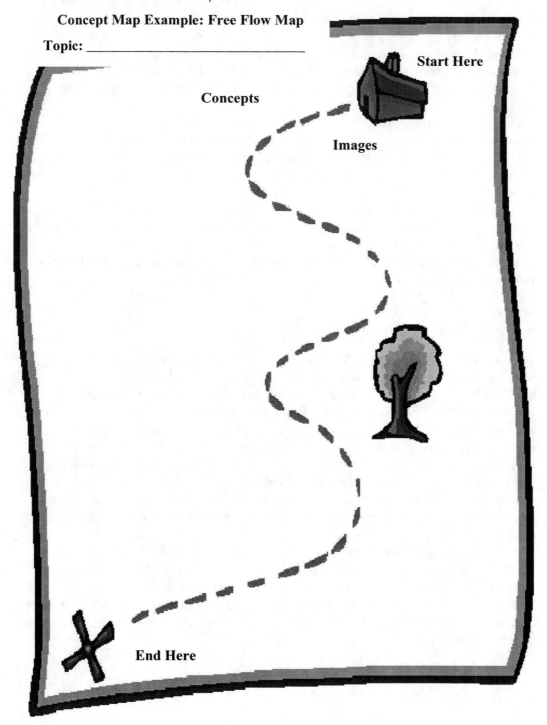

Concepts

Start Here

Images

End Here

Training from the BACK of the Room!

5. Timeline Map

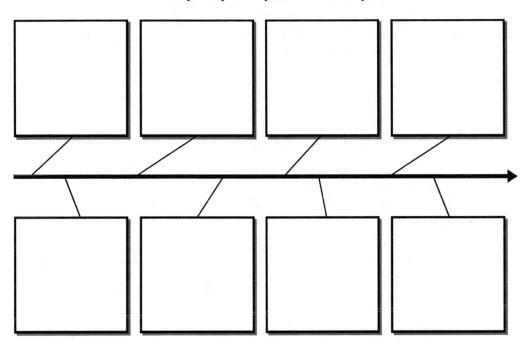

A Timeline Map represents information that is linear or time-dependent, such as procedural or historical information. A procedural example is the sequence of steps for a specific computer program. Another is the action sequence needed to resolve a particular problem. Historical examples are specific dates related to the stages of a company's growth or the past, present, or future models of a piece of equipment.

For a Timeline Map, say:

- *Turn a blank, note-taking page sideways in front of you, so that the longer side of the page is horizontal, rather than vertical.*

- *Draw a line along the middle of the paper, from left to right, so you have divided the paper in half. This is your timeline.*

- *As I lecture, you will be writing notes above and below this line, and then connecting your notes to the timeline with other lines. You will write the notes in a certain order* (depending on the topic information), *from left to right.*

- *Draw a colored box around each piece of information attached to the timeline.*

Your Turn

In the space below, experiment with your own Concept Maps, or reproduce ones you have seen other trainers use. You might take one or two ideas from this section and combine or change them to apply to the topics you teach. Or jot down other mapping ideas you've seen.

Concepts:
Interactive Lecture Strategies

What Is an Interactive Lecture?

"Interactive" generally means active participation *by the learner*. So an Interactive Lecture is a speech, presentation, or talk in which learners actively participate, instead of simply sitting and listening to the trainer talk. I stress this because often there is confusion about what is and is not interactive, For clarification, here is list of what Interactive Lecture strategies are *not*:

- Asking whether the learners have any questions
- Asking one question and having one learner answer it
- Asking a rhetorical question that needs no answer
- Having learners watch PowerPoint® slides whizzing on and off screen
- Telling a story or entertaining learners with jokes
- Having learners watch a video
- Saying, "Now we'll discuss . . . " and then doing all the talking while learners do all the listening
- Lecturing for over an hour and then following the lecture with a short group activity or game

Please understand: There is nothing wrong with doing anything on this list. Include any/all of them if you wish, but also include activities from this section in order to make your lectures truly participatory.

Listed below are the structural components that are common to all effective Interactive Lecture strategies:

- *Specific time limit*. Usually these strategies last from only one to three minutes so that you can insert them into your lecture material without sacrificing content. You'll use one strategy about every ten to twenty minutes of lecture so that learners will have been actively involved in a variety of ways at least three to six times during an hour of training.

- *Concrete goal.* You state the goal of the activity so that learners know what is expected.

- *Collaborative interdependence.* Learners work collaboratively together, either in pairs or small groups, to accomplish the goal. They cannot accomplish the task without working together.

- *Individual accountability.* Learners know what they are responsible for doing while the strategy lasts. Because the activity is so short, most learners have no problem staying on task.

What Does an Interactive Lecture Do?

When you use an Interactive Lecture strategy, you will

- *Keep* learners awake and involved during the lecture.

- *Hold* learners' interest in the material being presented.

- *Enhance* learners' comprehension of concepts being learned.

- *Lengthen* learners' retention of important information.

- *Increase* the energy level of the group during the lecture segment.

Getting Ready

- **Materials:** For most strategies, you will only need standard training materials. Any additional materials will be listed with the activity.

- **Setup:** No special setup is necessary.

- **Group Size:** Any size group is fine.

- **Time:** Most Interactive Lecture strategies last from one to three minutes, so they can be inserted into the direct instruction at any time.

Five Interactive Lecture Strategies

1. Rapid Response

Do the following:

- Pause during the lecture and instruct learners to think about the material just covered.

- Ask them to state a certain number of facts they feel are the most important. For example, say, *"Think about the information you just heard. As a group, let's come up with the five most important facts we need to remember from this material."*

- Wait for learners to state the facts. Accept all facts, unless they are incorrect.

- Add any facts that learners have not stated but that you think are also important.

- Correct any misconceptions at this time as well.

Other Rapid Response instructions:

- *Think about what you've learned so far. If you had to make up a test question about it, what would you ask? Write your question on an index card. (Later, as another Interactive Lecture strategy, have learners exchange cards and answer the questions).*

- *With a partner, take two minutes to write a quick list of all the facts you now know about the topic. Be ready to share your list with others later.*

- *Write a one-sentence summary of the information I've just covered. Compare your summary with someone seated near you. Are your summaries similar or different?*

- *If you had to explain to a colleague why you think this information is important, what would you say? Write it down in a sentence or two on an index card.*

- *If I stopped talking now and asked you a question, what might that question be? Take a moment to think about that. Let's hear five questions from the group.*

Be sure to change the Rapid Response instructions every time you use this strategy so that learners don't become bored doing the same thing the same way. Or vary this strategy with other Interactive Lecture activities.

2. Pass That Card

Instructions for this activity:

- Before the lecture begins, give each learner a half-dozen index cards or place a stack of index cards in the middle of each table.

  Before beginning the first lecture segment, say: *"On an index card, write three concepts that you think will be covered during the lecture. You will have a minute to do so. Then mark this card Number 1, and put it aside. We'll come back to it later."*

- After a ten- to twenty-minute lecture segment, stop and say: *"If you were to take a quiz about what we've just covered, what might one quiz question be? On another index card, write a sample quiz question, and mark this card Number 2. Pass this card to your right. Do not read your new Number 2 card yet."*

● After another lecture segment, stop and say: *"Now read the Number 2 card and write your own answer to the quiz question. Then take a new card, mark it Number 3, and write a question about the content we've just covered. Pass both 1 and 2 cards to the right. Do not read your new cards yet."*

● Continue with the next lecture segment, then stop and say: *"Now read the Number 2 card's question and answer. If you agree with the answer, write 'agree.' If you don't, write 'disagree,' and write what you think the correct answer is. Then read the Number 3 card's question and write your answer. Pass both cards to the right."*

● Again, lecture for a bit, then stop and say, *"Read card Number 3. If you agree with the answers write 'agree.' If not, write 'disagree' and add your own answer. Think of what you have learned about the topic from this lecture. Take a new card, mark it Number 4, and write a one or two sentence summary of the new information. Pass all cards to the right."*

● Finally, say, *"Read through all the cards. Add your own answers to cards 2 and 3, or your own summary statement to card 4. Be ready to share the summaries with the whole group."*

● After another lecture segment, ask for volunteers to read their card Number 4 summaries aloud to the group.

● You can have as many or as few card-passing rounds as appropriate for your lecture content and length and the size of the small groups.

● At the end of the total lecture time, ask learners to look at card Number 1—the card with the three concepts on it. Instruct learners to compare the material you have covered with what they wrote and to circle the similar concepts. If time allows, ask for a few volunteers to read their concept cards aloud. Take this time to talk about any concepts they wrote but that you didn't cover in the lecture.

Other suggestions for Pass That Card instructions include:

● *Title your card "True or False?" Write a true or false statement about the topic. The person you pass the card to will have to determine whether the statement you have written is true or false.*

● *Write a short opinion about the information we've just covered. Do you agree or disagree with the information, and why?*

- *Compare or contrast the information we've covered to what you knew about the topic before you came to the training. Write your comparison on a card.*

- *How can you apply this information to what you do? On a card, write your answer to this question.*

3. Stand, Stretch, and Speak

As I pointed out in the "Brain-Friendly Training" chapter, physical movement is crucial to effective learning. When learners stand and stretch, even for a minute, it enhances their ability to stay focused on the learning.

You have to decide whether this activity is appropriate for your training audiences. Many trainers use it with great success. Some choose not to use it because they feel their training participants would be uncomfortable with this much physical activity. The choice is yours.

Give learners these instructions:

- *We are going to take one-minute, topic-related stretch break to get more oxygen to our brains.*

- *Please stand up and form a pair or triad, making sure no one is left out.*

- *Decide which one of you will be the Stretcher and which one is the Mirror.*

- *If you are the Stretcher, you will lead a stretch* (demonstrate stretching a part of your body: arms, legs, torso, back, neck, hands, or feet). *If you are the Mirror, you will copy the stretch* (again, demonstrate the same stretch).

- *While you both stretch, the Stretcher summarizes what he or she has learned so far.*

- *Switch roles and repeat the process one more time.*

- *When you have finished the two stretches, thank your stretching partner and have a seat.*

Variations to Stand, Stretch, and Speak:

- Triads stand and stretch following the procedure for standing pairs, as described above.

- Table groups stand and each group member takes a turn leading a stretch while the entire small group mirrors the stretch.

- Table group members take turns leading a sitting stretch, that is, a movement the group can duplicate without standing up.

- One volunteer leads a stretch that the entire class mirrors.
- You lead a stretch, then ask for a volunteer to do one more.

4. Beat the Clock

This is a short, competitive activity that is timed, with the whole group competing against the clock.
   Do the following:

- Stop lecturing and say: *"You now have sixty seconds to quickly write down the ten most important facts you've just learned about the topic. The time starts now."*
- After the sixty seconds are up, tell learners to stop writing and ask whether anyone was able to beat the clock and write ten facts in one minute.
- If someone did, ask that person to read her list to the group. She receives a round of applause.
- If more than one person beat the clock, ask each person to read two or three facts from his or her list. Then they all receive a round of applause.
- If there are fewer facts to list, make the Beat the Clock time limit shorter than one minute.
- Participants can also work in pairs or table groups when doing this activity, and you can lengthen the time accordingly.

5. Bend, Breathe, and Write

Like Stand, Stretch, and Speak, this is another movement activity that helps oxygenate the brain. If you lead this activity with a humorous flair, learners will laugh as they participate. If you feel this is out of your own or your learners' comfort zone, then choose a different activity that will encourage learners to move and stretch, or make up one of your own.
   Some examples of humorous introductions to this activity:

- *Want an endorphin release? Here's how to get one!*
- *Let's do something crazy and energizing at the same time.*
- *Time for a serious review of what we have covered.*
- *We're going to do a little stretching to get some oxygen to our brains. Be glad I'm not asking you to do cartwheels.*

Your instructions to learners:

- *While seated, drop a pen, pencil, or other small object on the floor by your chair.*

- *As you bend down to pick up the object, exhale completely, blowing all the air out of your lungs with an audible "Whoosh."*

- *As you straighten up again, take a deep breath and think about a word or phrase that best summarizes what you have learned so far.*

- *Write that word or phrase on a piece of paper. Then compare what you wrote with what your neighbor wrote.*

Other variations:

- *Pick up the object, take a deep breath as you straighten up, then do a few shoulder shrugs and neck rolls. Now write a one- or two-sentence summary of what you have learned so far. Be ready to read your summary to your table group later.*

- *After you pick up the object and take a deep rejuvenating breath, stretch your arms in the air as if you are trying to touch the ceiling of the room. Now on the ceiling, pretend to write a one-word summary or one-phrase summary of what you've learned (demonstrate this by pantomiming the act of writing on the ceiling), Tell your neighbor what you pretended to write.*

- *As you straighten up and take a deep breath, pretend that you have your cell phone in your hand and a friend has just called you to ask you about this training. What would you tell your friend? Pantomime this conversation, then tell your neighbor what you pretended to tell your friend.*

Your Turn

Your own Interactive Lecture activities can go in the space below.

Training from the BACK of the Room!

Concepts: Jigsaw Activities

What Is a Jigsaw?

A Jigsaw is a collaborative instructional strategy in which learners are responsible for the direct instruction, acting as both teacher and learner, with some guidelines from you. The title of the activity comes from decades of cooperative learning research and is a metaphor for how the activity is structured. Basically, each person owns a piece of content—the "jigsaw puzzle piece" of the metaphor—and learners put the content (the puzzle) together by combining what they know.

More specifically, training participants are responsible for learning new concepts by using handouts, the Internet, or other printed materials as their information sources. Afterward, they teach what they learned to another participant, their own table group, or a different table group.

A Jigsaw is a powerful way to engage participants during the direct instruction. There are simple ways to do a Jigsaw and more complex ways that need more setup time beforehand. All Jigsaws are based on the same three structural components:

- *Learner as learner*. Training participants first learn what they will teach. Each participant or small group is responsible for a specific segment of content and becomes an expert on that material. The content to be learned can be on media such as handouts, worksheets, flashcards, books, charts, slide sets, and the like. Or learners can find the information through Internet searches, company manuals, other employees, or any other resources available. Learners work together in small groups to learn the material—discussing, questioning, agreeing on, and listing major facts; rehearsing how they will teach it to others; and planning their presentations.

- *Learner as trainer*. Learners form new groups (instructions for group formation are in the specific Jigsaw activities in this section). Each learner is now an expert on his content segment. Learners take turns teaching their new groups what they know about the content.

- *Trainer as observer*. As learners teach each other and learn from each other, the trainer walks around, observes the process, offers suggestions and guidance, and answers questions as needed. The trainer also checks for understanding, that is, asks individuals or groups what the major facts are from their respective content segments. The trainer's presence is a reminder to participants that they need to stay on task, seek help if they need it, and complete the Jigsaw assignment.

What Does a Jigsaw Do?

By participating in a Jigsaw activity, learners will

- *Teach* themselves and each other, instead of having content presented to them by the trainer.
- *Deepen* their understanding and mastery of what they teach.
- *Make* meaningful contributions to the content and the learning process.
- *Become* experts on one segment of the content.
- *Take* personal accountability for the material to be learned and taught.
- *Remain* focused and involved throughout the direct instruction process.

Getting Ready

- **Materials:** Depending on the activity, learners will need standard training materials, as well as any materials necessary for a specific Jigsaw activity, including resource material such as handouts, worksheets, books, manuals, access to the Internet, slide sets, and the like.
- **Setup:** There will need to be breakout areas, either in the training room (if it is large enough) or outside the room so that small groups can work together undisturbed. If this isn't possible, make sure there are enough tables and space around the tables in the training room to accommodate learner movement.
- **Group Size:** Any size group is fine, as long as there is enough space in the room for the groups to form and re-form. There should be about four to six learners in each of the small groups.
- **Time:** This will vary greatly, depending on the amount of new material participants need to familiarize themselves with. From beginning to end, a Jigsaw activity can last from thirty minutes to over two or three hours. If you

want to shorten the preparation time, assign some/all of the research and reading as an out-of-class activity. When learners return to the training, they will be prepared to discuss with their first Jigsaw group what they learned outside of class, before teaching the new content to the second group.

Five Jigsaw Activities

1. One-Person Experts

For this activity, learners will need all resource materials, as well as writing materials, chart paper, and markers. Do as follows:

- Assign each person in a table group a short paragraph, slide set, or worksheet to read that covers a segment of new information. All table groups will have the same information assigned to individual members. Suggest that the learners underline the main ideas and write short paragraphs summarizing the material. Give them about ten minutes to do the reading, underlining, and summarizing.

- If time permits, learners can list key words or draw a representation of the main ideas on a chart to use as a visual of the information they present.

- Each person presents her summary to her table group. To the best of her ability, she answers any questions the group may have about the material. If she doesn't know the answers, she defers to the trainer.

- Table groups give each Jigsaw expert a round of applause.

2. Table Group Experts

For this activity, learners will need all resource material, as well as writing materials, chart paper, and markers. Do the following:

- Assign each table group a segment of new information—each group will have information to learn that differs from the other groups. Give groups the reading material they will need to learn the concepts they will be teaching. In effect, each table group becomes an expert on a portion of the new content.

- Instruct group members to work together to learn the new material. They can divide it among members, read it aloud together, work in pairs, or do whatever feels best to them. Ultimately, they will discuss and agree on the main ideas and concepts they will be presenting to the whole group.

Allow from fifteen to thirty minutes for this step, depending on the length of the new material.

- Expert group members decide how they will present the information to the class: taking turns leading the presentation, assigning presentation roles, or choosing one or two people from the group to present. Allow about fifteen minutes for this step.

- If time allows, expert groups can make visual representations of the main ideas on chart papers or slides. They can include a short activity for the class to do, if they wish.

- Each expert group presents its content to the class and answers any questions the class may have. Or they may defer to you if they don't know the answers. At this point, you also add any information you feel is important.

- Expert groups receive rounds of applause when they finish their presentations.

- Make copies of all original material (the information that you passed out to each table group) available for all training participants to have when the presentations are finished.

Instructions for another variation of Table Group Experts are as follows:

- Each table group is called a "home group," with each person in the home group assigned a number: 1, 2, 3, 4, 5. You give each home group a different segment of content to learn and teach, as you did for the first set of Table Group Expert instructions above. In addition, each home group member must become a stand-alone content expert because that person will teach the new material to a new group of like numbers: 1s teach 1s, 2s teach 2s, and so on.

- Each home group reads, discusses, and agrees on what the main ideas and concepts are. Groups decide how each member will present this information to a new group. If the home group decides to use charts or other visual aids, each member must make his own charts. Allow about fifteen to thirty minutes for this step, depending on the amount of new material to cover.

- Home groups split up and form new groups with like numbers: 1s form a group of 1s, 2s form a group of 2s, 3s with 3s, and so on.

- Each expert presents his information to his new group. He answers any questions the group has or defers to you, if necessary. He receives a round of applause for his presentation.

- When finished, all learners return to their home groups for a final discussion about the Jigsaw activity: *"What did and didn't work? What else did you need to know? What questions came up? What have you learned from the Jigsaw?"*

- Again, make copies of all original material (the information that you passed out to each table group) available for all training participants to have when the presentations are over.

3. Concept Card Experts

For this Jigsaw, learners will need index cards and pens. Do as follows:

- Before the Jigsaw activity, create a set of cards, one set per table group. On each card print a different main idea or concept from the material to be learned.

- Each table group member chooses one card, then stands and finds others from the other table groups who have chosen the same card.

- Participants with the same concept cards work together to brainstorm important facts or details about the concept. They list what they already know, or you give them some handout material that goes with the concept cards they hold. Participants write the facts and details on the backs of their concept cards or on blank index cards. They can also write short summaries about the concepts. Allow about ten to fifteen minutes for this step.

- You walk around and listen to the concept card group conversations to make sure the important facts they list include details you consider important.

- At the end of the time limit, participants return to their original table groups. They take turns reading the concepts, facts, details, and summaries they listed while in their concept card groups. Group members who are listening to the presentations take notes.

- Finish the activity with a whole-group discussion about the major points learned from the Concept Card Jigsaw activity. If any important facts were left out, add them during the discussion.

4. Concept Clinic

The source of this Concept Clinic Jigsaw activity is organizational consultant and trainer Mimi Banta (www.netspeedleadership.com). For this activity, learners will need resource material, as well as chart paper or legal-size printing paper, writing materials, and markers. Instructions for this activity are as follows:

- Each table group chooses a team name for its group and prints its name on one large, blank piece of paper (chart paper or legal-size printing paper).

- Assign each group a specific segment of content. Each group brainstorms facts about its content segment, using the resources you provide as well. Groups write these facts on their team papers.

- Each group passes its paper to the group on its right (or in an order that you determine will ensure that, with each round, groups all receive new team papers).

- The groups read the information on the papers that were passed to them, then add more written information to that team's paper.

- Each time a group receives a new paper, the process is repeated: They read, discuss, write, and pass the papers again until the rounds are complete and all groups have their original team papers back.

- Each original group takes a few minutes to write a summary statement of the information on its team paper. If time allows, groups can also create chart papers with bulleted summary points or graphics to enhance the summaries.

- Each group then presents its summary statement and posts its team paper on a wall where everyone can review the posted information during the remainder of the training.

5. Jigsaw Choices

Give learners a list of concepts and the resources to learn about these concepts (handouts, slide sets, worksheets, websites, and the like). Or put the resources out on a Jigsaw resource table, along with presentation materials such as chart paper, craft items for three-dimensional representations, and perhaps some soft, throwable objects. Explain that they will become experts on one concept that they will present to the group when the study time is over. They can make the following choices:

- *Pairs, Triads, or Small Groups.* They can choose the participants they want to work with for the duration of the activity, as along as no one is left out.

- *Concepts and Materials.* Each small group can choose the concept it wants to study and the materials it will use, as long as no concept is left out (meaning that each group must choose a concept from the list and cannot repeat another group's choice, until each concept is covered by a group).

- *Where to Study.* Small groups can move within certain parameters set by you for the duration of the study time: breakout areas in the training room or in other rooms, hallways, or outside if weather permits.

- *Presentation Methods.* Small groups can choose how they will present their concepts to the whole group: lecture with visuals, game format, skit, role play, sculpture that represents the concept information, ball toss, and so on.

Set the duration of the study time and the presentation time. Post the instructions, time limits, and any other information learners will need for this Jigsaw. Be sure to walk around and check for understanding, monitor the small groups' progress, and make sure that the groups know the main ideas of the concepts they will be presenting.

Your Turn

Think about different ways you could have learners become the teachers. In the space below, draw a Concept Map of your own Jigsaw activities.

Concepts: Concept Centers

What Is a Concept Center?

A Concept Center is a table, wall, or designated area in the training room where participants learn or review a specific topic-related concept, or practice a topic-related skill.

You can have one or many Concept Centers set up around the room. Learners participate in the centers at designated times during the training day. Concept Centers can be part of the direct instruction, part of an active review, or a combination of both. If the centers are part of the direct instruction, they will be included in the Concepts step of the 4 Cs design and delivery model. If they are part of the active review or skills practice, they will be a Concept Practice step. This might sound confusing, but it illustrates the versatility of Concept Centers. You can easily have both direct instruction and concrete practice going on the room at the same time, especially if the training lasts a day or more.

With Concept Centers, as with most of the activities in this part of the book, you step aside as learners teach and learn from each other, with guidance from you, as needed.

Here are the major components of Concept Centers:

- *Content-related*. Concept Centers need to be relevant to the content being learned. They aren't fill-in activities, like fun but nonessential games. Instead, they are an integral part of the learning.

- *Posted purpose*. The purpose for each Concept Center needs to be clearly printed and visible so that learners know the reason why participation in the center is important. The purpose can be simple: "To review our company's history and growth." Or it can be more behaviorally specific: "To demonstrate competency in running the database program." The purpose can also be one of learning new content: "To be able to explain five important facts about our online security protocol" or "To list the steps of our company's billing process."

- *Learner interest*. In training, anything that arouses curiosity and sustains interest is beneficial. So Concept Centers should be visually interesting. Examples are wall charts or game pieces in bright colors, a variety of graphics, activity titles that create curiosity, or interactive worksheets that capture learners' attention.

- *Clear instructions*. Whether you post the instructions on a wall chart, a handout, a game card, or a worksheet, the instructions have to be easily understood and clear enough for learners to follow. This way, valuable training time isn't wasted while learners try to figure out what to do. Before including a new Concept Center, have a colleague read the instructions and explain them back to you so you know the instructions are clear enough.

- *Time limits*. Learners need to know how much time will be allotted for each center activity. If rotating centers, you can use an auditory signal (upbeat music, a bell, a chime, or horn) to signal starting, stopping, and rotating.

What Does a Concept Center Do?

By using Concept Centers as part of the direct instruction, you can

- *Introduce* new information in interactive and interesting ways.
- *Add* to what learners already know about the topic.
- *Provide* more resources for learners to explore on their own.
- *Keep* participants' interest and motivation high.
- *Review* what you have already taught during this, or previous, training.
- *Make* your training unique, engaging, and memorable for the learners.

By participating in Concept Centers, learners will

- *Explore* new concepts in hands-on ways.
- *Remain* engaged and alert during the direct instruction.
- *Review* information using a variety of interesting review formats.
- *Deepen* their understanding and levels of competency.
- *Increase* their interest, enthusiasm, and motivation to learn.

Getting Ready

- **Materials:** For most centers, provide standard training materials, in addition to the specific materials needed for some of the activities below.

- **Setup:** Ideally, Concept Centers should be set up on tables around the perimeter of the room, in designated areas, or scattered throughout the room. If there isn't enough space for this, use the tables at which participants are sitting. Another option is to put materials and instructions for each center in a bag, box, or manila envelope and pass these out to table groups during the scheduled center time.

- **Group Size:** Concept Center groups should be from four to six people. Larger groups than that are unwieldy and lessen the amount of individual participation. Smaller groups are fine, as long as the center isn't a game that needs more participants than two or three people.

- **Time:** If you are running a number of Concept Centers at the same time, allow about ten to twenty minutes for each activity. If there is only one center in the room, participants may have to take turns visiting it, so the activity may be only about five minutes in length. Or learners may choose to participate in the center at breaks or meals, when they have a longer period of time.

Five Concept Center Activities

1. Table Centers

You will need appropriate activity materials for each Table Center you create. You will also need posted instructions for each center. Do the following:

- Until you feel comfortable using Concept Centers in your training, make your first center a simple one, with one or two review games you create before the training. Set up a game table against one wall of the training room. It will be a Concept Center that learners can visit at different times during the training. For game suggestions, see the Learner-Created Games section in Part Three of this book (these games are simple ones using index cards and paper).

- Post a wall chart above the table that reads: "*Game Center—Try Your Luck!*" or something similar, which will pique participants' curiosity and interest.

- Instruct learners to visit the Concept Center during breaks or meals. They will choose a game and spend about five minutes playing it with colleagues in the training or with their table group. When they finish, they return the game to the center for other groups to play.

⊛ If you have enough review games at the Concept Center, you can designate a five- or ten-minute period of time during the training in which all table groups play a game of their choice at the same time.

Table Center variations include:

⊛ *Game Table Rotations.* Using the same review games as mentioned above, put the games at separate tables around the room instead of on one table. During a designated time, small groups gather at each table to play a game, then rotate to another table to play a different game.

⊛ *Centers with New Content.* Once you become comfortable enough with a Concept Center review activity, create a Concept Center that covers new material—some nice-to-know information about the topic. This is content that adds value to what you are teaching, but that you won't be covering in your lecture segments. It may be reading material, a short quiz with answers, or a self-correcting, fill-in-the-blank worksheet along with printed material. Encourage learners to visit the Concept Center during the training.

⊛ *Table Center Rotations.* If you decide to have learners rotate through a series of Concept Centers over an hour or two of training time, use the tables at which learners are already seated as the centers. Decide what activities will take place at each center, and have all necessary materials available on each table so that learners don't have to hunt for materials. You explain the guidelines to them:

  ⊛ *Stay with your center group and choose a group leader.*

  ⊛ *Read the center instructions and participate in the activity.*

  ⊛ *The center time lasts* (give length of time) *minutes. The signal to rotate clockwise is* (give signal).

  ⊛ *Clean up the center for the next group to use before you rotate to the next center.*

You may choose to have them do all the rotations sequentially, one after the other. Or learners can do a number of rotations in the morning, take a lunch break, then finish the rotations in the afternoon. Follow the entire center time with a whole group discussion about the centers. Ask:

⊛ *What were the most important facts you learned about the training topic from the Concept Centers?*

⊛ *What activity was most beneficial for you and why?*

⊛ *What are some topic-related questions you still have?*

- *What are some other topic-related areas you wish to explore?*

- *What other observations or comments do you have about the Concept Center activities?*

See the two specific examples of Table Center rotations at the end of this chapter for a more detailed look at how to use this Concept Centers variation.

2. Wall Centers

Do the following:

- Designate a wall area as a Concept Center, and create the center before the training.

- On the Wall Center, post charts with topic-related concepts, facts, questions, and so on. To make the posted information more interesting, you may want to give the Wall Center an interesting title such as: *"What You Didn't Know But Wanted to Learn* (about the topic)*"* or *"Believe It or Not"* or *"Little Known Facts* (about the topic)*."*

- If you want learners to do an activity using the information posted on the walls, also post the instructions for the activity. A training example: In an insect abatement class for a pest control company, the Wall Center contained a display of different household pests—photos, descriptions, habitats, invasive signs, etc. Also posted was a list of discussion questions, as well as blank charts for learners to write a summary statement after they discussed one of the questions. The posted questions included:

  - *After reading the information on this wall, what do you know about insect abatement that you didn't know before?*

  - *What can you do with this information?*

  - *In addition to this information, what else might be helpful to know?*

  - *What are other resources you can use to add to what you now know?*

- Explain the purpose of the center and invite learners to visit the center sometime during the training. Or visiting the center can be a mandatory part of the training.

Wall Center variations:

- *Learner-Created.* If the training lasts longer than a day, invite learners to create one or more Wall Centers. These can be simple displays of content they've learned from the training, or the Wall Centers can include content from Warm-Up activities and other resources (see Warm-Ups in Part One of this book).

● *Add to It*. Start a Wall Center with a concept title, graphic, and perhaps one or two pieces of information. Invite learners to add their own information charts to it during the training.

● *Concept Collage*. Invite learners to bring to the training anything related to the topic that can be hung on a wall: photos, newspaper or web articles, website URLs, topic-related objects, book titles, and so on. Ask for volunteers to create a wall collage from all these materials. Learners can add to the collage throughout the training.

3. Discussion Centers

Similar to the structure of The World Cafe (see the chapter titled "The World Cafe: An Innovative Process with Conversations That Matter"), Discussion Centers are areas of the room in which specific topic-related discussions take place among small groups of learners. Do the following:

● Designate one or more Discussion Center areas in the room.

● At each center, post one of the following: a question to answer, a concept to talk about, a problem to solve, application of the information learned or anything else that is relevant and topic- or concept-related.

● One learner in each group takes notes during the discussion and then tapes the notes to the Discussion Center instructions chart. Or each small group creates a short statement summarizing its discussion, prints the summary on chart paper, and hangs it on the wall.

4. Computer Centers

Do the following:

● Transform a computer lab into Concept Centers by designating a certain number of computers as Computer Centers.

● The center instructions can either be on the computer screen or posted on paper beside the computer.

● Learners form pairs or triads and rotate from computer to computer. At each Computer Center, they follow the posted instructions, discuss what they learned, and then reset the computer for the next rotation group.

Two examples of Computer Centers:

- For a training on a new database program, each Computer Center contains instructions for learners to do a practice activity with a segment of the program. Participants work in pairs and mentor each other while they practice.

- At an insurance company training, each Computer Center contains different policy coverage information. Working in pairs, learners read the information on the computer screens and then discuss and complete a short, computerized quiz that follows the information segment.

Computer Center variations:

- *Internet Searches.* If Internet access is available in the computer lab, have different topic-related Internet search activities at each center. For example: At one center, learners search for topic-related web articles; at another, book titles; at a third, topic-related blogs; at a fourth, Wikipedia information. Learners summarize and report their findings to the class after the centers end.

- *Blogs.* Short for "web log," a blog is an online journal entry to which readers can add their own comments. You set up the first blog entry at the Computer Center; then learners add their own comments. Your blog entry can be a topic-related question or opinion. Learners' comments would be answers to the question or comments about your opinion. To find out how to set up a blog, do an Internet search for "set up a blog" or log onto www.blogger.com.

- *Pop Quizzes.* Post a quiz question for which learners have to find a web-based answer. If you want them to log onto a specific website to find the answer, post that as well.

- *Learner-Created Quizzes.* Post a topic-related question on the computer screen. The first group discusses and prints their answer to the question. They post a second question. The second rotation group reads the first question and answer, adds to it if they wish, and then answers the second question. They post a third question. The sequence continues until all rotating groups have posted questions and answers.

- *Wikis.* A wiki is an online encyclopedia. It differs from a blog in that anyone can post entries on a wiki, whereas only one person posts an entry on a blog—all others post comments to the first entry. Log onto www.wikipedia.com or www.wikidot.com to find out more about wikis. At a wiki center, learners add their own topic-related information.

5. Learner-Created Centers

These are Table Centers with a twist: Learners create the Table Centers and then rotate from table to table. Instructions:

- Each table group chooses a piece of training content from a list of possible concepts.

- Make sure all necessary content resources are available at each table: handouts, slides, web access (if necessary), worksheets, and the like. In addition, besides standard training materials such as markers and index cards, each table group has tape, chart paper, construction paper or card stock, extra CDs for a computer center if desired, and so on.

- Table group members familiarize themselves with their specific content segments. Before groups create their center activities, you make sure that they are covering the main ideas of their respective content segments.

- Each group designs and creates a center to teach the content segment to the other groups. Each group chooses a different way to do this: a table game, flashcards, discussion topics, handouts to read, quiz questions and answers, or charts to read. You may decide to post a list of possible center activities and have table groups cross off the ones they choose to make so that all groups don't choose the same activity. (See Learner-Created Games in Part Three of this book.)

- When all table groups are ready, they rotate tables and do the various center activities created by the other table groups. If time allows, they do enough rotations to visit all centers, other than their own. If time is short, they may only rotate once or twice.

- When the rotation time is over, facilitate a whole-group discussion (or assign one small group to do this) about what they learned, what questions they still have, and any other information they need to know about the content.

Your Turn

Make a Concept Map for Concept Center ideas. Write or draw your ideas here.

Table Center Examples

Example One

The following six Concept Centers were part of a full-day, train-the-trainer program I facilitated. The centers were a combination of two of the 4 Cs steps: Concepts and Concrete Practice. Groups of five or six training participants rotated through all six centers during two hours in the afternoon. Each center rotation lasted about twenty minutes, with a few minutes to clean up and rotate between each activity. The centers were as follow:

- *Center One: Using Your Body and Voice.* A visiting guest speaker led a series of short, interesting exercises about using effective body language in training. This was new information for the learners.

- *Center Two: How Much Do You Know?* Learners worked collaboratively on fill-in worksheets that reviewed major concepts covered during the morning. They checked their answers against an answer key. This was a review of previously learned material.

- *Center Three: Grab and Gab Game.* Learners participated in this competitive game (see Learner-Created Games in Part Three of this book) as an active review of learning styles concepts.

- *Center Four: Myth or Fact Game.* Individually, learners read a short handout about new instructional design concepts that weren't part of the content they learned earlier. Afterward, learners played a collaborative Myth or Fact Game (see Learner-Created Games in Part Three of this book) to review the material.

- *Center Five: Your Best Practices.* Learners participated in a small-group discussion about their best training practices and how to use what they learned earlier in the day with their own training topics.

- *Center Six: Strengths and Stretches.* This center covered an individual self-assessment that evaluated each learner's personal training strengths and stretches, with an action-planning section to help turn stretches into strengths. Each participant worked by himself as he read and scored his self-assessment worksheet.

Example Two

The source of this Concept Center example is Amy Perry, sales trainer for Hallmark Cards, Inc. The centers were part of the introduction to new product

lines for the newly hired sales representatives. These employees needed
to become familiar with all aspects of the products they would be selling:
appearances, prices, manufacturing processes, as well as background information
on the development of each product. In the past, this introduction was a one-day,
product-by-product, lecture-based event.

There were nine table centers set up around a conference room, with one large
tri-fold cardboard display at each table for one product line. The product lines
included cards, party, stationery, gift wrap, books, movies, music, gifts, and
albums. Posted on the product displays were photos and key facts or statistics
about the products. Product samples were placed at each center, along with
catalogs and supporting documentation about the products.

The employees rotated around the room in groups of three (they could also
work individually, if they preferred). They visited each product center and filled
out self-directed worksheets at their own pace. They were able to touch and
feel the products and read the most recent catalogs they'd actually be selling
from. They also gained thorough, in-depth information to support their selling
efforts. The Concept Center time lasted for most of the day and allowed for
plenty of employee interaction with co-workers and the trainer. The trainer was
accessible the entire time—to answer questions and clarify information about the
products.

Before the training ended, the trainer gathered the new employees together for
a whole group discussion and summary of what they learned about the product
lines. The trainer answered final questions, employees evaluated what they
learned, and the trainer thanked them for their efforts before they headed out
the door.

part THREE

Concrete Practice

What You Need to Know About Concrete Practice

*Without concrete experience,
the [information] may have little meaning,
no matter how much someone explains it to you.*

Patricia Wolfe
Brain Matters, 2001, p. 137

Timeline Concept Map for This Chapter

As you read the chapter, add what you learn to the concepts below.

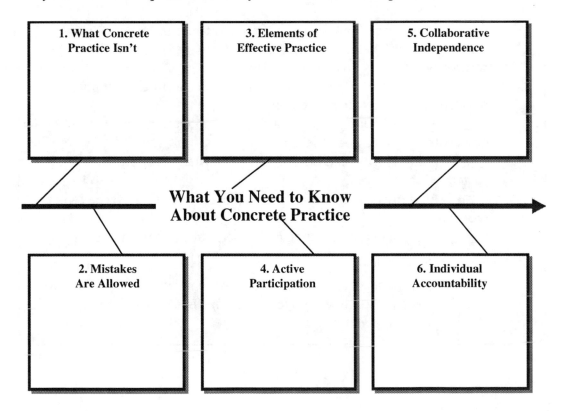

1. What Concrete Practice Isn't

3. Elements of Effective Practice

5. Collaborative Independence

What You Need to Know About Concrete Practice

2. Mistakes Are Allowed

4. Active Participation

6. Individual Accountability

CONNECTIONS

One-Minute Connection: Fast Pass

Practice takes many forms. Rate the following items B for
Best Practice and W for Worst Practice strategies:

1. _____ Participants sit and watch a video demonstration of the computer database entry steps they need to follow.
2. _____ At a safety meeting, and with real equipment, each learner teaches another learner how to safely set up, hold, climb, and dismount a ladder.
3. _____ Paired at computer stations, participants take turns practicing the steps for creating a new spreadsheet while their partners coach and advise them.
4. _____ One person from each of two teams competes for points in a review Jeopardy® game while all the other team members watch the competition.
5. _____ In an insect abatement class, learners take a written test about how to check for termite infestation.
6. _____ In a retail outlet training, participants watch someone demonstrate how to operate the cash registers.
7. _____ With a partner, each learner role plays what to say and do if a customer is dissatisfied.
8. _____ All learners read through the employee guide to learn call center procedures.
9. _____ The trainer asks whether the learners have any questions.

Check your answers against the ones below:

1. **Worst.** Participants sit and watch a video demonstration of the computer database entry steps they need to follow. *What is needed is hands-on practice with real computers.*

2. **Best.** At a safety meeting, and with real equipment, each learner teaches another learner how to safely set up, hold, climb, and dismount a ladder. *This is skills-based practice at its best.*

3. **Best.** Paired at computer stations, participants take turns practicing the steps for creating a new spreadsheet while their partners coach and advise them. *This is another example of concrete, skills-based practice.*

4. **Worst.** One person from each of two teams competes for points in a review Jeopardy® game while all the other team members watch the competition. *Only two people are doing the active review here.*

5. **Worst.** In an insect abatement class, learners take a written test about how to check for termite infestation. *A written test checks knowledge comprehension; a skills-based demonstration by the learners is still needed.*

6. **Worst.** In a retail outlet training, participants watch someone demonstrate how to operate the cash registers. *Good for a start, but learners still need to do it themselves.*

7. **Best.** With a partner, each learner role plays what to say and do if a customer is dissatisfied. *This is practical and experiential.*

8. **Worst.** All learners read through the employee guide to learn call center procedures. *Reading isn't practice.*

9. **Worst.** The trainer asks whether the learners have any questions. *Neither is a question/answer session.*

In this part of the book, you will discover what is and isn't concrete practice and the elements of effective practice. This part also includes fifteen concrete practice strategies that strengthen learners' retention of skills and knowledge.

Imagine That . . .

The training is over. Participants have left the room. You are sitting down for the first time all morning, feet up, and reflecting on what everyone accomplished. Thinking back over the three hours, you realize that the best part of the entire learning experience was the hour during which learners participated in practice activities that gave them opportunities to apply what they had learned.

You had posted a list of activities on the wall, and you directed each table group to pick one activity that sounded interesting to them. On the list were activity titles such as Table Teach Back, Rounds and Repetition, Grab and Gab, Ball Toss, Table Demonstrations, Circle Teach Back, Cooperative Jeopardy, and Group Scavenger Hunt. You then gave each small group the printed instructions for the practice activity chosen by that group. Depending on the activity, some groups practiced the skills with their group members. Others created a whole-group review activity that everyone participated in. The hour was filled with active practice and review, conversation, collaborative work, laughter, and learning.

As participants left the room, you heard many comments about how much they learned and what a good time they had. "A very effective and satisfying hour of concrete practice," you conclude, as you stand and close up the training room.

● ●

CONCEPTS

Practice, by definition, means doing something. Obviously, concrete practice is exactly that: learners repeatedly performing a skill until they become competent doing it. If there are no skills to be learned, then concrete practice refers to the active review of information learned. Either way, *all* learners are actively involved during the practice time, not just a few.

What Concrete Practice Is *Not*

Because concrete practice is the training segment that is often the most challenging, it helps to know what effective concrete practice is *not*. Effective concrete practice is *not*

- Watching the trainer demonstrate the skill.

- Reading about or watching a video of people performing the skill.

- One or two learners competing in a review game while all others watch.

- Being part of a competitive team in which only the team leader participates in the competition.

Training from the BACK of the Room!

- Review activities or games that are not topic-related.
- A paper/pencil test, although that may be one component of the practice.
- A question-and-answer session before the training ends.
- Performing a skill in a high-risk situation, where mistakes can lead to serious consequences.

In addition, there is sometimes a blurry line between concrete practice and a concept review. If there are no real-life, behavior-based skills to practice, then the concrete practice step actually becomes an activity-based concept review. This, in turn, leads to knowledge-based competency rather than skills-based competency. Sometimes knowledge-based competency is the goal of training.

Mistakes Are Allowed

Think about some of the physical skills you have and the amount of practice it took for you to learn how to perform them well. Driving a car, playing a musical instrument, cooking a gourmet meal, or playing sports all come to mind. The mistakes you made along the way were an important part of the learning. And while you learned, it was also important that you were encouraged; competition was kept to a minimum until you could demonstrate confidence and competency in performing the skill.

Concrete practice is about *approximation*, meaning that making mistakes (and learning how to correct them) is part of the practice. So perfection isn't a goal of concrete practice; skill-building or knowledge-building toward a certain level of competency is.

Knowledge-building also requires concrete practice in a collaborative, low-risk learning environment, until learners can demonstrate knowledge-based competency. Some work-related examples of knowledge-based competency are: using a computer program, dealing effectively with customers, working a call-center hotline, filling out forms, interpreting data, making sales calls, creating employee schedules, managing staff, communicating with co-workers, building a team, solving problems, and so on. We could call these either cognitive or interpersonal skills, to differentiate them from physical skills such as operating equipment, following safety procedures, performing an inspection, or constructing a building, to name a few.

Whether practicing skills or acquiring new knowledge, mistakes are an integral, and sometimes necessary, part of concrete practice. I emphasize this because many trainers still assume that once learners hear information or see a skill demonstrated, they will be able to use it or do it correctly the first time around. When approximation is accepted as an important part of effective concrete practice, learners move toward competency more quickly.

> **Try This**
>
> **Learner-Created Practice.** Instead of setting up a practice activity and telling learners how to do it, invite them to create the activity. Give them a few minutes to come up with one practice strategy that they can do in their small groups or with the whole group. Or ask volunteers to create a practice activity for the whole group. The guidelines are that the activity must include everyone, it must reinforce skills or knowledge, and it must take place within a time limit that you set.

Elements of Effective Practice

Here are three important concrete practice elements that will increase either skills-based or knowledge-based competency:

- *Active participation by all learners.* Each learner needs to have multiple opportunities to demonstrate the skill or to participate in the active review.

- *Collaborative interdependence among learners.* When learners work cooperatively together to learn a skill, more learning takes place than if learners compete with each other.

- *Individual accountability.* Learners need to know what it is that they are expected to do or know—and how they will determine their own level of competency.

Let's take a closer look at each of these three important elements.

Active Participation

As I mentioned earlier, one of the most common mistakes trainers make when they create practice activities is to assume that, if a few learners demonstrate a skill while everyone else watches, then everyone is learning. Instead, all learners need to participate in the concrete practice, even if they take turns while doing so.

Active participation doesn't have to have to take place all at once. Skills-based practice can be divided into smaller practice segments following each of the concept segments. This way, learners practice one small part of a multi-step procedure at a time. For example, in a safety training on the Heimlich maneuver for choking victims, learners pair up and do each procedural step as the trainer explains it. Then they practice doing all the steps until they can demonstrate the procedure correctly.

If a training is knowledge-based, then learners can participate in an active review of what was learned, using a game, presentation, Teach-Back, and the like. The more physically active the review game is, the better. For example, in a customer service training, table groups create skits using real-life customer service issues they've encountered and demonstrate appropriate ways of handling these issues.

Collaborative Interdependence

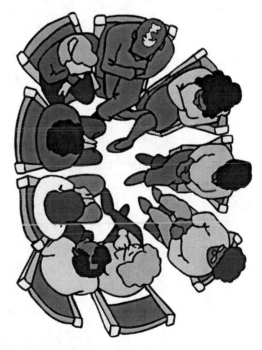

Current brain research emphasizes the importance of collaboration in learning. When a learning community works together in positive ways to help its members learn, and when it provides support and encouragement among its members, learning increases. According to Jay Cross, "We humans exist in networks. We are part of social networks. Our heads contain neural networks. Learning consists of making and maintaining better connections to our networks" (2007, p. 7).

In contrast, competition "focuses on [learners] increasing their own achievement and on preventing [other learners] from achieving higher than they do" (Barkely, Cross, & Major, 2005, p. 17). This is not to say that competition is a bad thing. The research simply points out that, for many people, learning increases when the emphasis is on collaboration and not on competition. Competition seems to sharpen skills already learned, but only for those personality types who feed on the adrenalin rush competition provides. Many learners shut down when competition kicks in. The trick is not to avoid competition, but instead to de-emphasize it, make it more collaborative, or include it as a small part of the entire practice period.

Individual Accountability

Learners need to be clear about what it is they are expected to do or to know, as well as how they will determine their own level of competency. If they have had opportunities at the beginning of the training to become familiar with the learning outcomes and to discuss and write their own learning goals, individual accountability is easier. The learning outcomes and personal goals will help learners stay focused on what they will be held accountable for. Dave Meier reminds us that "Unless what is learned is applied, there is no learning" (2000, p. 101). So concrete practice needs to be tied to the learning outcomes of the training. A practice activity or game unrelated to the learning outcomes is a waste of valuable learning time.

Make a List

Quickly now: Without looking back, list the three elements of effective concrete practice. Write them down, then look back in the chapter to check your answers.

1.
2.
3.

CONCRETE PRACTICE

For concrete practice with your own training programs, choose one or more of the fifteen activities from this part of the book. Some are short, quick practice activities that you can insert into your training right after each concept segment. Others combine all the information and/or skills taught into longer practice sessions. Use them in ways that work for you and your learners.

The activities are divided into three sections. Here are the section and activity titles and brief summaries:

- *Five Teach-Back Strategies: Paired Teach-Back, Table Teach-Back, One-Legged Teach-Back, Improv Teach-Back, Circle Teach-Back.* With these collaborative strategies, learners teach, coach, encourage, and give each other positive feedback and suggestions.

- *Five Skills-Based Activities: In-Room Mentoring, Each Teach, Rounds and Repetition, Table Demonstrations, Skills-Based Game Shows.* While on-the-job training (where a learner is apprenticed to an experienced professional) is the best way of learning and practicing a skill, the activities in this section will give you ways to include this kind of mentoring in a classroom setting.

- *Five Learner-Created Games: Card Games, Grab and Gab, Cooperative Jeopardy, Ball Toss, Group Scavenger Hunts.* Although competition is usually a major game element, the games in this section lessen the emphasis on competition and strengthen the emphasis on collaboration.

One-Minute CONCRETE practice

Change It

Now that you know the elements of effective practice, how would you turn the following Worst Practices into Best Practices? After each statement, write a sentence that describes the changes you would make. Then check your answers against mine.

1. Participants sit and watch a video demonstration of the computer database entry steps they need to follow. *Changes you would make:*

_____

_____

(continued)

2. One person from each of two teams competes for points in a review Jeopardy game. All the other team members watch the competition. *Changes you would make:*

_____

_____

_____

3. In an insect abatement class, learners take a written test about how to check for termite infestation. *Changes you would make:*

_____

_____

_____

4. In a retail outlet training, participants watch someone demonstrate how to operate the cash registers. *Changes you would make:*

_____

_____

_____

5. All learners read through the employee guide to learn call center procedures. *Changes you would make:*

_____

_____

_____

6. The trainer asks whether the learners have any questions. *Changes you would make:*

_____

_____

_____

(continued)

Here are my answers. Your answers might differ, but they should include one or more of the three elements of effective practice, as described in this chapter.

1. After watching the video, participants pair up at computers and mentor each other as they practice the database entry steps.
2. Each team's members collaborate to come up with the team's answers. The team leader position rotates so each person has the opportunity to speak for his or her team.
3. After finishing the written test, learners take turns describing how to check for termite infestation. They also physically demonstrate how to use the pest abatement equipment.
4. After watching the demonstration, learners take turns operating the cash register and mentoring each other.
5. Learners teach each other the call center procedures and then practice the procedures while coaching each other.
6. Each table group creates a set of test questions on index cards. Groups exchange sets and write or state answers to the card questions they received.

● ●

CONCLUSIONS

In order for concrete practice to be effective for *all* learners, the strategies you use must include active participation, collaborative interdependence, and individual accountability. Concrete practice is the "proof of the pudding," if you will—the observable evidence that learners are moving toward skills-based or knowledge-based competency.

You don't learn to swim, or play the piano,
by reading a book about it.

Patricia Wolfe
Brain Matters, 2001, p. 101

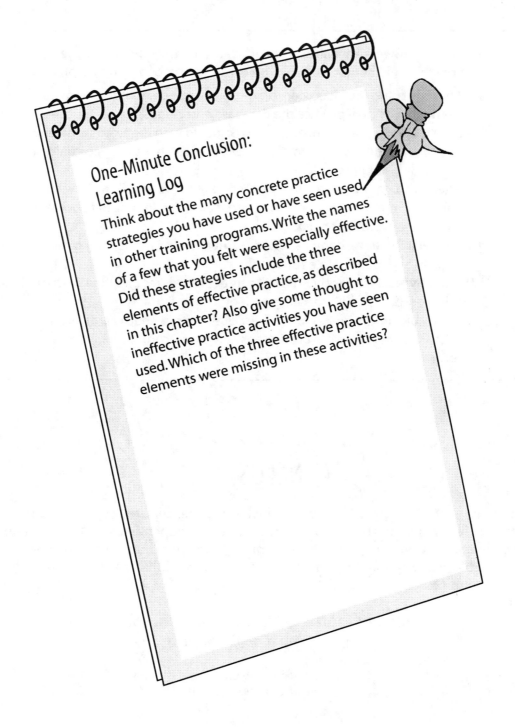

One-Minute Conclusion: Learning Log

Think about the many concrete practice strategies you have used or have seen used in other training programs. Write the names of a few that you felt were especially effective. Did these strategies include the three elements of effective practice, as described in this chapter? Also give some thought to ineffective practice activities you have seen used. Which of the three effective practice elements were missing in these activities?

Trainer's Toolbox

Write down the useful ideas from this chapter and flag this page.

Concrete Practice:
Teach-Back Activities

What Is a Teach-Back?

A Teach-Back is an activity in which learners teach each other what they have learned. They can do this many ways—verbal explanations, demonstrations, skits, and skills coaching, to name a few.

Besides helping participants learn and remember new information, a Teach-Back is an excellent way for a trainer to check for understanding. You don't truly know how much your learners understand or remember until they explain, demonstrate, or teach what they have learned. With a Teach-Back, you obtain a clear idea of their level of understanding and whether or not you have to re-teach certain concepts.

A Teach-Back differs from a Jigsaw activity (see Part Two) in that the former reinforces material that has already been learned, whereas the latter is a method for introducing and learning new material. In both the Teach-Back and the Jigsaw, the trainer steps aside and allows learners to teach and learn from each other.

A Turn and Talk (see Part One) is a mini-version of a Teach-Back, with a one- or two-minute timeline to the verbal exchange of information.

What Does a Teach-Back Do?

For learners, participating in a Teach-Back can

- *Deepen* their understanding of information already learned.

- *Increase* their long-term memory of important facts.

- *Clarify* any misconceptions or confusion about the information.

- *Make* them aware of how much they have learned and what they still need to know.

- *Increase* their confidence as they teach someone else what they have learned.

- *Help* them to master what they teach.

By observing learners as they participate in a Teach-Back, a trainer can

- *Check* for understanding and *clarify* what learners know and don't know.
- *Assess* what areas of learning need more direct instruction or more review.
- *Give* constructive and encouraging feedback to individuals and groups when necessary.
- *Make* notes on the progress of each learner and tailor some of the later review to specific learning needs.

Getting Ready

- **Materials:** Provide standard training materials. For specific activities, see the instructions for additional materials.
- **Setup:** There must be enough space in the room so that learners don't get in each other's way as they do Teach-Backs. Use breakout areas in addition to the training room, if possible.
- **Group Size:** Any size group is fine.
- **Time:** This will vary, depending on the amount of information or the complexity of the skill being practiced. Usually, Teach-Backs last from five to twenty minutes.

Five Teach-Back Activities

1. Paired Teach-Back

Ask learners to stand, find partners (triads are acceptable if there is an odd number of participants), and do one of the following:

- Take turns explaining the need-to-know information from the training.
- Take turns demonstrating the skill being learned and giving each other positive feedback, suggestions, and encouragement.
- Take turns asking each other questions about the material covered.
- Together, create a short, one- or two-minute skit demonstrating the need-to-know information or skill learned, and then perform the skit for the whole group.

2. Table Teach-Back

Do the following:

- Assign each table group one specific content segment to teach to the class.

- Each group prepares a short presentation of the material. These can be summaries of about one to three minutes in length or longer presentations of five or ten minutes, in which table groups use different media: visuals, slides, charts, interactive strategies, or demonstrations.

- Table groups make their presentations and receive rounds of applause from the class.

3. One-Legged Teach-Back

Learners form standing groups of three to five people per group. Each learner summarizes what he has learned, but there is a fun twist to the summaries: The person speaking must stand on one leg while talking. This ensures that the summaries will be short and adds a note of humor to the Teach-Back.

4. Improv Teach-Back

Improvisation is a role play, jazzed up with more spontaneity and less structure. When you say to learners *"We're going to do Improvs"* you won't hear the groans that you might when you say, *"We're going to do role plays."* The Improv Teach-Back instructions are as follows:

- Explain to learners what an Improv Teach-Back is and that, as a whole group, they will need to have eight Teach-Backs done in two minutes. This means that each Teach-Back should last between ten and fifteen seconds.

- Choose a timer who will signal when fifteen seconds are up.

- One participant volunteers to begin the activity by standing and talking about what he has learned so far. While talking, he can be as dramatic as he wishes, using gestures and voice tone to emphasize the information and to add humor to it.

- In the middle of a sentence (or when the timer signals that fifteen seconds have passed), he abruptly stops talking and calls out another learner's name.

- This next participant stands and immediately picks up the Improv where the first participant left off. The second learner talks for ten or fifteen seconds, then stops mid-sentence and calls out another name.

- The rounds continue until the number of Improv Teach-Backs has been reached within the time allowed, or until the two minutes end.

For an Improv Teach-Back with skills practice, do the following:

- Again, establish the number of Improv Teach-Backs the whole group must accomplish within a certain time limit. Choose a timer.

- One volunteer begins to demonstrate the skill.

- She stops in the middle of the demonstration, and the next person has to continue the demonstration where the first one left off.

- If learners can demonstrate the skill in two or three rounds, the skills demonstration starts over, with the next learner repeating the beginning of the skill. Rounds continue until learners have demonstrated the designated number of Improv Teach-Backs or until the timer signals to stop.

- For skills practice, learners can choose to be quite dramatic in their demonstrations, which adds humor to this type of Improv Teach-Back.

5. Circle Teach-Back

Do the following:

- Learners stand in a circle around a volunteer. If the whole class is large (twenty or more), learners form smaller standing circles of about ten people each.

- The person in the middle of the circle holds a soft, throwable object (such as a Koosh® or Nerf® ball). This person gives a quick summary or demonstration of what he learned, then tosses the ball to someone else.

- The next person moves to the middle of the circle (the first one joins the circle and the activity repeats itself).

- If the circle is small enough, everyone has a turn to stand in the middle and do a Circle Teach-Back. If the circle is large, or if there is only a short amount of time to do the activity, you can limit the number of Teach-Backs to just a few.

Your Turn

Make a Concept Map of your own Teach-Back ideas. I've included one on the next page for the Teach-Backs in this section.

Concept Map for
Teach-Back Activities

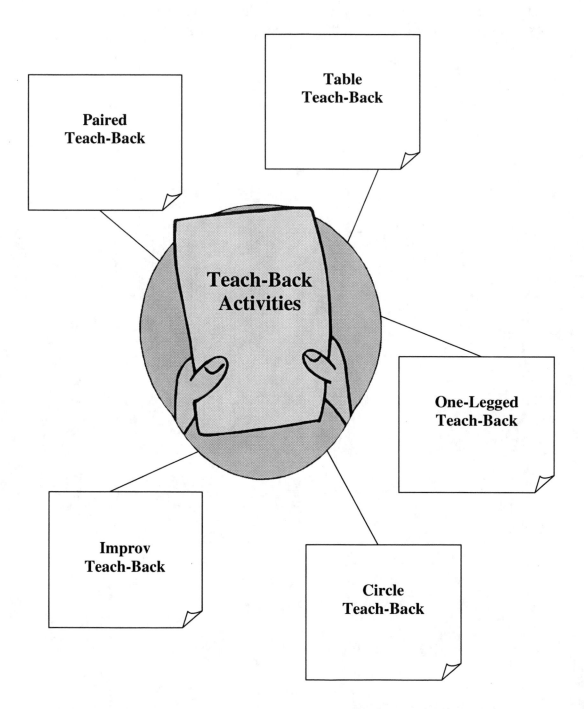

Training from the BACK of the Room!

Concrete Practice: Skills-Based Activities

What Is a Skills-Based Activity?

A skills-based activity is an actual skills practice during which training participants *physically* practice the skills they are learning. A skills-based activity can also be a simulation, that is, a "pretend" way to practice skills. An example of practicing an actual skill is driving a car during a driver's training class. A skill simulation example is using a computerized driving program instead of a real car.

It seems pretty obvious that if the training involves actual skills, learners should, at some point, practice those skills. Yet many training programs do not include enough time for practice. One problem is that it takes a great deal of time to master a skill. Another is that sometimes it is difficult for a trainer to know how to set up and monitor a skills-based activity. However, even with these constraints, concrete practice is the only way for training participants to learn a skill well enough to be able to *do* it once the training is over. Of course, concrete practice also significantly increases learners' long-term retention of knowledge and skills.

The skills-based activities in this section are easy to set up and monitor, while giving learners quality practice time during training.

What Does a Skills-Based Activity Do?

When learners participate in a skills-based activity, they

- *Practice* the skill, with guidance and encouragement from the trainer and their peers.
- *Can make* mistakes safely, without the fear of adverse consequences.
- *Self-correct* as they practice.
- *Peer-correct* each other's practice.

- *Gain* confidence in their ability to demonstrate or perform the skill they are learning.

- *Reach* a degree of skill mastery they wouldn't have without the skills-based practice.

Getting Ready

- **Materials:** Depending on the activity, you will need standard training materials, as well as any materials mentioned in the activity instructions.

- **Setup:** Most activities require little special setup, with the exception of enough open space in the room, or extra space outside of the room, for learners to be able to move around if necessary. If using real-life work areas (offices, call centers, equipment areas, and the like), you will need to make these arrangements beforehand.

- **Group Size:** Any size group is fine, as long as there is enough room space for the activities.

- **Time:** This will vary greatly, depending on the activity. Usually a skills-based practice will last from fifteen to sixty minutes.

Five Skills-Based Activities

1. In-Room Mentoring

The most powerful skills practice is what has been done for thousands of years: actual on-the-job practice with an experienced mentor—in other words, an apprenticeship. It is worth the time and effort set up this type of skills-based practice during the actual training time, if possible. Do the following:

- Ask that learners form mentoring pairs, with a more-experienced learner (the mentor) pairing up with a less-experienced one.

- If all learners are less-experienced, check to see whether you can bring in other experienced people from outside the class (employees, supervisors, previous class participants, experts in the field) for the In-Room Mentoring time. These people will be the mentors for the training participants.

- The practice becomes a simulation of what would occur in real life, with the less-experienced learner demonstrating the skill, and the mentor offering coaching suggestions, advice, encouragement, and feedback.

It is helpful to remind mentors how to give positive feedback to the less-experienced learners. You can post phrases on the wall for the mentors to use: *"You did that well. Try it this way instead. In addition, you might want to do this. You almost hit the mark. You are closer this time. Let's change this step to this one. Let's review it again. You got it."*

2. Each Teach

This is like the Paired Teach-Back, except that, in this case, one learner pretends she knows nothing about the skill, and the other learner in the pair must demonstrate and teach the entire skill to the first. Then they reverse roles.

The Each Teach activity works well when learners are at about the same skill level. It is also helpful with technology training in computer labs. Even if each learner is seated at her own computer station, it still makes sense to have learners work in pairs for the skills practice, teaching and learning from each other.

3. Rounds and Repetition

This activity works well if the skills practice involves a series of procedural steps. Do the following:

- At each table group, post the procedurals steps of the skill on chart or printer paper.
- Each learner in the group takes a turn demonstrating one of the procedural steps while the other group members act as mentors.
- Learners continue to take turns demonstrating the procedural steps until each group member has had one or more turns.

Here is a Rounds and Repetition variation:

- Before the training, print the skills on a set of index cards (one set per table group and one procedural step per card).
- Each learner in a table group takes a turn choosing a card and demonstrating that procedural step.

4. Table Demonstrations

Do the following:

- Each table group prepares a skill demonstration.

- The demonstration may include how *not* to do it, then how to do it correctly. Or the group may break the skill down into its procedural steps, with each group member demonstrating one step.

- Each group presents its demonstration in front of all the other groups and receives peer feedback and applause.

5. Skills-Based Game Shows

A game show activity is a popular way to review and memorize new information. With a Skills-Based Game Show, learners demonstrate skills instead of answering questions. The emphasis is on skills practice rather than verbal replies.

- Explain the game show format—one of your choosing, or learners can choose a format. Some formats are: Jeopardy®, Concentration®, Let's Make a Deal®, and Who Wants to Be a Millionaire®, to name a few.

- Ask for volunteers to be the game show host, referee, timer, and any other roles needed.

- Participants or table teams will demonstrate skills, or specific procedural steps, instead of answering questions. Or the activity could be a combination of questions, information sharing, and skills practice.

- The referee awards points to the participant or table team that correctly demonstrates the skill or the procedural step.

- Make sure everyone has a chance to participate in the Skills-Based Game Show.

- Award small prizes to the winning learners or teams.

Your Turn

Make a Concept Map of your own skills-based activities.

Concrete Practice:
Learner-Created Games

What Is a Learner-Created Game?

A Learner-Created Game is a review activity, usually in a game format, in which learners take the roles of creators, leaders, hosts, players, timers, and referees. As obvious as this type of concrete practice may seem—yes, learners *can* create and lead their own review games—it's interesting to note how often the trainer ends up creating and leading the game.

Even though most trainers know the value of participatory games in reviewing learned material, it is still difficult for many of us to step aside and hand over the game creation and leadership to the learners. Sometimes that isn't our fault. Learners expect us to take the leadership role in a review game; after all, we know what the game will be—they don't.

If trainers were totally honest, though, we would probably acknowledge that it's fun (and an ego boost) to be the game leader and call the shots, so to speak. Again, the challenge for us is to break our own long-held habits, step aside, and let the learners create—and lead—their own games.

In his book *Design Your Own Games and Activities* (2003), corporate trainer and gaming guru Sivasailam (Thiagi) Thiagarajan calls learner-created games "framegames." He defines framegames as "templates for the instant creation of a performance-improvement activity" (p. 8). As such, this template or frame becomes the game's structure, which learners use when they create their own games. Thiagi's book abounds with framegames.

Most of television's game shows are examples of framegames as well. In the United States, some of these game shows are: Jeopardy®, Hollywood Squares®, Wheel of Fortune®, Family Feud®, Who Wants to Be a Millionaire?®, and Deal or No Deal®. The structures of these game shows are general enough to be used with just about any topic.

Of course, you need to set some guidelines for Learner-Created Games so that participants have a structure that makes the game work better for everyone. Here are a few suggested guidelines:

- *Game purpose.* Make sure learners know the purpose of the game and how it ties to the learning outcomes of the training. This means that you need to think about how effective a particular game will be as a *learning* tool for *all* learners before you decide to include the game.

- *Frame the game.* Explain to learners the general structure of the game (examples: game-show format, pencil-paper, card game, collaborative versus competitive, or team versus individual). The frame also includes what will be expected of the participants and the group or individual accountability.

- *Leadership rotation.* Instruct learners to rotate game roles (leader, host, referee, timer, players) so that everyone has a turn to both play a role and play the game.

- *Collaboration versus competition.* As I mentioned in the chapter "Brain-Friendly Training," when collaboration is emphasized and competition is de-emphasized, most people learn better, at least at the beginning of a learning experience. This is not to say that competition should be eliminated from concrete practice. Instead, it means that, whenever possible, use some elements of collaboration as part of the competition. For example, when participants compete as teams instead of as individuals and team members are allowed to collaborate on game-show answers, everyone participates and learns.

- *Game duration.* Before the game, determine how long the game will last, the level of participation (for example, everyone participates at the same time or learners rotate participant roles), and the criteria for "winning" the game. Often, games can have many winners, instead of just one person or group.

- *Post-game discussion.* Create a list of questions that learners will discuss after the game is over. During the post-game discussion, learners reflect on and talk about what they learned from the activity itself. Examples of post-game discussion questions:

  - *What was the most important thing you learned from playing the game?*
  - *What was something that surprised you during the game?*
  - *What was a pattern or interesting element that you observed?*
  - *What did you learn about the game content that you didn't know before?*

- *What information from the game can you use after the training ends?*
- *What suggestions do you have that would make the game a better learning experience?*
- *What are some variations to this game that would be useful if you played it again?*
- *How could you use a game like this at work to help you remember new information/skills?*

What Does a Learner-Created Game Do?

When learners create, lead, play, host, and referee their own learner-created game, they

- *Increase* their understanding of the content learned.
- *Translate* what they know into practical application.
- *Create* unique ways to move the knowledge or skills into long-term memory.
- *Help* others review important information or skills in a wide variety of ways.
- *Self-correct* and *peer-correct* any misconceptions or mistakes.
- *Own* the game and the content the game is based on, meaning that they have more of a reason for wanting to learn and use it than just the trainer telling them that it is important to know.

Getting Ready

- **Materials:** Provide standard training materials, as well as any other materials specified by the table groups. Most groups will need index cards, writing materials, markers, construction or other colored paper, card stock, chart paper, and other game-making materials.
- **Setup:** Learners will determine what the setup is for each game.
- **Group Size:** Learners also determine the size of groups playing the game.
- **Time:** The amount of time needed to create and then play the game may vary from group to group. You can determine the time allotted, or learners can do this, within the general time frame of the training.

Five Learner-Created Games

1. Card Games

Before learners or table groups create their own card games, give them examples of games, either on a printed list (see below), a chart list, or verbally. Learners then do the following:

- They work in pair, triads, or table groups to create the card games.

- Each pair, triad, or table group creates a different card game using index cards as the game pieces.

- Each group also makes a game instruction card and an answer key card. When the groups finish creating their card games, they exchange games with other groups (or with pairs/triads).

- The groups play each other's games and exchange games again, if time allows.

- After the games are over, each group holds its own post-game discussion. Or you can ask for a volunteer to lead a whole-group discussion about the games.

Listed below are some Card Game examples for learners to read and use:

- *Twenty Questions.* Prepare a set of about a dozen game cards. On each card, print a topic-related question and answer and the number of points the card is worth. The instruction card reads: *"Choose a game leader. The leader reads each question and calls on the person who first raises his hand to answer it. If the answer is correct, that person is awarded the points. At the end of the game, the person in the group with the most points wins. You can rotate the leader role so everyone has a chance to play."*

- *Myth or Fact.* Prepare a set of about two-dozen game cards. On each card print a topic-related statement. Some of the statements are myths and others are facts about the topic. On a separate index card print "MYTHS" and on another print "FACTS" in large letters. Make an answer key card, or print the word MYTH or FACT on the back of each card. The instruction card reads: *"As a group, discuss and sort the statement cards into two piles: MYTHS and FACTS. After you sort the cards, use the answer key (or turn the cards over) to see whether you sorted them correctly. Give your group a point for each correct card. Let the whole group know your score at the end of the game."*

- *Put Them in Order.* On each card, print a statement that describes separate steps in a topic-related procedure. Make an answer key card too. The instruction card reads: *"As a group, discuss and agree on the order in which the steps occur, as described on each card. Put the cards in order. Then check your group's choices with the answer key. Give your group a 'high five' if you put the cards in the correct order."*

◉ *Fill-in-the-Blanks.* On each card print one factual statement but with one or two important words left out. Put a point value on each card. On the back side of each card, print the word or words that were left out of the statement. The instructions card reads: *"Lay the cards, statement sides up, on the table. Each person in the group takes a turn choosing one card and verbally reading and completing the statement by saying what words he thinks go in the blanks. He turns the card over and checks the printed answer against his own. If he is correct, he is awarded the points. The person with the most points wins."*

2. Grab and Gab

This is a variation of the game Grab That Spoon in *The Ten-Minute Trainer.* For this game, each table group creates a printed list of a dozen or more items. The listed items can be

◉ *Questions and answers* and point values for each topic-related question.

◉ *True and false statements* about the concepts learned and point values for each statement.

◉ *Concepts that are topic-related* and point values for each concept.

The game procedure is as follows:

◉ Place an object in the middle of each table group and within easy reach of all the game players at that table. Besides being an important part of the game, the object will be the final prize for the person in the group with the most points. Objects can be topic-related or metaphorical. Some examples are a company baseball cap or tee-shirt, a mouse pad for a computer class, a small bag of candy for a customer service class (a metaphorical reminder to be "sweet" to customers), a toy that represents something used by the company, a stuffed animal, a rubber brain (Grab That Brain?), a Koosh® or Nerf® ball, or other objects.

◉ One person in the group volunteers to be the game leader (group members can rotate this role). The leader reads the question, statement, or concept.

◉ After the leader reads the item, the first player to grab the object must do one of the following:

- *For a question*—Answer the question.

- *For a statement*—Decide whether the statement is true or false. If it is false, give a reason why or reword it so that the statement is true.

- *For a topic-related concept*—Verbally define, explain, or give an example of the concept.

- After the person who grabbed the object finishes talking, the reader (or the group) decides whether his answer, his true/false assessment, or his definition/explanation is correct. If he is correct, the leader awards him the points.

- The player puts the object back in the middle of the table and the next round begins. The group plays the game until time is called. After the game is over, the participant with the most points wins the Grab and Gab object as a prize.

3. Cooperative Jeopardy

The problem with traditional Jeopardy® (as played on the television game show) is that only one person from each team actually plays the game. And the traditional game is a contest of speed more than knowledge; the person who hits the buzzer the soonest gets to state the answer. Traditional Jeopardy also has the players stating the question in response to a reading of the answer.

With Cooperative Jeopardy, everyone in the teams plays, and every team has a chance to answer the questions and win the game. Furthermore, two or more teams can win. Instructions:

- All learners create the question and answer cards for the game and give the cards point values for the difficulty of the questions.

- Three learners volunteer to be the host, timer, and referee. The referee will walk around the room and check each group's written answer.

- The host collects the cards and begins the game by reading aloud one of the questions.

- All table groups will have fifteen seconds (twenty or thirty seconds, if the question is a difficult one) to discuss the question, agree on an answer, and write the answer on an index card.

- Once each group finishes writing, one person stands up at each table (this person has to be a different person each round, and the person may not stand until the card has been completed).

- When the timer calls "Time," only those standing with a card to read can read their cards aloud.

- The referee makes sure that the cards have the answers written on them. The standing players take turns reading their cards aloud. The host tells them whether or not their answers are correct and awards points to the table groups with the correct answers.

- If there are any disagreements about what is or is not a correct answer, the referee has the final say. For each round, there can be more than one table group with the correct answer, and these groups are all awarded the same number of points.

- If an answer is partially correct, the referee may decide to award that group partial points.

- One member of each table group needs to keep track of the group's points. At the end of the game, the group(s) with the most points wins.

- The host gives out small prizes, if available. Or, in lieu of prizes, the winning group(s) receive standing ovations or rounds of applause from the other table groups.

4. Ball Toss

Learners can create all sorts of review games with any kind of small, soft, throwable objects: Koosh® or Nerf® balls, beach balls, stuffed animals, bath sponges, small pillows, and balloons, to name a few. Plus, a Ball Toss is a great way to get participants up and out of their seats when they have been sitting too long. Here are three Ball Toss variations:

- *Ask, Answer, Toss.* Learners work in collaborative groups. Each group creates three or four topic-related questions, each with a certain point value. One group asks another group a topic-related question. The second group works collaboratively to answer the question. If the answer is correct, a group member tosses the ball into a container of some sort (trash can, bowl, bucket, bag, or small hoop) in order to win the card points. If the answer is incorrect, another group may have an opportunity to answer the question and toss the ball. Groups take turns asking questions of each other. A different person in each group tosses the ball each time so that everyone participates. The group with the most points wins the game.

- *Ask, Toss, Answer.* This variation is similar to the one above, except that there is no container in the Ball Toss activity. Instead, one group asks a question and tosses the ball to a second group. If the second group answers the question correctly, the group is awarded the points. Then the second group poses a question for a third group. Rounds continue until each group has had a turn at asking and answering questions and tossing the ball.

- *Answer, Toss, Ask.* As in traditional Jeopardy, each group creates three or four topic-related answers, each with a certain point value. The Ball Toss continues like the variation above, with the difference being that groups must state the question that goes with the answer.

5. Group Scavenger Hunts

Learners can do this activity during the training, or between training sessions if the training lasts more than one day. The activity can also be a Warm-Up variation (see Warm-Ups in Part One of this book). Instructions:

- Each table group makes a scavenger hunt list of ten (more or less, depending on time) topic-related items to find.

- Table groups exchange lists and the game time begins. Groups can work together or can divide up the list to find the items within the time allowed.

- The group (or groups) that finish finding/doing all the items before time is called are the winners.

Scavenger Hunt item examples:

- *Find a person outside of this training room (or in another table group) who knows five important facts about the topic. The person must state the facts and then write his or her name here:*

  _____

- *Find an object in this room (or in an office, board room, staff room) related to the topic. Write its description and who found it here:*

  _____

- *Do an Internet search for one important topic-related concept, and write the URL where the information was found:*

  _____

◉ *Ask someone in the room who is not in your group to demonstrate a topic-related skill you just learned. After the demonstration, have that person sign his/her name here:*

_____

◉ *Find someone from another table group to help you compose a short poem, jingle, rap, or slogan that will help you remember important topic-related facts. Write your composition here:* _____

_____

_____

_____

_____

_____

◉ *Using any materials in the room, create a small, three-dimensional representation or metaphor of one important concept. Be ready to explain your creation to the whole group. Give your creation a title and write it here:*

_____

Your Turn

Try your hand at a Concept Map of your own Learner-Created Games.

part FOUR

Conclusions

What You Need to Know About Conclusions

What the learner thinks and says and does
is more important than
what the instructor thinks and says and does.

Dave Meier
The Accelerate Learning Handbook, 2000, p. 91

Burger Concept Map for This Chapter

As you read the chapter, write a few facts in the burger parts about each concept.

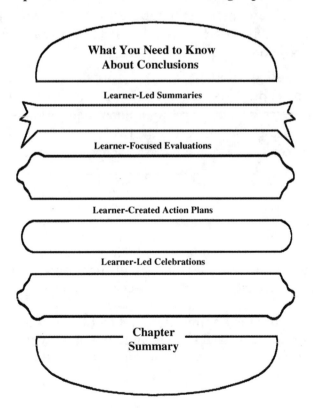

What You Need to Know About Conclusions

Learner-Led Summaries

Learner-Focused Evaluations

Learner-Created Action Plans

Learner-Led Celebrations

Chapter Summary

CONNECTIONS

One-Minute Connection: Fast Pass

The training program you conducted is just about over. You have five minutes left. Circle what your learners will do during the last five minutes of the program.

The learners will

A. Fill out the evaluation forms.

B. Clean up their table areas and gather their books and materials.

C. Listen while you summarize what they have learned and thank them for attending.

D. Summarize what they learned and describe how they will apply what they learned.

E. Tell their table groups what they appreciated about working together.

F. Take part in a celebratory activity that ends the training on a positive, high-energy note.

This is a trick question because all of the above items need to be accomplished before the training ends. However, items D, E, and F are the ones that learners will do *during the last five minutes* of your program. Items A, B, and C will happen earlier. You'll discover why in this part of the book, and you'll find fifteen activities that will help you create effective and memorable conclusions.

Imagine That ...

Ten new ski resort employees just finished their company's "Safety in the Workplace" training, where they learned about such concepts as hazardous materials, emergency procedures, first aid, accident reporting, snow and ice issues, and so forth.

Fifteen minutes before the training ended, they filled out the company's standard evaluation form, as well as the mandated paperwork signifying their successful completion of the training. After finishing these tasks, employees formed a standing circle. The trainer, Mel, tossed a white Koosh® ball—he called it a snowball—to one of the employees. He told the group that the person holding the ball had to tell the group the most important fact he or she learned about workplace safety before tossing the ball to another employee. After a half-dozen of these quick Ball Toss summary statements, Mel instructed everyone to form standing pairs or triads. While upbeat music played in the background, Mel explained the final training activity, a Walk and Talk, in which standing groups walked around the room while talking about how they planned to apply the safety tips when they returned to their jobs. When everyone had completed the Walk and Talk, Mel thanked them for their participation in the training, and the training ended. Employees left with the learning fresh in their minds and a commitment to use what they learned.

- -

CONCEPTS

Conclusions are short, learner-focused closing activities in which learners

- *Summarize* what they have learned.
- *Evaluate* what they have learned.
- *Make* an action plan—a commitment to apply what they have learned.
- *Celebrate* the learning experience.

Like connections that engage learners from the moment they walk into the training room, conclusions engage learners up until the moment they leave. With conclusions, learners leave with a positive feeling about the training. Furthermore, conclusions help learners focus on what they learned and how they can use the knowledge or skills in real life.

Here is a closer look at each of the four elements of effective conclusions.

Learner-Led Summaries

In most traditional training programs, it is the trainer who summarizes the major points of the training. By now you know that learners need to be doing their own summaries so that they deepen their understanding and long-term retention of what they learned.

Learner-led summaries are much more effective as *learning* strategies than a trainer-led summary. And, let's face it, learners are more interested in what *they* say they've learned than in what the trainer says they've learned. Dave Meier explains that the trainer's role is to "Get the learners to think, say, and do . . . in ways that will help them integrate [learning] into their existing structure of knowledge, meaning, and skill" (2000, p. 91).

An example of a learner-led summary is the Ball Toss, described above. Here is another example: Each participant in a database class writes one fact about the database program on a piece of paper. Everyone exchanges papers. Each writes another fact on the new papers. They exchange papers and write one more fact each. Finally, they summarize the three facts on their final papers and read these summaries aloud.

Learner-Focused Evaluations

Obviously, learners need to assess their own learning. Additionally, your company, school, or training department may need to do an assessment as well. It's not an "either/or" but a "both/and" proposition. However, in most traditional training programs, learners evaluate *the training*, but not necessarily *their own learning*. Or, if there is any learning assessment, it's usually in the paper/pencil form of a written test. There is nothing wrong with a test, nor with a learner evaluation of the training. All that is lacking is the learner's personal evaluation of his or her own learning.

An example of a learner-focused evaluation is when training participants discuss what they've learned in comparison to what they knew before the training. A more specific example is this: Participants in a call service training rank their own comfort levels with the new call service procedures by standing along an imaginary continuum that signifies a degree of confidence, from "need more practice" on one side to "can use it with ease" on the other side. If time allows, they discuss their choices and the next steps they will take to improve their standings.

The Four Levels of Learning Evaluation. Most trainers have some working knowledge of Donald Kirkpatrick's learning evaluation model, which, as I've mentioned before, assesses the following four levels:

1. Learners' feelings about what they learned
2. Knowledge learned
3. Improved performance
4. Return on training investment

If you're not familiar with Kirkpatrick's evaluation model, do yourself a favor and read through some of the web articles about his research—valuable information that gives you a big-picture perspective of evaluation. Browse through the selection of Kirkpatrick's books on www.amazon.com, or other websites that offer these useful resources.

The Four-Square Levels of Learning activity in the Evaluation section of this part of the book gives you a simple tool that incorporates the concepts from the Kirkpatrick's model.

Learner-Created Action Plans

When learners make public their commitment to use what they have learned, they are more likely to make good on that commitment. An action plan is a learner's public commitment, either verbally or in writing, to use what was learned in the training.

In addition to simply stating their action plans, training participants can create *ongoing* plans in which they assess their performance improvement at future intervals, perhaps in two weeks or a month after the training. They may report to a supervisor or a colleague who attended the training, or email a short report to the trainer about how they have put their new knowledge/skills to work.

Action plans are usually included in the summary, evaluation, or celebration parts of the conclusion step of the 4 Cs. You'll find action plans imbedded into many of the fifteen activities in this part of the book.

Learner-Led Celebrations

The final element of conclusions, and perhaps the most important, is the celebration. Because of time constraints, many trainers eliminate this element, which is unfortunate because it is the element that is often the most memorable. A celebration during the closing is the emotional counterpart of a connection during the opening. It is the feeling of positive energy that rounds out the entire learning experience. Connections created a learning community for the duration of the training; celebrations acknowledge the journey the learning community has taken and the emotional connections shared among learners.

In addition, by ending a training with a celebration activity, you are applying the Primacy-Recency Principle (as described in Part One), thereby ensuring that the learning sticks longer in the minds of the participants. Celebrations that are learner-led create a release of endorphins, the brain's pleasure chemicals, which means that training participants leave feeling good about the learning experience and will want to attend another like it.

The celebration activities should be meaningful and relevant to the learners. Each learner's attention and energy is turned toward *the group* and not the trainer. In other words, you step aside and let the learners lead the activity, or you participate in the activity as one of the learners, not as a trainer leading a celebration.

An example of a learner-led celebration is when table groups each create a sound and movement that represent what they learned or how they feel about what they learned. They present their sounds/motions to the whole group and receive rounds of applause. Another specific example: At the end of a train-the-trainer certificate program, each participant takes a turn handing out another participant's certificate, while the whole group applauds and cheers.

Box It In

Put a box around the correct phrase in each sentence below:

A. An important element of conclusions is (*learner-led summaries; the trainer's summary statements*).
B. Conclusions help learners (*evaluate the trainer and the training; evaluate what they have learned*).
C. During the conclusion, (*learners celebrate their learning journey; learners celebrate getting passing scores on the final test*).
D. Conclusions are really about (*filling out an evaluation form and heading out the door; allowing learners to summarize, evaluate, and celebrate the learning*).

The sentences should read:

A. An important element of conclusions is *learner-led summaries.*
B. Conclusions help learners *evaluate what they have learned.*
C. During the conclusion, learners *celebrate their learning journey.*
D. Conclusions are really about *allowing learners to summarize, evaluate, and*

● ●

CONCRETE PRACTICE

Choose one or more of the fifteen connection activities in this part of the book to use in your training. Vary the activities you choose until you are familiar with them. Decide which ones work best for your topics and participant groups. Then make them a regular part of your programs.

The activities are divided into three sections. The section and activity titles and brief summaries are listed below:

● *Five Learner-Led Summaries: Learning Logs, Stand and Deliver, Table Talk, Card Exchange, Round Robin.* These activities help learners deepen their own understanding of what they learned. Some include learner-created action plans, in which learners make a commitment to use what they learned.

- *Five Evaluation Strategies: Where Do You Stand?, Four-Square Feedback, Four-Square Levels of Learning, May We Quote You?, Email Blast.* These are alternative ways for learners to evaluate their own learning, besides the traditional "strongly agree/disagree, 1-to-5" scale. Learner-created action plans are also part of the evaluation strategies.

- *Five Celebration Activities: Make and Take, Certificate Car Wash, Circle Celebration, I Like My Neighbor, Walk and Talk.* Fun, yet still content-related, these activities end training with positive energy and put the learners center-stage in the celebration.

· ·

CONCLUSIONS

Conclusions help training participants pause, reflect on, and summarize what they have learned. Learners also assess their own learning, and make action plans to apply their new knowledge/skills after the training ends. And most importantly, they celebrate the learning journey they've taken together. The connection and conclusion segments of a training are related to each other and bracket the entire training experience.

Closure is usually the last opportunity the learner has to attach sense and meaning to new learning.

David Sousa
How the Brain Learns, 2006, p. 276

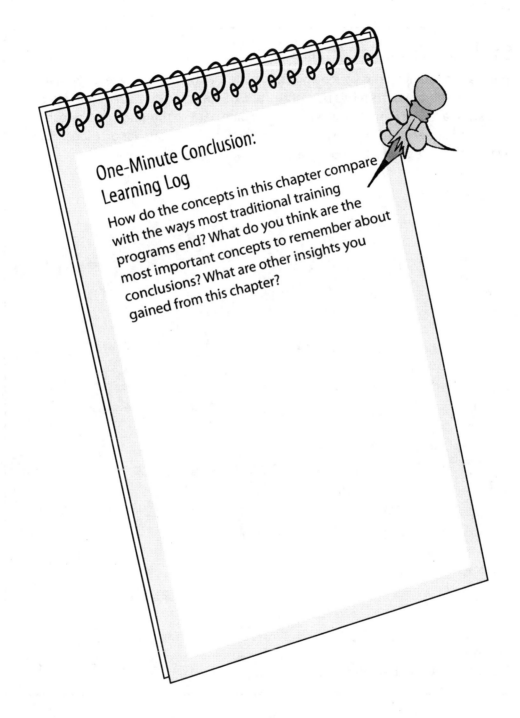

One-Minute Conclusion:
Learning Log

How do the concepts in this chapter compare with the ways most traditional training programs end? What do you think are the most important concepts to remember about conclusions? What are other insights you gained from this chapter?

One-Minute Conclusion: Action Plan

In the space below, write your own action plan, that is, what you are making a commitment to use from this part of the book. Sign and date your action plan. Also write a future date on the page. You'll come back to this page and reread it then to see how you did. Take it a step further and make your action plan public by telling a colleague what your plan is and when you will apply it

My Action Plan

My Signature:
The Present Date:
The Future Date to Reread My Plan:

Training from the BACK of the Room!

Trainer's Toolbox

Write down the useful ideas from this part of the book. Don't forget to flag this page for later use.

Conclusions: Learner-Led Summaries

What Is a Learner-Led Summary

A Learner-Led Summary is a discussion or series of statements, led by the training participants, that summarizes what they have learned. Remember: *You* are not doing the summary; the *learners* are.

Besides being an effective way for learners to review content and to assess their own learning, a Learner-Led Summary also gives you—the trainer— an opportunity to evaluate what learners know. For example, during a learner's summary statements, if you hear erroneous information, you can make a mental note to meet with that learner after the training, or at another time, to address the misconceptions. You would not even know there was a misunderstanding if you did the summarizing for the participants.

What Does a Learner-Led Summary Do?

For training participants, a Learner-Led Summary is an opportunity to

- *Think* again about what was learned and its impact on what they do.

- *Focus* on the most important information, and what was most meaningful to them.

- *State* what they learned, either verbally or in writing.

- *Decide* how they plan to use what they learned.

- *Discuss* the learning with others in the training.

- *Deepen* the relevancy of the topic and concepts to their own work.

Getting Ready

- **Materials:** Check the summary activities for the needed materials, other than standard training materials.

- **Setup:** No special setup is necessary.
- **Group Size:** Any size group is fine.
- **Time:** This will vary, depending on the large- and small-group sizes. The time range will be from ten to thirty minutes for most of the activities.

Five Learner-Led Summaries

1. Learning Logs

A Learning Log is a written summary—a short paragraph or two (somewhat like a journal entry)—that learners create. A Learning Log helps learners keep a record of their own learning journey: what they know that they didn't know before, what they feel are the important concepts, and how they might use these concepts in their own training. These summaries can also include action plans, which are the learners' commitments to use what they have learned. Usually Learning Logs are written, but learners can draw, doodle, flow chart, or create a Concept Map as well.

Do the following:

- Before the training, print the Learning Log instructions on a worksheet, index card, chart paper, or slide. Use one of the following Learning Log instructions or make up your own:

  - *Compare and contrast the knowledge and assumptions you had about this topic before the training with what you now know. Write a paragraph summarizing your comparisons.*

  - *For you, what are the most important concepts and insights from this training? How do you plan to use what you've learned?*

  - *In what ways does this information change previous perceptions you've held about these concepts? How do you think you might use this information?*

  - *If you were a newspaper reporter and were asked to summarize this training for a news article, what would you say? Write your short article here.*

  - *What would you tell a colleague about this training and what you learned here that will help you at work (or in your life)?*

  - *Describe the benefits from this training for you or your company?*

  - *What do you know now that you didn't know before? How will you use this knowledge?*

- Ask learners to take a few minutes to write their responses to the Learning Log. If you wish, play quiet, instrumental background music to set a reflective mood as they write.

- Learning Logs can be private reflections of the learning, in which case learners do not share what they have written. Or, if learners wish and time allows, they can read their Learning Logs to each other. Or you can ask for a few volunteers to read their logs to the group.

- Training participants usually keep their Learning Logs as reminders of what they learned.

Variations to Learning Logs:

- *Group Logs.* Each table group creates a collaborative Learning Log and then reads the log aloud to the class. After the training is over, collect and post these logs to a website, intranet site, or blog.

- *Concept Logs.* In addition to Learning Logs written during the training conclusion, learners can also write shorter logs after each concept segment. In effect, learners are creating an ongoing Learning Log of the entire learning experience.

2. Stand and Deliver

This is a kinesthetic summary that includes movement as well as learners' action plans. Do the following:

- Post one or more of the following questions where everyone can see them:

  - *What are the most important concepts you learned from the training?*

  - *How will you use this information?*

  - *What behavior changes will you make as a result of what you learned?*

  - *What other steps can you take in order to learn more about this topic?*

  - *Who can you share what you learned with and what will you tell him or her?*

  - *What is one question you still have about the topic? How will you find the answer to this question?*

  - Ask learners to write their answers to one or two questions of their choice.

  - Instruct learners to form standing groups of three to five people with participants from other table groups.

- Learners read their written answers aloud while in their standing groups.
- If time allows, ask for a few volunteers to read their answers to the class.
- When finished, learners thank their standing groups and return to their seats.

3. Table Talk

A variation of Stand and Deliver, Table Talk uses the same questions and instructions, but participants stay with their table groups to talk about their responses to the questions. They may remain seated, or stand if they wish.

4. Card Exchange

Learners do the following:

- On index cards, they print how they plan to apply what they learned.
- They also print their names and work email addresses on the cards.
- They exchange cards with other participants, forming pairs of Card Exchange Partners.
- They make a commitment to email each other every week for the first month after the training is over. In the emails, they tell their Card Exchange partners information such as:
  - *This is how I've used what I've learned. . . .*
  - *These are the challenges I've encountered . . . .*
  - *This is a question I still have about the training topic. . . .*
  - *Here is another goal I've set for myself regarding what I've learned. . . .*
- In the email, they can include notes of encouragement for their Card Exchange partners. Or they can give their partners feedback related to the specific challenges or questions their partners may have written.

5. Round Robin

Post the Stand and Deliver questions. Then instruct learners to do the following:

- Each learner in a table group prints one of the questions on a piece of blank paper. Each group member must choose a different question to print.

- They pass their papers to the right. The next members write their responses to the questions.

- They pass the papers again to the right. The next members write their responses.

- The rounds repeat until all table members have responded to all printed questions.

- When group members receive their original papers back, they read all the responses and then write summaries of what they have read.

- During the whole-group discussion that follows the activity, volunteers read some of the summaries aloud and the class adds any final comments to the discussion.

Your Turn

This space is for a Concept Map of your own Learner-Led Summaries.

Conclusions:
Evaluation Strategies

What Is an Evaluation?

An evaluation is a way for learners to assess what they learned and, by extension, how they plan to use what they learned. An evaluation is also a way for the trainer to assess the level of learning that has taken place and for the company to assess the benefits of its investment in training.

You are probably already familiar with author Donald Kirkpatrick's learning evaluation model, in which he identified four levels of evaluation. Very briefly, the four levels are listed below, along with a question specific to each level:

1. *Level One—Emotions (feelings)*: "How do participants feel about what they learned?"

2. *Level Two—Knowledge (information)*: "What do participants remember about what they learned?"

3. *Level Three—Behavior (skills)*: "Can participants use what they learned?"

4. *Level Four—Return on Investment (benefit to the company)*: "How does the company benefit from what participants learned?"

The evaluation strategies in this section fall under the first three levels listed above. Put another way, these strategies, for the most part, are not about evaluating the return on training investment after the training is over. Instead, these strategies give you various ways to conduct an in-training evaluation so that you don't have to use the same format over and over.

In addition, these evaluation strategies give learners opportunities to become more actively involved in assessing their own learning. Most research indicates that, when learners take a more active role in evaluating what they learned and making a commitment to apply this information at work, the transfer of knowledge and skills to the workplace is greater than if they just fill out and evaluation form and then head out the door.

Obviously, there are many ways to conduct an in-training evaluation. A paper/pencil type of evaluation is probably the most widely used method, but even a written evaluation can be made more interesting and relevant to the learner than what most traditional training programs use. In addition, there are many ways to physically engage learners in the evaluation process.

You will note that the evaluation strategies in this section focus on the *learner*—on what he learned and what he plans to do with what he learned. These strategies do *not* focus on the trainer's skills nor presentation techniques. They do not ask, "Was the trainer prepared? Did she give time for questions?" Nor do they focus on the training logistics: "Were the facilities adequate? Was there enough air to breathe?" (Just kidding on the last one.) Learners can add those comments at the end of a written evaluation or in an email later. Because the primary purpose for doing an evaluation is to assess *learning*, the activities in this section will serve that purpose.

What Does an Evaluation Do?

By participating in an evaluation strategy, learners will

- *Think* about the entire training experience.
- *Assess* their own cognitive (knowledge-based) learning.
- *Assess* their behavioral (skills-based) learning.
- *Make* a commitment to use what they learned.
- *Create* an action plan that states their commitment to apply the learning.
- *Leave* feeling positive about the learning experience and confident about their new knowledge and skills.

Getting Ready

- **Materials:** Provide standard training materials, as well as any materials specifically needed for the activity.
- **Setup:** No special setup is necessary, other than space in which to move around, if needed.
- **Group Size:** Any size group is fine.

- **Time:** This will vary, with most strategies lasting about five to fifteen minutes.

Five Evaluation Strategies

1. Where Do You Stand?

This is a physically active evaluation strategy that generates both discussion and a higher level of physical energy than simply sitting and writing. Do the following:

- Explain that three areas of the room represent three levels of training application:
  - *One side of the room represents "Not quite yet."*
  - *The middle of the room represents "On the way."*
  - *The opposite side of the room represents "Ready to roll."*
- If you wish to create a visual of the three levels, you can post the following on a slide, or label the three areas of the room with charts that read:

  Not quite yet————On the way————Ready to roll

- Ask learners to think about what they have learned from the training, and assess their level of readiness to use what they've learned.
- Instruct them to move to the part of the room that represents their readiness.
- Once they have chosen where to stand, learners form standing pairs/triads, and answer the following questions:
  - *If you are standing at the "not quite yet" place, what will it take for you to be able to move to "on the way"?*
  - *If you are standing at the "on the way" place, what will it take for you to be able to move to "ready to roll"?*
  - *If you are standing at the "ready to roll" place, what will it take to keep you there or to help you continue learning?*
- Allow about five minutes for the pair/triad discussion, then ask for volunteers to give verbal summaries of what they discussed.

2. Four-Square Feedback

Do the following:

- On a chart paper or slide, post the Four-Square Feedback example shown below:

1. **Connections:** My feelings about what I have learned are	2. **Concepts:** The most important concepts I learned are
3. **Concrete Practice:** What I plan to do with what I learned:	4. **Conclusions:** A final comment, suggestion, or question I still have is

- Explain to learners that they will each make an evaluation sheet like the one posted and finish the sentences.
- Learners will give you their papers when finished. The evaluations can be anonymous, if you wish.

Four-Square Feedback variations:

- *Ongoing Feedback.* If the training is more than a day in length, ask learners to sign the Four-Square Feedback forms, then collect them. Before the next training day, read them and be prepared to answer any questions written on them. The next day, verbally respond to the questions and comments from the forms. Then hand the forms back to the learners so that they can take their evaluations with them when they leave.
- *Database Feedback.* Using a computer database, tabulate the Four-Square Feedback responses. Then send each learner an emailed compilation of his/her responses after the training is over. That gives learners an opportunity to

Training from the BACK of the Room!

once again think about the topic and concepts, read what others learned, and review ways of using the knowledge and skills.

3. Four-Square Levels of Learning

A variation of Four-Square Feedback, this evaluation form is an adaptation of Kirkpatrick's model. You will follow the instructions for Four-Square Feedback, but post the following form instead:

1. Emotions: How do I feel about what I learned?
2. Knowledge: What did I learn that will help me do my job better?
3. Behavior: How will my on-the-job behavior change as a result of what I learned?
4. Return on Investment: How will my company benefit from what I learned?

Direct learners to create a page like the one posted, then start at the top of the page, answering the questions and working to the bottom of the page.

4. May We Quote You?

Do the following:

* Before the training, create an evaluation form that states: *"We would like to know how you plan to use what you've learned— and we would like to be able to quote you when we offer this training again. Please take a few moments to*

complete the statements below. By filling out your contact information, you give us permission to quote you. Thank you so much for attending!"

Include the following statements on the form:

- *I gained these valuable insights about this topic:*
- *Three adjectives or phrases that describe this training are:*
- *What I plan to do as a result of this training:*
- *What I would say about this training if a reporter quoted me:*
- *Other comments and/or suggestions:*
- *My contact information (name, department, email):*

- Leave enough space between statements for participants to write their responses. If possible, make the evaluation page visually interesting with a graphic or cartoon.
- You may wish to play some quiet, instrumental background music while participants fill out the form, to set a reflective mood.
- When participants have finished, collect the pages.

5. Email Blast

This evaluation is a post-training strategy that goes beyond the training experience into the work lives of the participants. Do the following:

- Create a group email list of all the participants, and obtain their permission to circulate the list among the entire group.
- One week after the training, send out a group email to all participants, letting them know that they will be expected to check in with everyone else at least twice during the next month. Your email will say: *"Greetings to all! You will be checking in via email with everyone to let them know how you are applying the information you learned, or if there are any insights or questions related to the training topic that you want to share with the group. Please make a note on your calendar to send our group an email twice in the next month. Use these check-in times to*

  - *Share a topic-related best practice, suggestion, or insight.*
  - *Let the group know how you are applying what you learned.*

- *Let the group know any changes you've made as a result of what you've learned.*

- *Share a question you want an answer for or a challenge you want help with."*

- Two weeks after the training, send out a group reminder that participants need to do the above.

- Four weeks after the training, send one final email to the group, thanking those who sent their emails to the group.

Variations to the Email Blast:

- *Table Group Blast.* Learners can do an Email Blast with their table group members, instead of the whole class. Or they can form partners or triads to exchange emails with.

- *Blog Blast.* Create a blog site for learners to access and write comments. Explain that each participant needs to visit the blog and write a comment at least once during the next month.

Your Turn

Have more evaluation ideas? Create a Concept Map of them here.

Training from the BACK of the Room!

Conclusions: Celebrations

What Is a Celebration?

A Celebration is a closing activity that ends the training on a positive note, often with a burst of physical energy and enthusiasm. Ideally, a Celebration comes at the very end of the conclusion step, right before learners walk out the door. That way, they leave feeling emotionally positive about the training, reconnected to the learning community, confident about their new knowledge or skills, and committed to using what they have learned.

With a Celebration, you step aside as learners celebrate their own learning experience. You may decide to participate in the Celebration, but you aren't the focus of it. For example, if there are certificates of completion to hand out, give them to the participants to hand out to each other. If congratulations are in order, learners congratulate each other. Instead of bringing learners' attention back to you before the training ends, they focus on each other, applaud each other, and celebrate each other.

Ultimately, you must decide whether or not these Celebration activities are appropriate for your training group, the time allowed, and space available. Or you can use these ideas to help create other Celebration activities that might be more suited to your specific training topic or group.

What Does a Celebration Do?

A Celebration gives learners the opportunity to

- *Connect* with each other once again, in a positive, affirming way before the training ends.
- *Acknowledge* the training journey and the group they traveled with.
- *State* what they appreciated about individuals, about the small groups they worked with, and about the class as a whole.
- *Recommit* to using what they learned after the training is over.
- *Leave* the training feeling positive and enthusiastic about the learning experience.

Getting Ready

- *Materials:* Depending on the activity, you will need standard training materials as well as any materials specifically required for specific Celebrations (examples: small bags of craft items for the Make and Take, certificates for the Certificate Car Wash, a soft throwable object for the Circle Celebration).

- *Setup:* For physically active Celebrations, you will need more space in the room. For some activities, you will need to use a breakout area, a hallway, or go outside, if possible.

- *Group Size:* Any size group is fine.

- *Time:* Most of these activities take from ten to thirty minutes.

Five Celebration Activities

1. Make and Take

In this Celebration, learners create souvenirs of the training to take with them when they leave. Souvenirs are three-dimensional representations or metaphors that remind them of training concepts. Do the following:

- Place a small bag of craft items (pipe cleaners, Play-Doh®, small dowels, TinkerToys®, Legos®, or other three-dimensional objects) at each table.

- Explain that each group is to share the craft items among members. Members will create individual, three-dimensional sculptures that represent:

  - *A training concept or concepts*

  - *How the learner plans to apply what he has learned*

  - *A metaphor for the entire training experience*

Some examples:

- In a customer service training, a participant makes a pipe cleaner flower in which petals represent the various ways to "grow" customers.

- In an effective communication skills training, a participant constructs an ears-and-mouth Play-Doh sculpture as a reminder to listen before speaking.

- In a safety inspection workshop, an employee makes a construction paper job aid—in the shape of a hard hat—with the three most important safety reminders listed on it.

- In a database program, a learner makes a card stock bookmark with the program codes printed on it.

- When all table group members have completed their Make and Take sculptures, instruct them to take turns explaining their sculptures to their groups or to the class. A round of applause follows each explanation.

- Participants take their sculptures with them when they leave.

Make and Take variations:

- *One for the Learner.* Instead of a variety of craft items, each learner receives one item (e.g., one pipe cleaner, one small Play-Doh container) with which to create a small, individual sculpture. Learners tape or glue these sculptures to construction paper and then label the paper with a title or explanation of the sculpture. For example: A safety training participant makes a pipe cleaner outline of a footprint. He tapes this to a paper that he titles "Steps to Safety." He prints the safety procedure steps around the footprint.

- *One for the Table.* Each table group receives a bag of one craft item (pipe cleaners at one table, Legos at another, Play-Doh at a third). Table groups create collaborative sculptures and then present them to the entire class. Example:

  - In an insurance training, one table group uses pipe cleaners and paper to create a timeline of the application process, with paper labels explaining each step on the pipe cleaner timeline. Another group creates a Play-Doh representation of troubleshooting solutions, with each clay shape standing for a different solution.

2. Certificate Car Wash

This is high-energy Celebration that is especially effective when you have certificates of completion to hand out. Although it is popular with many trainers, if you don't think it would be appropriate to do with your training participants, consider doing the Toot That Horn variation below, or choose a different Celebration activity. For this activity, do the following:

- Clear a large space running the length of the training room (a wide aisle in the middle of the room, for example), or use a long hallway or a walkway outside.

- Instruct participants to form two standing lines, facing each other (about the same number of people in each line). If your group size is small (fewer than twelve), you may want to have them form one line instead.

- To begin the activity, you stand at the head of the two lines, holding the certificates. Call out the name of the person on the first certificate.

- This person walks to the opposite ends of the lines from where you are and then walks between the lines until she is standing in front of you. As she walks between the lines, the other participants give her high-fives, handshakes, pats-on-the-back, applause, congratulations, shouts, and so on (think "car wash" metaphor here).

- When she stands in front of you, give her the certificate and congratulate her. Also hand her the pile of remaining certificates and let her know it is now her turn to call out the name on the next certificate. At this point, you join one of the lines as a Certificate Car Wash participant.

- The person to whom you gave a certificate calls out a name, hands out a certificate, and gives the remaining pile to the next person. The procedure continues, with participants taking turns handing out the remaining certificates.

- Ultimately, each learner will have walked through the Certificate Car Wash to applause from the group and will have handed out a certificate to another learner (with the exception of the last person to receive a certificate—he won't have one to hand to someone else).

- When everyone has received a certificate, lead a group round of applause, and the training ends.

Certificate Car Wash variations:

- *Two by Two.* If your training group is really large (twenty or more), or you have a very short time to do the activity (under twenty minutes), then call out two names at a time. Two participants walk between the Car Wash lines together to applause from the group. They will, in turn, call out two more names, and the procedure continues until everyone has received a certificate.

- *Jump and Shout.* If your training group has been together for longer than a day, or if they are particularly outgoing, you might suggest they add a gesture, dance movement, or shout to their Car Wash walk. Many folks will do this anyway, but sometimes it's fun to suggest that they do it purposefully.

Training from the BACK of the Room!

Toot That Horn. Instead of Car Wash lines, participants can form a large standing group or circle. Give each participant a small noisemaker (a whistle, toy flute, hand clapper, small bell, or the like). When they pass out the certificates to each other, they applaud by using the noisemakers.

3. Circle Celebration

This activity is similar to the Ball Toss in Learner-Created Games in Part Three of this book. For the Circle Celebration, the whole group will need a soft, throwable object (Koosh®, Nerf®, beach ball, stuffed animal, bath sponge, or the like). Do the following:

- Instruct learners to form a standing circle in a cleared space of the room. You join the circle too.
- Explain that whoever has the ball must tell the group:
  - *What he enjoyed about the training.*
  - *What he appreciated about the group.*
  - *How he plans to use what he has learned.*
- Toss the ball to one participant to begin the activity.
- Participants toss the ball randomly around the circle until everyone who wishes to speak has had a turn to do so. If the group is large (twenty or more), or if time is short, limit the ball toss repetitions, with some volunteers speaking and the rest of the group watching and listening.
- End the Circle Celebration with a round of applause.

Circle Celebration variations:

- *Seated Circle.* If the group is large and space allows, have learners arrange their chairs in a large circle. They participate in the activity sitting down, instead of standing.
- *Small Group Circle.* Again, if the group is large (thirty or more), you may suggest that they do the Circle Celebration with their table groups instead. They have the choice of staying at their tables or using breakout areas in the room. They can choose to sit or stand. Each table group will need its own ball for the activity.

4. I Like My Neighbor

This activity is physically energizing and highly kinesthetic. It works best with a training group that has been together longer than two days and that is from fifteen to thirty participants. Allow a specified length of time for the activity— usually from ten to twenty minutes. This activity also works best with a younger group (twenties and thirties) or a group that is outgoing or enjoys physically active exercises. Ultimately, you decide whether this activity is appropriate for your training. If not, choose a different Celebration instead.

Think of this activity as the child's game of musical chairs, but with an adult twist. Do the following:

- Before the Celebration activity, prepare a list of printed statements and give a copy to each participant. Sample statements:

  - *I like my neighbor, who will use a specific idea from this training at work tomorrow.*

  - *I like my neighbor, who feels he or she can teach someone else at work what was learned here.*

  - *I like my neighbor, who thinks that the most important thing he learned was* (follow this with a topic-related fact).

  - *I like my neighbor, who still wants to know* (follow this with a topic-related question).

  - *I like my neighbor, who plans to attend another training like this in the near future.*

  - *I like my neighbor, who will use this skill* (name the skill) *right away when he gets back to work.*

  - *I like my neighbor, whose favorite part of the training was* (state your favorite part).

  - *I like my neighbor, whose least favorite part of the training was* (state your least favorite part).

  - *I like my neighbor, who worked with* (name a person) *in a table group.*

  - *I like my neighbor, who worked with everyone in this room.*

  - *I like my neighbor, who took some risks during this training.*

  - *I like my neighbor, who talked a lot during the training.*

  - *I like my neighbor, who worked with me during the training.*

- *I like my neighbor, who wrote a lot during the training.*

- *I like my neighbor, who was very surprised by some of the content.*

- *I like my neighbor, who says this training has changed his/her life.*

- Have learners help you put chairs in a circle in a large space in the room (away from the other furniture). There must be plenty of space within the circle to accommodate movement from the entire group.

- Ask learners to bring their statement copies with them and to sit in the circle. Once everyone is seated, remove any extra chairs. There should be only one chair for each participant.

- Because you will be participating too, and because there is NO chair for you, ultimately there will be one less chair than participants in the activity. In other words, during the activity, one person will always remain standing.

- Begin the activity by explaining that you will read a statement from the paper (the statements do not have to be in order). You say, *"If this statement applies to you, you must stand and exchange places with another person who is also standing."*

- Caution participants that the activity can get very lively, so they need to move carefully, so as not to trip or bump into others as they move from chair to chair. Participants can choose to watch the activity and not participate, if they wish.

- Read a statement aloud. As soon as some participants stand, you move to one of their chairs and sit down. When the dust settles, and those standing find new places to sit, there will be one participant left standing in the middle of the circle.

- Explain that it is this participant's turn to either make up a statement or read one from the paper. Again, participants to whom the statement applies must stand and trade seats with others who are also standing.

- Another person will be left standing in the middle of the circle. This person reads or makes up another training-related statement. The activity continues with a different person left standing in the middle each time.

- Stop the activity while the enthusiasm and excitement are high. Have the group give itself a round of applause, and the training ends.

5. Walk and Talk

This is another highly kinesthetic activity, which generates a lot of noise and positive energy before participants leave the training. I have used this activity with dozens of training groups in both corporate and educational programs. Although groups both large (over one-hundred) and small (fewer than ten) have enthusiastically participated in this activity, you must decide whether Walk and Talk is appropriate for your training. Do the following:

- Ask learners to stand and form pairs or triads with one or two other participants.

- Explain that they will walk around the perimeter of the room (or outside and back inside, if possible). While they walk, they take turns talking about what they enjoyed about the training, what was meaningful to them, and how they plan to use what they learned.

- Play upbeat music to add a feeling of celebration and liveliness to the activity.

- When learners get back to the place they started, have them give each other high-fives or a round of applause before they leave.

Your Turn

List your Celebration activities here, or add to the Concept Map on the next page.

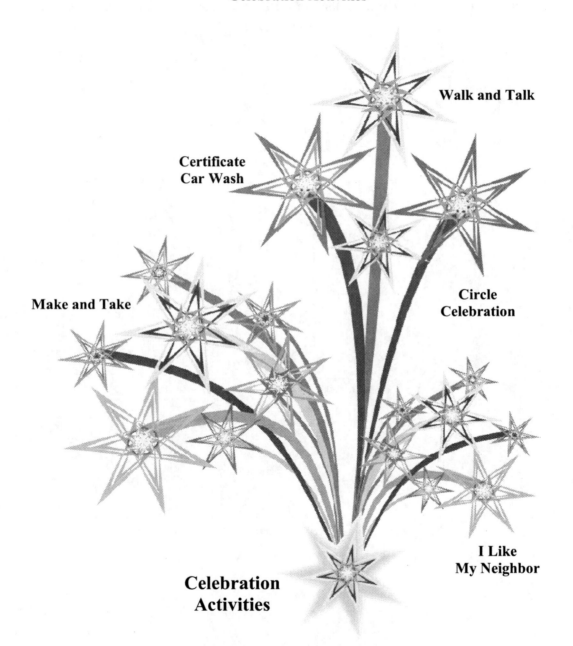

Concept Map for
Celebration Activities

Walk and Talk

Certificate
Car Wash

Make and Take

Circle
Celebration

I Like
My Neighbor

Celebration
Activities

Training from the BACK of the Room!

Nice-to-Know Information from the *Back* of the Book

The Secret of
Adult Learning Theory
It's NOT About Age!

All learning is self-directed.

Dan Tobin

You already know a lot about how adults learn. As an adult learner yourself, you've experienced it "up close and personal." Furthermore, as a trainer, you've observed adult learning in action. And this book is full of information about this topic. What else can you discover about how adults learn that you don't already know?

Before I answer that question, let's begin with a list. Read the following sentences and check off the ones that you think apply to adults:

- ❏ They want to or need to learn.
- ❏ They learn in different ways.
- ❏ They learn best in an informal environment.
- ❏ They see themselves and self-directed and responsible.
- ❏ They learn best when they have hands-on practice.
- ❏ They bring their own past experiences to the learning.
- ❏ They learn best when they can relate new information to what they already know.
- ❏ They have their own ideas to contribute.

You probably checked off most or all of the statements. You're right—they *all* apply to adults.

Now think about the children you know, the children you've raised, or the child you once were. Think about what you know about how children learn and how you learned as a child. With those thoughts in mind, read the following list, and check off any of the statements that you think apply to children:

- ❏ They want to or need to learn.
- ❏ They learn in different ways.
- ❏ They learn best in an informal environment.
- ❏ They see themselves and self-directed and responsible.
- ❏ They learn best when they have hands-on practice.
- ❏ They bring their own past experiences to the learning.
- ❏ They learn best when they can relate new information to what they already know.
- ❏ They have their own ideas to contribute.

You're probably thinking, "What's going on? It's the same list." Yes, it *is* the same list, and you've probably checked off most or all of the statements in this list too. The point is this: Adult learning theory is *not* about age! This chapter will explain why. In addition, it will give you a different perspective of adult learning theory, and some suggestions for using this information in your training.

Once Upon a Time

In the early 1960s and 1970s, a U.S. college professor noticed that the ways most adults were being taught—through lecture-based classes—didn't work very well. In fact, in terms of remembering and using the information they were being taught, many adults were learning very little from lectures, assigned readings, drills, quizzes, rote memorization, and examinations. This professor felt so strongly about what he observed that he wrote a number of books about the perceived learning needs of most adult learners.

The author's name was Malcolm Knowles, a Boston University associate professor of adult education. His writings spanned four decades, from the 1950s to the 1980s, and he was almost solely responsible for making two words household items in the worlds of teaching, training, and adult learning: *pedagogy and andragogy.*

Pedagogy Versus Andragogy

For better or worse, Malcolm Knowles changed the beliefs about adult learning in the United States. I say "for better or worse" because the effects of Knowles' lifelong work had both positive and negative consequences.

Basically, Knowles defined two different ways of learning. First, he said that children learn best through "pedagogy," which he defined as teacher-centered instruction, where the focus is on lecture-based learning. Second, he said that adults learn best through "andragogy," that is, learner-centered instruction, where the focus is on experiential learning. Thus, the word pedagogy became synonymous with learning environments in which learners sit passively while teachers deliver information via lectures, books, and tests. The word andragogy became synonymous with informal, hands-on learning environments in which learners are actively engaged in learning.

Adults Versus Children

In the United States, Knowles did adults a huge favor: He significantly changed the perceptions of educators and trainers as to what adults need in order learn effectively.

In one of his most famous books, written in the early 1970s, *The Adult Learner: A Neglected Species*, Knowles emphasized the need for andragogical learning in adult classes and training—a radical departure from traditional methods of adult instruction at the time.

Unwittingly, Knowles did a drastic disservice to children. He permanently cemented the old paradigm of teacher-centered instruction for non-adult learners. He made the assumption that, because children had been taught with lecture-based methods since the early 1800s, it must be the way children learn best. Because that was the way it had been done for decades, it must be effective. Circular "chicken and egg" thinking, to be sure.

Knowles' mistake regarding how children learn was understandable. At the time, there wasn't much research about how the brain is hardwired to take in information, remember, and retrieve it later. This type of brain research really began in earnest during the late 1970s, with the majority of the most relevant research appearing from the 1990s to the present.

When Knowles realized that traditional methods of instruction weren't working for adults, he assumed that it was a matter of age difference, not a matter of ineffective instructional methods to begin with. He didn't have the research indicating what we now know: Most people, regardless of age, do *not* learn best when passively sitting and listening to a lecture.

From Adult Learning to Human Learning

The brain research from the past two decades proves that human beings learn best when they are actively involved in the learning process—experiencing a variety of meaningful, motivating, self-directed learning methods in an informal, hands-on learning environment. This kind of brain-based learning describes *human learning*. It is *not* based on age, gender, culture, generation, or other such assumptions. True, these variables all play into the mix, but they are not as important as the underlying research that supports human learning.

The irony regarding adult learning theory is that, forty years after Knowles' research, much of adult instruction is *still* pedagogical in nature—lecture-based, teacher-centered. Although a lot of lip service is given to Knowles' theories and most train-the-trainer programs cite Knowles' work, lecture-based instruction is still the order of the day in the majority of adult learning environments—even in those classes that teach about adult learning! Old habits die hard.

Because you already know a lot about how *humans* learn, let's do two exercises. First, read the list below, paraphrased from Malcolm Knowles' work. I've changed one word in each sentence—and what a difference that one word makes:

- Humans want to or need to learn.

- Humans learn in different ways.

- Humans learn best in an informal environment.

- Humans see themselves as self-directed and responsible.

- Humans learn best when they have hands-on practice.

- Humans bring their own past experiences to the learning.

- Humans learn best when they can relate new information to what they already know.

- Humans have their own ideas to contribute.

Now read a second list, and mark each sentence M for Myth or F for Fact. Careful—this isn't True or False:

1. Humans learn best by listening and taking tests.
2. Most learners like to be self-directed and actively involved in learning.
3. Both children and adults have their own preferred ways of learning.
4. Both children and adults learn better when they feel good about learning.
5. Humans learn differently depending on their ages.
6. Past experiences are important to the human learning process.
7. Regardless of their ages, humans have their own ideas to contribute.
8. Informal learning environments detract from the learning experience.
9. Relating new information to what they already know is confusing to learners.

Check your answers against the ones below:

1. Humans learn best by listening and taking tests. *MYTH—Very few people, regardless of their age, learn well by passively listening, then taking tests.*
2. Most learners like to be self-directed and actively involved in learning. *FACT*
3. Both children and adults have their own preferred ways of learning. *FACT*
4. Both children and adults learn better when they feel good about learning. *FACT*
5. Humans learn differently depending on their ages. *MYTH—You know now that age is not an important factor in human learning.*
6. Past experiences are important to the human learning process. *FACT—While children may not have as many past experiences to draw on as adults do, they often have some knowledge of the topic, even if it's only through observation or hearsay.*
7. Regardless of their ages, humans have their own ideas to contribute. *FACT*
8. Informal learning environments detract from the learning experience. *MYTH—Most learners, regardless of age, do better in informal learning environments.*
9. Relating new information to what they already know is confusing to learners. *MYTH—Linking new information to old is important to all learners.*

It feels good to retire the old paradigm of pedagogy and andragogy, especially since pedagogy never worked well for most learners, regardless of their age. Chances are pedagogy didn't work well for you either. And it probably doesn't work well for most of *your* learners in your classes and training programs.

Bringing It Home to What You Do

Now you're going to apply these concepts to your job as a trainer. Based on the characteristics of how *humans* learn, what will be your choices when designing and delivering your next training, class, or presentation? Read the following list and circle the action items that describe what you will do:

A. I will make sure I present the important concepts clearly and concisely, while learners listen quietly so that they learn it all.

B. I will include a variety of instructional strategies that involve learners so that they are talking, writing, and doing topic-related activities.

C. I will give learners choices of discussion topics and review activities as part of the learning.

D. I will begin by explaining the goals, learning outcomes, and agenda for the learning experience.

E. I will begin by facilitating a discussion about what learners already know about the topic.

F. So that the environment doesn't distract from the learning, I will set up the room with desks, tables, or chairs in orderly row in which learners all face the front of the room.

G. I will arrange the room informally, with round tables or chairs in small cluster groups so that learners can participate in topic-related discussions and learn from each other.

Of course, you will do items B, C, E, and G, because you know how humans learn best.

If you have read previous chapters of this book, you don't need to read the following material. It serves as a review of a number of important points that I made earlier. However, if you are a reader who reads the *back* of a book first, then the following points are suggestions to help you shift from *adult* learning to *human* learning:

- *Take time to find out what learners know.* At the beginning of the training, give learners a few minutes to discuss what they know or have heard about the training topic. Throughout the training, encourage them to share comments, ideas, insights, and opinions with the whole group. Use Part One of this book as a resource to start.

- *Use a variety of active learning strategies to involve learners.* Examples are paired and small group discussions, quick games (more collaborative than competitive), Teach-Backs in which learners teach each other what they've learned, quizzes that learners make and take, learner presentations, large group discussions, projects, simulations, and skits, to name a few. Parts Two and Three of this book contain many other activities.

- *Give learners choices.* From a list of review tasks, let learners decide which they wish to do and let them work in pairs, triads, or small groups to accomplish the tasks. Again, Parts Two and Three will help you with this.

- *Create an inviting, friendly, informal learning environment.* Cluster learners into small groups, using round tables or chairs arranged in circles. On the tables, put plenty of markers, colored paper, Post-it® Notes, index cards, and the like. On the walls, hang colorful charts with topic-related information on them. If possible, provide snacks and beverages, or ask learners to bring their own. The chapter titled "Brain-Friendly Training" at the front of this book will give you more ideas.

In summation, your greatest challenge as a trainer is to let go of the old pedagogical paradigm of trainer-led, lecture-based instruction and to embrace brain-friendly, andragogical instruction instead. Because you are reading this chapter (and this book), you have already begun this shift. By using the strategies in *Training from the BACK of the Room!*, you will become a master at helping humans learn.

> *"Andra" is the "gogy" to go with for all.*
>
> Jay Cross
> *Informal Learning*, 2007, p. 247

Begin with the End

A Fresh Approach to Learning Outcomes

If they didn't learn it, you haven't taught it.

Benna Kallik

Let's start with a quick connection exercise. You've begun reading this chapter. What is it you want to take away from the reading? More specifically, what do you hope to be able to either *explain or do* once you have read this? Think about this for a moment, then write a sentence or two in the box below.

As the author (you could call me the instructional designer of this chapter), I hope that you will be able to *explain* what effective learning outcomes are, should someone ask you. I also hope that you will be able to *write* effective learning outcomes, thus further demonstrating what you've learned. Let's see whether we can work together toward these ends.

When author Stephen Covey penned this phrase, "Begin with the end in mind," he was, perhaps—without realizing it—giving educators and trainers the definition of learning outcomes. Often called learning objectives, the outcomes are the end results you have in mind *for the learners* when you train. What should they be able to demonstrate, perform, or *do* after the training ends? And, if knowledge is the goal, what is it that they can now define, explain, answer questions about, or *teach to others?*

What You *See* Is What They *Learned*

A learning outcome is an action, an observable behavior demonstrated by the learner when the training is over. The learner does it; the trainer (or another person) can see it being done. It's not guesswork. It's pretty clear to the learner as well as to anyone else observing.

For example, if an employee attends a training about a company's new database program and correctly enters customer information into the database afterward, she is demonstrating what she learned. On the other hand, if a new filing clerk who attended a training about federal filing regulations still inaccurately files dozens of forms, he is demonstrating that he didn't learn anything from the training. It's clearly observable when it comes to specific skills.

When looking at people-to-people skills, also called soft skills, the same applies, although it may be a bit more difficult to observe. For example, when a manager finishes a class on leadership and then imperiously orders her employees around, she hasn't learned the new leadership skills, as evidenced by her lack of skill performance. Oh, she may have *heard* what was said about the topic, but she didn't really *learn* anything because her behavior didn't change. Conversely, after attending a problem-solving workshop, when a supervisor actively listens to a complaining customer before commenting or offering solutions, he is demonstrating what he learned from the workshop.

When training is about the memorization of information, with no skills being taught or practiced, then the learning outcomes in that training will focus on a learner's ability to explain, define, list, write, or repeat that information later. For example, a hotel desk clerk demonstrates his understanding of the hotel's amenities by explaining them to a hotel guest. Another example: A financial planner who attended a basic investment class demonstrates what she has learned by explaining a variety of investment options to a potential client. On the other hand, if a manager goes to a retail tax update workshop and can't even list the changes to the retail tax laws afterward, he probably didn't learn much.

Let's stop here for a moment and look at three learning outcomes. Read them, and then decide for yourself whether they describe observable behaviors that learners can demonstrate and that you, or someone else, can see happening:

1. After this security training, security guards will know the proper way to lock up the building.

2. Learners in this systems analysis program will understand the process used in updating the company's computer systems.

3. Call center employees will learn how to refer callers to the appropriate departments.

Chances are you spotted three verbs that are *not* observable: *know, understand,* and *learn.*

Many trainers still use these words when they write learning outcomes, even though these words do *not* describe what learners will be able to *do.* In fact, they don't describe any observable behaviors at all, because you can't *see* knowing, understanding, or learning. What you *can* see are changes in behaviors as a result of knowing, understanding, or learning.

Let's rewrite these three outcomes to make them observable:

1. After this security training, security guards will *demonstrate* the proper way to lock up the building.

2. Learners in this systems analysis program will *perform* the process used in updating the company's computer systems.

3. Call center employees will *refer* callers to the appropriate departments.

These learning outcomes now describe changes in behaviors the learners will make as a result of attending training. If the learners don't make these changes, they haven't learned what they were supposed to have learned, and further training, remediation, one-on-one coaching, mentoring, or a job change may be necessary.

Here is a list of action words—observable behaviors—to consider using when you write learning outcomes. For practice, choose two or more and, in the spaces beside the words, write outcomes for your training topics that include these words. You can also add your own action words to this list:

- *Demonstrate*
- *Perform*
- *Show*
- *Present*
- *Use*
- *Apply*
- *Choose*
- *Do*
- *Act*
- *Design*
- *Make*
- *Create*
- *Discuss*
- *Identify*
- *Explain*
- *State*
- *List*
- *Describe*
- *Define*
- *Pass a test*
- *Teach someone else*

What They Need to Know

As trainers, we also need to be clear about *what* it is learners need to know in order to be able to *demonstrate* their learning of it. This seems simple enough. The knowledge it takes to do something is inseparable from the doing. The challenge for us arises in separating need-to-know from nice-to-know information, and not becoming sidetracked teaching content that has little to do with the learning outcomes. If some of the content isn't tied to the learning outcomes, we can include it as resource material for learners to read later, come back to it if there is time to do this before the training ends, or delete it from the training altogether. (See Part Two of this book for more about this topic).

I'll use the three learning outcomes stated earlier to show examples of the difference between need-to-know and nice-to-know information (keep in mind that the nice-to-know information may be relevant to the training as a whole, just not to these specific learning outcomes):

1. *After this security training, security guards will demonstrate the proper way to lock up the building.* For this outcome, guards need to know the key and door locations, locking sequence, security codes, and the exact procedural steps to follow in order to properly secure the building. Nice-to-know but unessential information might be the telephone numbers of support services: police, fire department, and the building maintenance manager.

2. *Learners in this systems analysis program will perform the process used in updating the company's computer system.* Analysts will need to know the company's computer logins, codes, acronyms, passwords, and step-by-step procedures. Unessential to this outcome is information about the origins of the company's system or past problems with the system.

3. *Call center employees will refer callers to the appropriate departments.* Employees will need to know the exact questions to ask a caller and the phone codes for the specific departments. Unessential to this outcome are the steps the department will take once a call is referred.

In order to separate the need-to-know from the nice-to-know information, ask yourself:

- *What is the essential information learners need in order to effectively perform this learning outcome?*

- *What is the information that is related to this learning outcome, but that is not essential to learners' performance of it?*

- *If the training time were cut in half, which concepts would I choose to include and which concepts could I put in a reference handout for later use?*

- *Which concepts, if employees don't learn them, will adversely affect their job performance?*

- *Which concepts do learners need to remember in order to pass the test or to become certified?*

Use the Formula, Baby

Once you are clear as to what information is necessary for learners to know in order to be able to do what they are supposed to do, you can use a simple formula to write the learning outcomes (LOs). This formula is short and quick—a fresh look at longer, more traditional methods. I call it the basic LO formula:

Behavior + Concept or Skill = Learning Outcome

What could be more simple? You can fancy it up, if you want to. But all learning outcomes boil down to these two important elements: action and information or skill. Another way of writing the formula is:

Action word plus information or skill equals learning outcome.

Below, I've listed eight concrete examples of the basic LO formula. Can you recognize the observable behaviors and the concepts or skills? For practice, put a box around the action words and underline the phrases that describe the concepts/skills. Then check your answers against mine.

1. Machinery operators will demonstrate how to use the assembly line safety equipment.

2. Hotel reservation employees will describe the five steps that they need to follow when taking a new phone reservation.

3. Each employee will teach another employee how to enter information into the company database.

4. Supervisors will list three problem-solving strategies that will help them deal with difficult customers.

5. Train-the-trainer participants will divide their lecture material into segments of about ten to twenty minutes in length.

6. Managers will explain the differences between the old and new Americans with Disabilities Acts.

7. Restaurant waiters will set tables and take orders in the manner described in the employee binder.

Training from the BACK of the Room!

8. Call center operators will use the new phone procedure with all customers.

Here are my answers. Yours may be slightly different, but they should include what I have boxed and underlined.

1. Machinery operators will $\boxed{\text{demonstrate}}$ how to use the assembly line safety equipment.

2. Hotel reservation employees will $\boxed{\text{describe}}$ the five steps that they need to follow when taking a new phone reservation.

3. Each employee will $\boxed{\text{teach}}$ another employee how to enter information into the company database.

4. Supervisors will $\boxed{\text{list}}$ three problem-solving strategies that will help them deal with difficult customers.

5. Train-the-trainer participants will $\boxed{\text{divide}}$ their lecture material into segments of about ten to twenty minutes in length.

6. Managers will $\boxed{\text{explain}}$ the differences between the old and new Americans with Disabilities Acts.

7. Restaurant waiters will $\boxed{\text{set}}$ tables and $\boxed{\text{take}}$ customer orders in the manner described in the employee binder.

8. Call center operators will $\boxed{\text{use}}$ the new phone procedure with all customers.

Now try your hand at correcting learning outcomes that *don't* describe learners' observable behaviors. Read the list below and make the changes needed in each outcome. Then check your answers against my suggested ones.

A. Employees will *know* the updated database security codes.
   Change this to:

B. Train-the-trainer participants will *understand* the importance of active learning when designing and delivering training.
   Change this to:

C. Technology specialists will *learn* the hard drive replacement procedure.
Change this to:

D. Bank tellers will *understand* the record-keeping system for deposits and withdrawals.
Change this to:

E. Learners will *know* all the concepts.
Change this to:

F. *The trainer will teach* new employees the company regulations regarding sexual harassment laws.
Change this to:

I've listed my answers below. Your responses might differ, but they should describe observable behavior.

A. Employees will *know* the updated database security codes.
Change this to: *Employees will <u>list and explain</u> the updated database security codes.*

B. Train-the-trainer participants will *understand* the importance of active learning when designing and delivering training.
Change this to: *Train-the-trainer participants will <u>demonstrate active learning strategies</u> when designing and delivering training.*

C. Technology specialists will *learn* the hard drive replacement procedure.
Change this to: *Technology specialists will <u>perform</u> the hard drive replacement procedure.*

D. Bank tellers will *understand* the record-keeping system for deposits and withdrawals.
Change this to: *Bank tellers will <u>demonstrate</u> the record-keeping system for deposits and withdrawals.*

E. Learners will *know* all the concepts.
Change this to: *Learners will <u>state examples</u> of all the concepts.*

F. *The trainer will teach* new employees the company regulations regarding sexual harassment laws. (Note: This isn't a learning outcome at all, because it describes what the trainer will do, not the learners.)
Change this to: *<u>New employees will explain</u> the company regulations regarding sexual harassment laws.*

Real Outcomes for Real Training

There is no reason to write learning outcomes if we just put them on a slide or in a handout and then forget about them. Nor is there any reason to write them if we don't give learners time to read, think about, and discuss them. As Michael Allen tells us, "Many [trainers] hope objectives will not only help learners organize their study, but also motivate them to want to learn the content" (2003, p. 159). This can't happen if learners don't actively review the outcomes, or if the outcomes are irrelevant to the learner.

In order to make the LOs truly meaningful and an effective part of instruction, we must make them a prominent part of the entire training program. Parts Two and Four of this book will help you do this. Here are a few reminders from those parts—suggestions that help weave the learning outcomes into the entire fabric of the learning experience:

- *Post the learning outcomes.* They need to be highly visible for everyone to see. Besides putting them in a handout or on a slide, use large letters and dark markers to print LOs on chart paper and hang them on the training room walls. Make sure learners can read the charts from wherever they are sitting.

- *Begin with a learning outcome activity.* Once you post the LOs, learners must do something besides just reading the charts. The LO activity can be as short as a minute or two—just enough time to familiarize learners with the LOs in an active and interesting way. For example, learners can put check marks or sticky dots beside the charted outcomes that are most important to them. They can discuss the outcomes, vote as a group on the most important ones, or rank order the top two or three. Or they can write the most important one on an index card and refer to it later.

- *Have learners create and post their own learning outcomes.* This is really important for relevancy, as well as for learner motivation and buy-in to the training. Learners can add their own outcomes to the ones printed on the charts or write theirs on sticky notes and post them on another chart. Either way, the learner-created outcomes become their benchmarks both during and at the end of the training. Allen sums this up by saying: "Don't list objectives . . . put the learners to work" (2003. p. 161).

- *Refer to the outcomes during the training.* At the end of each major section of the training, come back to the charted lists and have learners discuss what they have learned related to the posted outcomes. They can also refer to and discuss their own posted outcomes as well. Sometimes you might want to change the printed outcomes, adding or deleting items, if the focus of the training changes. In this way, the LOs become the guideposts along the way.

- *End with a learning outcome activity.* Bring the learners full circle by allowing time for them to assess their own learning: Did they meet the learning outcomes—or not? Can they demonstrate their competency, both in the training and back on the job?

Back to the Beginning

Let's go back to the beginning of this chapter. You wrote what you wanted to be able to take away from reading the chapter. Also, it was my hope that you would be able to explain what learning outcomes are and write your own learning outcomes, using what you learned from this chapter. Did you accomplish what you set out to learn? Can you explain what learning outcomes are to a family member, friend, or colleague? Can you write learning outcomes with an acceptable level of competency? Try it now. On the lines below, jot down two or three learning outcomes for one training program you teach. Be sure to use the basic LO formula when you do.

_____
_____
_____
_____
_____
_____
_____
_____
_____
_____
_____
_____
_____
_____
_____
_____

Learning outcomes help us stay on track as we tie everything in the training to these observable results. They become guideposts for ourselves as well as our learners. Instead of being a mere PowerPoint® list, to be lectured about and forgotten, they become an integral part of the training itself. In effect, learning outcomes become as important to the learners as they are to us. In addition, learning outcomes make training effectiveness easier to observe and assess. When all training steps—Connections, Concepts, Concrete Practice, and Conclusions—are tied to the learning outcomes, long-term training success is a pretty sure bet.

*Each learner must buy into the value of the learning—
not just in general, but for specific, meaningful benefits.*

Michael Allen
Michael Allen's Guide to e-Learning, 2003, p. 154

The World Cafe

An Innovative Process with Conversations That Matter

Authentic conversation is our human way of thinking together.

Juanita Brown and David Isaacs
The World Cafe, 2005, p. 204

Welcome to The World Cafe

Note: The graphics in this chapter are copyrighted by Nancy Margulies, www.nancymargulies.com, and used with permission.

Imagine that you are an employee of a large retail company and are about to attend a two-hour training that will deal with some common customer service problems that have cropped up at a number of company stores.

You walk into a training room that looks very different from the traditional classroom environment. The trainer, Ross, has transformed the room into an informal, cafe-like setting: white paper "tablecloths" cover round tables scattered throughout the room, colorful markers fill glasses set at each table, and bright posters of some of the company's products decorate the walls. There are four chairs around each table, and morning snacks and beverages are available along one side of the room. Upbeat music plays in the background.

You grab some coffee and a bagel and settle yourself at a table, as do the other forty employees. You notice there is a question printed on each paper tablecloth. Because there are five questions and ten tables, each question is repeated once. All the questions refer to aspects of customer service that the company wants to address during the training:

1. *What is a customer service problem or concern you've experienced or heard about? If it was solved, what was the solution?*

2. *What is one customer service policy that is working well for you and your customers?*

3. *In your opinion, what is one customer service policy that needs to be changed, and how would you change it?*

4. *What can the company do to further support your customer service efforts?*

5. *What are other customer service questions, concerns, or suggestions you have that you would like to have addressed?*

Ross begins to speak and the room quiets down. He explains that you will be participating in a modified version of The World Cafe, a learning activity designed to help employees have meaningful conversations about topics that matter. He takes a few minutes to share Café "etiquette" and describe what will take place:

1. *You will stand and find a question that you'd like to discuss and sit at that Cafe table for about twenty minutes.*

2. *Explore the question with the others who have also chosen to sit at your Cafe table. Using markers, your group will share its answers, comments, and ideas, including visual images, on the paper tablecloth.*

3. *When time is called, thank your table group and find a new Cafe table with a different question and a different mix of participants. One volunteer at your table will remain as the "host" for the new group that will form the second round. The host is the person who welcomes the new Cafe members and shares the essence and key insights of what has been discussed at that table so far. The host invites the new group to build more ideas that link to the ones already written on the tablecloth.*

4. *The second round continues for about another twenty minutes, repeating the entire process. When time is called, the table host may remain at the table for another round, or a new host can volunteer to welcome the new members and summarize the information. All others rotate tables for the third round.*

5. *During the third round you'll be asked to synthesize key themes, insights, or deeper questions emerging from the conversations as a whole.*

Ross finishes explaining that you will only have time to respond to three of the five questions, based on which most interest you, but all five questions will be sent out via email to everyone for final comments later. Also, the department office will collect, tabulate, and post all the tablecloth responses so that employees can read them on the company intranet site. The company will make future revisions and updates to the customer service policy, based on employee responses from The World Cafe.

After the Cafe rounds are over, Ross asks each group to create a short verbal summary of the tablecloth responses. Groups present their summaries, and then Ross facilitates a general discussion about customer service. The summaries and discussion last about thirty to forty minutes.

During the final time remaining, Ross suggests that each person create an individual customer service action plan, based on some of the ideas and suggestions from The World Cafe. You share your action plan with your table group. Then Ross thanks you for your participation in the Cafe, and the training ends.

What Is TWC?

Although The World Cafe (TWC) appears to have a structure similar to Concept Centers (in Part Two), with participants rotating from table to table as they collaborate through discussion or some other form of active participation, the purpose of The World Cafe is very different. While Concept Centers are primarily training tools, used to teach new information in active ways, TWC is more of an idea-building process used to strengthen the work community, discover common values, explore mutual organizational concerns, consider new concepts and strategies, develop creative opportunities, and generate ideas for action. As authors Juanita Brown and David Isaacs state in *The World Cafe* (2005), "A Cafe dialogue sets the stage for more traditional ways of action planning" (p. 38).

For training purposes, The World Cafe is especially effective when a training group or company wants to

- *Generate* new ideas around a topic.
- *Develop* creative possibilities.
- *Deepen* communication and working relationships.
- *Build* a stronger learning community or work team.
- *Engage* in creative problem-solving.
- *Discover* a variety of creative solutions to key issues.
- *Explore* unexpected ways to connect, converse, and transform the individual, the group, the training, the company, the world.

The Cafe process is probably not an optimal learning tool if the learning outcomes are predetermined and very specific, the training is lecture-based, the training time is short (less than ninety minutes), the issues are highly charged emotionally (which would require greater facilitation expertise), or if the training focus is the acquisition of specific skills. Nor is it as effective if the number of participants is under a dozen.

According to Brown and Isaacs, "The World Cafe is designed primarily to generate collective knowledge-sharing, webs of personal relationships, and new possibilities for action" (2005, p. 38). In other words, TWC is a process of meaningful and collaborative conversations, as well as a metaphor for an inclusive way in which to invite people to begin these conversations. What other metaphor is more useful for a friendly chat about things that matter than a cafe?

Origins of TWC

How The World Cafe came about and its global impact on hundreds of thousands of people are the topics of both the book *The World Cafe: Shaping Our Futures Through Conversations That Matter* (Brown, Isaacs, & The World Cafe Community, 2005) and the website www.theworld cafe.com. The most important fact about the origins of TWC is its global roots. People from all over the world have had a hand in creating and influencing the original concept of using "cafe conversations" to effect business, community, and global change. Cafe groups have sprung up in dozens of countries and in thousands of small and large community, business, and education groups world-wide. This Cafe network is connected through the website and shared bulletin boards, blogs, wiki sites, and the like. The web of Cafe connections grows daily, as do the variations on its use. The impact of the Cafe process is profound, especially when people want to do strategic thinking, project development, educational or healthcare reform, and whenever people address critical issues that make a difference to the future of their group, company, organization, and lives.

Cafe Design Principles

The World Cafe founders, together with the global community of practitioners, have discovered seven core principles that make TWC the collaborative, world-wide success it is. These seven Cafe Design Principles are summarized here. However, to really understand the richness and diversity of the Cafe process, as

it is used by practitioners all around the world, I strongly suggest reading Brown and Isaacs illuminating book.

1. *Set the context.* Clarify the Cafe purpose. Decide what the topic or theme will be, and the questions that matter. Envision the possible outcomes. Invite the people who need or want to be there. Allow enough time for the Cafe conversations to take place. Here is a training example: An electronics company is creating new, interdepartmental teams, with sales, accounting, marketing, manufacturing, and retail employees working together on teams of five or six people. The purpose of The World Cafe is to gather suggestions from the employees for forming effective teams, in which people work successfully together, with a minimum of problems between departments.

2. *Create hospitable space.* The setting should be informal, welcoming, visually pleasing, and with enough creature comforts so that everyone feels physically relaxed and ready to take part in the conversations. Suggestions: paper tablecloths and large colorful markers with which to write, snack food and beverages, simple table decorations, soft background music, colorful posters, and anything else that creates a cafe-type ambiance.

3. *Explore questions that matter.* The questions need to be relevant to the group and worded in such a way as to elicit creative responses and energy. TWC encourages groups to move away from "What's wrong? Who's to blame?" questions and focus instead on "How can we make this better? What is possible here?" questions instead. TWC reminds participants that "People grow in the direction of the questions they ask." For the training example with the electronics company that I mentioned earlier, here are the questions employees will focus on:

   - *What are the greatest benefits to the company and its employees, as well as to customers, that can result from interdepartmental teams?*

   - *What are some of the challenges teams will face as they begin working together?*

   - *What are important ground rules that will help solve any team problems that arise?*

   - *What are some things that need to be done before the teams form?*

   - *What can the company do to support the teams once they begin working together?*

4. *Encourage everyone's contributions.* Each person in the group is an important part of that group's collective intelligence. Because of this, the group needs to make sure that each person has an opportunity to talk and is encouraged

by the group to do so. In the example, the electronics company asks for volunteers to be table hosts for each Cafe round. The table host will stay at his/her Cafe table, welcome the next groups, and summarize the conversation from the previous groups. The host also encourages participation from each group member and helps maintain a positive, inclusive tone.

5. *Connect diverse perspectives.* As conversations progress, patterns, themes, or connections begin to emerge from the web of perspectives. Many times a general consensus of opinion becomes apparent, even within the diversity. Brown and Isaacs call this "the creative cross-pollination of people and ideas" (2005, p. 117), which often produces surprising results that could not have happened otherwise. To continue with our earlier electronics company training example, it becomes apparent that the team members need to learn more about what the different departments actually do and how each department impacts the others. So they decide to schedule weekly lunch-and-learn meetings to deepen their understanding of their own interconnections and departmental responsibilities.

6. *Listen together for insights.* The success of TWC rests on each individual's ability to respectfully listen to other group members. A Cafe suggestion is for listeners to pretend that the person speaking is very wise (It may be so!), and that this person's ideas are an important part of the collective intelligence, much like each instrument is an important part of an orchestra. Effective listening also involves hearing what *hasn't* been stated, along with what *has* been shared. To continue with the electronics company example, the Cafe groups realize from the discussions that each department has a different timeline for product delivery, which makes working together on interdepartmental teams really challenging. The timeline issue must be solved company-wide before the interdepartmental teams can work successfully together.

7. *Share collective discoveries.* This is where all the rounds of conversation are leading—to the point at which participants stand back, reflect on what the conversations have uncovered, and find the common threads among the entire group. Coming up with the essence of the experience—the learning, insights, solutions, next steps, and deeper questions—is the most powerful part of the process. Action comes out of the collective discoveries of the group. TWC suggests questions like the following as a starting place for a whole-group discussion of the Cafe conversations:

   - *What is emerging here?*

   - *If there were a single voice in the room, what would it be saying?*

- *What deeper questions are emerging as a result of these conversations?*
- *Do we notice any patterns, and what do those patterns point to or how do they inform us?*
- *What do we now see and know as a result of these conversations?*
- *What are our next steps in this process?*

List reprinted with permission from The World Cafe Community Foundation at www.theworldcafe.com.

Coming back once more to the training example, the electronics company employees now summarize all the discussion question responses and, from these summaries, create an action plan outlining the next steps they plan to take as they form their interdepartmental teams and get down to business. They also assign each team a specific step of the action plan to be responsible for. And it is during this last principle—sharing collective discoveries—that employees make a formal commitment to contribute to their teams' efforts to the best of their ability.

Where to Begin

If you have never included Concept Centers in your training programs, or if you have never taken part in a collaborative learning activity like The World Cafe, the following suggestions will help you begin. If you are already familiar with these strategies, experiment with other variations as described in Brown and Isaacs' book and in Part Two of this book. Combine your own creativity with the Cafe principles as you adapt the process to your programs.

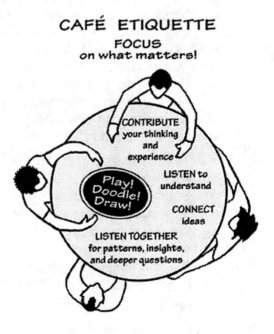

- *Start with a simple Cafe.* Set up the Cafe within your standard training room environment. Keep the table questions simple and related to the training topic. You can even begin with just one question for all Cafe groups to discuss. A single question allows participants to go more deeply into the connections and patterns as they begin to listen for other patterns or different questions that emerge from the first. Try for a total of three rounds of table conversations, if time allows. At the end of all the Cafe rounds, hold a whole-group conversation focused on key insights and learnings.

- *Explain the process to the group.* Let them know what to expect and what the Cafe principles are. Emphasize the focus on positive conversations that feel inclusive and respectful of all. Allow time for questions before beginning the Cafe rounds.

- *Ask for volunteers to be table hosts.* The job of a table host is not that of a formal facilitator, but rather a "conversation steward," that is, the one who encourages participation, asks open-ended questions, and also participates. More importantly, the table host stays at the same table during the Cafe rotations to welcome the new groups and to share the essence of the previous conversations for the new table members during each round. Ask for a volunteer at each Cafe table to be the table host. If there are several Cafe rotations, hosts may choose to rotate during the second or third rounds, with a new host volunteering to be the conversation steward for the following round.

- *Be the Cafe host/hostess.* While the Cafe discussions take place, move among the table groups. Be available to respond to any questions, listen to the conversations, add a relevant comment or two, if required, and then move on. It is your presence and interest that forms one of the important background pieces of the Cafe, much like a good host does at a restaurant.

- *Allow enough time for small group conversations.* Even though there may not be enough time for all participants to visit all Cafe tables during the activity, you still need to make sure that the conversations aren't cut short by an unrealistic time deadline. The average length of discussion time is about twenty minutes per Cafe round. Thirty is often better, fifteen is generally too short. It takes people time to relax and settle in to the conversations, reflect on what is being talked about, offer their opinions, and write their responses on the tablecloths.

- *Allow enough time for whole-group processing.* This is the most important segment of the entire Cafe process. Once in a while, you can let it go until another time if there is excellent documentation from the original conversations. However, in most cases, it works better if the whole group has an opportunity to discuss the insights from the Cafe experience immediately after the table conversations. Your questions during this whole-group dialogue can be simple:

- *What did you learn that you didn't know before?*
- *What are your insights into the topic now?*
- *What are other questions or concepts you wish to explore?*
- *Where should we go next with this information?*

- *Follow up with summaries and action plans.* So that participants know their conversations were meaningful, it's important to have a follow-up plan to the Cafe experience. Here are three examples:

  - If the training is with a group of learners who work together, each table group creates a written summary of the comments printed on each tablecloth. They email these summaries to all Cafe participants or post them on an intranet website or blog.

  - The whole training group decides what the next steps are. Then individual participants volunteer to oversee each step and to report back to the group the progress being made.

  - If the training group does not work together, the trainer collects the table group summaries and sends them out to all on a participant email list. Action plans and next steps become the responsibility of individual participants at their own job sites.

Final Reminders

Any time you entertain the notion that learners do, in fact, know a lot already about the topic at hand and that learners can, in fact, create effective solutions for issues and concerns that are important to them, you have the beginnings of The World Cafe. Whether you decide to use this learning tool or not is up to you. Brown and Isaacs remind us that "The World Cafe is not a technique. It is an invitation into a way of being with one another that is already part of our nature" (2005, p. 218). In training, The World Cafe is a way to allow learners the time and space they need in order to engage in creative, meaningful, transformative conversations.

If you decide to experiment with The World Cafe, here are few final reminders:

- *The process is as important as the product.* TWC isn't necessarily about producing a tangible result. The Cafe process is more about the synergy, creativity, and synthesis of the collective intelligence of the group and the possibilities that can emerge from that creative combination. Set up the Cafe experience, trust the process, and step aside to let it work its magic.

- *It's about progress, not perfection.* Don't expect the Cafe participants to come up with the one right solution to concerns and issues. The solutions often lie in the process itself, not in any final decision. Each Cafe round builds on the one before it, and each Cafe experience does the same—building the connections, community, and finally the consensus of the whole group as it moves toward a desired goal.

- *Go with the flow.* Often, the Cafe conversations generate a whole new perspective about the questions being asked and toward possible solutions. Be open to exploring unforeseen directions the conversations may take. Allow the explorations to continue, and remind the participants to do the same. Instant rejection of a new idea is the opposite of what this process is about.

- *You never know where its influence may go.* Whenever a small group of people come together in informal, relaxed ways to discuss topics that are important to them, the energy and vision of the group has a far-reaching impact that cannot be predicted at the time of the conversations. This is the way whole companies—and countries—have been changed for the better: from small groups of dedicated people who teach and learn from each other.

One word to sum up The World Cafe conversations is "possibilities." All things are possible when groups of committed people get together in informal gatherings to discuss things that matter to them. Training is no exception—it *is* an informal gathering of committed people who are learning about things that matter to them. "Optimum learning and development occur in systems in which there is a rich web of interactions" (Brown & Isaacs, 2005, p. 112). So the combination of training and The World Cafe has the potential for being a powerful catalyst for learning, change, and growth.

> *Is it too big a stretch of our imaginations*
> *to envision a world engaged in conversations*
> *that have real heart and meaning for us all?*

> Juanita Brown and David Isaacs
> *The World Cafe*, 2005, p. 112

Wake 'Em Up!

Ten Tips for Interactive e-Learning

If they like it, they will play.

Clark Quinn
Engaging Learning, 2005, p. 17

Many trainers consider interactive electronic learning (e-learning) to be an oxymoron, in that the words "interactive e-learning" cancel each other out. e-Learning *can't* be interactive, they say. After all, most training done via computers or phones usually consists of lectures or self-study manuals, sometimes combined with PowerPoint® slides and maybe a question-and-answer period or test at the end of the program. Even though there are now many computer software programs available for training that include interactive features—whiteboards, chat rooms, breakout areas, polling and signaling features, and the like—most of what people call e-learning, also called computer-based training, is still predominantly lecture or self-study.

e-Learning means many things to many people. Here, we'll define e-learning as information that is electronically delivered in one or more of the following ways:

- *Teleconferences.* These are auditory only, using phone lines as means of information delivery. Participants dial into a specific teleconference number that supports multiple callers. There is usually no computer-based component to a teleconference call.

- *Webinars.* These are both auditory and visual, using phone lines, computers, and the Internet to deliver training. The actual delivery is done in real time, with a trainer and participants in attendance via voice and Internet components. There are a number of webinar software programs available, some that have interactive features and some that don't.

- *Synchronous or distance learning.* These are live, televised programs that have both auditory and visual components, usually delivered over televised or satellite networks. A trainer facilitates the face-to-face training in one city, while numerous other sites around the country receive the training at the same time it is being delivered. If the other sites have auditory and visual components, the trainer may be able to see and hear the participants while they see and hear the trainer. This type of e-learning is also done with computer cameras, software programs, and Internet hosts as an alternative to television or satellite components. Whatever electronic media are used, the training happens in real time, with trainer and learners meeting in "virtual" classrooms that can be in many places at once.

- *Asynchronous or self-directed computer-based training.* These are training programs that have been created and uploaded to a website, web host, or company intranet site. The training is usually in the printed form of worksheets, slides, tests, and other written material to be read by the learner using her own computer at a time of her own choosing. Sometimes there are pre-recorded voice-over components or short video segments as well. There is no trainer and no class. This e-learning format is also called computer-based self-study.

While some of the ideas in this chapter may apply better to one form of e-learning than another, I am including all of the above electronic information-delivery systems under the term e-learning.

Let's begin with two false assumptions about e-learning:

- *e-Learning is boring (it doesn't have to be).*
- *e-Learning is not interactive (it should be).*

As with classroom instruction, boring and non-interactive e-learning programs are design and delivery issues, not content or learner issues. Even the most complex, technical material can be made both interesting and interactive. And even the most passive learners can be invited to participate in short, relevant learning activities.

So how can you go about creating interesting, interactive e-learning programs? Here are ten simple ways to begin.

1. Send Out Warm-Ups with Built-In Accountability

Warm-Ups are pre-program instructions, sent via email, detailing a variety of simple, topic-related activities that learners do before the e-learning class begins. You can apply the Warm-Up activities listed in Part One of this book to e-learning as well as to face-to-face instruction.

For teleconferences and synchronous distance learning, participants can report their Warm-Up findings verbally to the training group. For asynchronous training, learners can email their findings to their supervisors, instructors, or to other persons whose names and email addresses are part of the course.

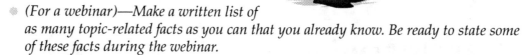

Following is a list of some of the Warm-Ups from Part One that work especially well with e-learning programs:

- *(For a webinar)—Make a written list of as many topic-related facts as you can that you already know. Be ready to state some of these facts during the webinar.*

- *(For a teleconference)—Interview an "expert" (someone who knows more than you do about the topic), and be ready to tell the teleconference group what you learned.*

- *(For a webinar)—Do an Internet search about the training topic and be ready to use the chat room feature to share what you learned from your search.*

- *(For all e-learning)—Ask co-workers what they know or have heard about the topic and make a list of facts and opinions. Email a summary of this information to the other class members.*

- *(For all e-learning)—Make up a short, pre-training quiz with some questions you want to have answered during the training. Email these questions to the instructor before the e-learning class begins.*

Give learners choices: They can do one or two, or do all but one, or make up one of their own.

2. Create an Interesting Graphic Organizer

Create a note-taking page (called a graphic organizer) and email it to the e-learning participants before the training begins. Use Adobe Acrobat PDF format, which is the most stable for email attachments.

The note-taking page should be visually interesting, with plenty of space for writing and doodling. It should *not* be a PowerPoint® handout with slide images and lines to write on—use these as resources only. Instead, the note-taking worksheet should have topic-related graphics, shapes, forms, and writing spaces. In Part Two of this book are five Concept Maps, which are examples of graphic organizers.

Send out an email reminder before the class, instructing participants to print the note-taking page and have it and a pen/pencil ready when the class begins. During the program, be sure to stop and direct learners to write important words, phrases, or concepts. *Don't* assume they are writing just because they have the page in front of them. Instead, say, "This is profound, so write it down!" and then *stop speaking* to give them time to do so.

For asynchronous training, include a graphic organizer in the computerized materials with instructions that the learner download, print, and use it as he or she works through the course.

3. Begin with a Fast Pass

At the beginning of an e-learning class, participants are expecting introductions, technical information, program agendas, learning objectives, and any other housekeeping details that most training starts with. Imagine their surprise when you direct them (via voice, slide, or other visual) to jot down the three most important things they learned from the Warm-Ups they chose and to be ready to report this to the class. You give them a minute or so to do this, then you begin the class with their reports. If the class is large, you might ask for only a few reports.

There are five Fast Pass activities in Part One of this book. When adapted to e-learning, these Fast Pass strategies engage learners from the moment they log onto the e-learning experience. The immediate involvement and novelty motivate learners to pay attention.

For a teleconference Fast Pass, you verbally state what you want learners to do. For synchronous distance learning, post the Fast Pass on the computer, camera, or television screen and instruct participants to report to their site's groups. For asynchronous training, have printed instructions that direct learners to write a short summary of what they learned in the Warm-Ups.

Here are a few more specific examples of e-learning Fast Pass instructions:

- *(For a webinar)—Using the chat room feature, print a topic-related question that you want answers for.*

- *(For a teleconference)—When I call your name, please state one thing you want to learn from this program.*

- *(For a webinar)—On the whiteboard, print a word or phrase that you associate with this topic.*

- *(For distance learning)—With the other participants at your learning site, brainstorm what you already know about the topic, and be ready to report back some facts from this list.*

- *(For self-study)—On blank paper, make a list of five facts you know or have heard about this topic. Come back to your list after you finish the course and check your facts for accuracy. Correct any that are incorrect.*

4. Follow the Ten-Minute Rule

Regardless of the type of e-learning class you are facilitating, *always* use the ten-minute rule, meaning that you will divide your slide show, lectures, or printed material into segments of about ten minutes in length. In between each ten-minute segment, insert a short, one-minute review activity that gives learners the opportunity to review the information just presented. Both the chapter titled "Brain-Friendly Training" and Part Two of this book give you the rationale for using the ten-minute rule, as well as a variety of quick review strategies. Listed below are a few e-learning adaptations of some of these strategies:

- *Think and Write (for all e-learning)—On your note-taking page, write one sentence summarizing what you just learned.*

- *Pair Share (for webinars)—In the chat room (or at your distance learning site) pair up with another participant and share the two most important facts from the lecture.*

- *Shout Out (for teleconferences)—As a group, we need to state eight new things we now know about the topic.*

- *Whiteboard Writing (for webinars)— We'll now take one minute for everyone to quickly write a word or phrase related to the information just covered.*

For an asynchronous course, insert the short review activities as printed instructions between information segments. Examples:

- *Write four main ideas from this chapter.*

- *Write eight facts you now know about this topic. Look back through the chapter to see whether you listed them correctly.*

- *Write a review question that could be on a test.*

- *Think of how you might use this information. Write this down.*

- *Think of what you just learned. Write down a question you still have. After reading the rest of the material, come back to this question and see whether you can answer it.*

5. Build in Body Breaks

Stop reading this book now and do the following one-minute Body Break: *Stand, stretch, and take a couple of deep breaths. Walk one time around your chair, the room you are in, or down the hall and back. Return to this book and continue reading.*

The paragraph above just instructed you to stand and move. Could you instruct your e-learning participants to do the same? Of course you can! There is no rule that says they have to be sitting during the entire class. When training participants stand and stretch, even in e-learning classes, they wake up their bodies and minds.

Will they do it? You have no way of knowing for sure, but they probably will. After all, you are the "teacher" and they are used to doing what teachers tell them to do. Besides that, they'll feel better standing and stretching after sitting a while. The chapter "Brain-Friendly Training" in this book give you more information about the physical benefits of learners standing, stretching, and moving during training.

Here are some adaptations for e-learning:

- *Stand, Stretch, and Speak—Stand up, stretch your body, and then state a topic-related fact you have learned that you didn't know before.*

- *Mini-Walkabout—Stand up and walk one time around your chair, breathing deeply as you do so.*

- *Micro-Macro Stretches—A micro stretch is a small stretch such as in fingers and toes. A macro stretch is a stretch such as arms and legs. We need a volunteer to verbally lead us in a micro or macro stretch, telling us all what part of the body to stretch as we stand.*

For teleconferences, webinars, and distance learning, ask for a volunteer to verbally lead a whole-group stretch. For asynchronous self-study, print the Body Break instructions into the material, as I did at the beginning of this section. You can also put the Body Break instructions on a note-taking page. Or include a page of suggested Body Breaks with instructions to choose one to do every ten to twenty minutes.

6. Become Familiar with Interactive Features—And Use Them

As I stated earlier, many webinar software programs have a number of interactive features built into them. Explore the ones that are available to you and become familiar enough with them that you don't have to learn them "on the fly," that is, while you are training. Such interactive features may include whiteboards, chat rooms, hand icons, polling, applause, and other visual signals. You can also have participants circle important concepts with the electronic pencil, draw doodle representations of important concepts on the whiteboard, or fill in the blanks. The point is to make learners *use* these interactive features and, to ensure that they do, *you* have to be comfortable using them as well.

Listed below are examples of interactive instructions using these features:

- *Raise your hand by using the hand icon if you agree with this statement . . .*

- *Let's take a poll to see how many of us agree or disagree with the following . . .*

- *Using the electronic pencil, circle the most important bulleted fact on the screen.*

- *Using the highlighter, mark the question that is most important to you.*

- *In the chat room, write a one-sentence opinion about the usefulness of what you've learned.*

- *On the whiteboard, draw a doodle representing one important concept.*

- *When you're ready to answer this question, signal with the button icon.*

7. Lengthen the Learning with Follow-Up Action Plans

Action Plans are the learners' written or verbal commitments to use what they have learned. Action Plans help learners review and evaluate the new information as they decide how they will put it all to practical use back on the job. Action Plans can also have an accountability piece built into them as well, meaning that learners must report their plans to someone else. Part Four of this book contains a variety of Evaluation and Learner-Led Summaries that also include Action Plans.

Here are a few e-learning adaptations:

- *(For all e-learning)—On your graphic organizer, write one or two sentences describing how you plan to use this information at work. Also write the name of one other employee (or your supervisor) with whom you will discuss your Action Plan.*

- *(for webinars)—In the chat room, write your Action Plan for how you plan to apply what you've learned. Put your name beside your plan. We'll copy the Action Plans and email them out to all participants when the class is over.*

- *(For all e-learning)—On an index card, write one thing you can do immediately with what you have learned. Tape this index card to your desk or bulletin board at work. Send an email to the instructor in a week letting her know how your Action Plan is going.*

8. Follow Up with Blogs or Wikis

A blog is an online web log where you post information and learners can respond by commenting on the posted material. A wiki is an online encyclopedia where you and the learners can both post and respond to posted material. If you know how to set up a quick blog or wiki site, these can be ways to lengthen the learning as well. If you're not sure how to begin using these follow-up tools, do an Internet search for "setting up a blog or wiki" and browse through the free instructions. For wikis, you can also log onto www.wiki.wetpaint.com, which is a wiki about creating wikis. Or skim the many books at www.amazon.com that give how-to instructions for both electronic tools. Many Internet blog and wiki hosting sites are free. Two examples of free hosting sites are www.blogger.com and www.wikidot.com.

Make sure that e-learning participants know how to access the blog or wiki so that they can post their after-training insights, questions, best practices, responses, comments, and the like. For self-study, include an access instruction sheet at the end of the computerized materials.

9. Give Them Changes and Choices

As noted in the chapter on brain research earlier, habituation is when the human brain begins to ignore anything routine, repetitive, or boring. Whether you are conducting a classroom or e-learning training, the trick is to keep habituation from kicking in. Any changes you make that help hold learners' interest and curiosity will work: activities, graphics, sound, movement, stories, video segments, and colors and images in printed material, to name a few. In addition, any time you give participants choices during the training, you enhance their motivation to learn. Examples: choosing from a list of quick review activities, choosing a way to report back to the group, choosing what to write, choosing a question to answer, choosing someone to work/partner with, or choosing whether or not to participate in the interactive segments.

10. Go with the Flow

Nothing works all the time. Be okay with the fact that no e-learning experience runs perfectly. There will always be technical, program, participant, and content challenges (not unlike classroom-based training). Even the best plans—and interactive strategies—can occasionally crash—in more ways than one. So be patient with yourself and your e-learning participants, start with baby steps, and give yourself plenty of kudos for creating e-learning experiences that are interesting, participatory, and memorable.

Putting the Tips to Work

Look back through this chapter now and circle one or two tips that you will include in your next e-learning program. When you have time, redesign an entire e-learning training using three or more interactive strategies from this chapter. Or adapt three or more strategies from other parts of this book.

Let's do a quick check of what you have learned about interactive e-learning. A list of training-related sentences follows. Underline the correct phrase in each sentence, then check your answers.

1. e-Learning should be *(lecture-based; activity-based)*, with *(short; long)* periods of direct instruction.

2. *(Standing and moving; sitting for a long while)* helps e-learning participants learn better.

3. Accountability means learners have to *(just show up; show they did the activity or assignment)*.

4. An effective graphic organizer is *(an interesting, visual note-taking page; a copy of the PowerPoint® slides)*.

5. Learners must *(remain standing, remain seated; do some sitting and some standing)* during an e-learning class in order to remain alert.

6. To create interest, send out pre-program *(Warm-Ups; tests)*.

7. Begin with *(introductions, agendas, and technical information; a Fast Pass)* that will engage learners right from the start.

8. Divide your lecture material into *(thirty-minute; ten-minute)* segments.

9. End with participant-created *(Action Plans; training evaluations)*.

If you underlined the correct phrases, the sentences should read:

1. e-Learning should be *activity-based*, with *short* periods of direct instruction.

2. *Standing and moving* helps e-learning participants learn better.

3. Accountability means learners have to *show they did the activity or assignment*.

4. An effective graphic organizer is *an interesting, visual note-taking page*.

5. Learners must *do some sitting and some standing* during an e-learning class in order to remain alert.

6. To create interest, send out pre-program *Warm-Ups*.

7. Begin with *a Fast Pass* that will engage learners right from the start.

8. Divide your lecture material into *ten-minute* segments.

9. End with participant-created *Action Plans*.

Be creative! Experiment with these tips, make up your own, and share what you have discovered. Begin to design e-learning programs that capture and hold the interest and involvement of your learners from the moment they log on until the moment they log off.

You'll "wake 'em up" and keep them interested, learning, involved, and wanting more.

> *The extraordinary power of interactivity*
> *is to get people thinking through doing and doing*
> *well by thinking.*

Michael Allen
Michael Allen's Guide to e-Learning, 2003, p. 312

The Author's Epilogue

If [people] can't learn the way we teach,
maybe we should teach the way they learn.

Ignacio Estrada

The Orange Juice Cure

According to an elementary school psychologist and friend of mine, there once were two concerned parents who talked to my friend about their seven-year-old daughter, who still wet the bed at night. My friend listened to the problem, then asked the parents to explain the pre-bedtime routine. "Well," the father said, "We have dinner around 6 p.m., and then our daughter does her homework. After that, she plays or watches television until about 8:30. Then she changes into pajamas, drinks a glass of orange juice, brushes her teeth, and goes to bed." After the father finished his narration, my friend sat quietly for a moment and then gently suggested that they skip the orange juice. The problem resolved itself immediately, and their daughter no longer wet the bed.

Often, the "cure" is pretty straightforward. Do this—and this is the result. Do something different—and a different result occurs. When it comes to teaching and training, one of the cures to the sickness of boredom that ails much instruction today seems obvious: When instructional strategies change, the responses to learning will change. When trainers change how they teach, learners will change how they learn.

Be the Change You Seek

Mahatma Gandhi was one of the 20th century's major political and spiritual leaders of India and of the world. He is credited with reminding us that we must be the change we seek in the world. A simple story about Gandhi serves to illustrate his words. A mother brought her son to Gandhi. She told Gandhi that her son ate too many sweets and asked him to please tell her son to stop eating sugar. Gandhi instructed her to go home and come back in two weeks. When she and her son returned two weeks later, Gandhi looked at the boy and said, "Stop eating sugar." The mother protested, "Why couldn't you have told him that two weeks ago?" Gandhi replied, "Because two weeks ago I hadn't stopped eating sugar."

As teachers and trainers, we have to walk our talk. In order to change how our students and training participants learn, we must change ourselves first—and change what we think effective teaching and training is.

When we make the paradigm shift from "trainers talk; learners listen" to "when learners talk and teach, they learn," a myriad of opportunities begin to appear, as if by magic. We discover new books, workshops, and friends who are already walking the talk and who are willing to help us. We receive accolades that reaffirm the effectiveness of the changes we are making. Colleagues ask us to teach *them* how to do what we are doing. All the personal experiences that appear as a result of changing how we train are, in effect, *our teachers*—they help us become the change we seek.

Teaching *Is* Learning, Learning *Is* Teaching

At some point in this journey, we finally understand, on a deeply personal level, that we master *what* we teach, *when* we teach it. The same holds true for our learners. When they teach and learn from each other, they move toward mastery of the material as well.

Let me put it another way: When we teach, we learn; when we learn, we teach. It's a natural cycle of human learning that affects every moment of our lives, because the human brain cannot help but learn. In everything we do, we are the learners as well as the teachers. No exceptions. Once we've really put our heads around this, stepping aside and encouraging learners to teach and learn from each other becomes easy—and an immensely effective and rewarding way to train.

I'll end with a wish for abundant blessings for you and your learners, as you teach and train from the *back* of the room, allowing your learners to take center-stage and truly *learn*.

Learning is finding out what you already know.
Doing is demonstrating that you know it.
Teaching is reminding others that they know it as well as you do.
We are all learners, doers, and teachers.

Richard Bach

Sharon Bowman
Lake Tahoe at Glenbrook, Nevada
August 2008

Great Resources

Author's Note

With a few exceptions, the research that forms the foundation of this book is from the 21st century, meaning that it is no more than ten years old (up to this book's publication date). I point that out because those of us who train and teach for a living may be unfamiliar with the most current updates to research about human learning. This is unfortunate because, in the last decade, a whole new area of science (called "cognitive neuroscience" or how the brain takes in, stores, and retrieves information) has virtually exploded with information that is of practical use to anyone who helps others learn. While the information found in this research may not be new, the application of it is.

There are many excellent resources from the 1990s as well. I've included a number of them in this bibliography, in a separate section. Beyond that, when we stretch back earlier than the 1980s, much research, while still relevant in light of what we now know about the human brain, lacked practical application, especially for teachers and trainers. Put another way, it was more difficult then to translate the research into instructional behaviors that would positively affect learners.

The 21st century brain research has opened up new possibilities for trainers, teachers, and learners—if we become familiar with the research and apply it to what we do. In this book, I have attempted to help with the practical application of some of the useful research. This book is by no means complete. Neither is this resource section. Both the book and the research upon which it is based are only a beginning. A decade from now, this book will probably seem obsolete, as we move faster and faster into whole new ways of approaching learning—ways we can't even imagine right now. Author Jay Cross asks, "If we lived in a world with no schools, what would we build in their place?" (2007, p. 55). The 21st century research points us to the answer:

[Let's] return to the natural way people learn:
through conversations with one another, trying things out,
and listening to stories.

Jay Cross
Informal Learning, 2007, p. 12

Need-to-Know Books: The Author's Top Five

I am often asked, *"Which training books do you recommend?"* Since we are all busy people, and even those of us who read the resource books probably do a lot of skimming and little cover-to-cover reading, I've selected a few favorites—for usefulness of information and for practicality in the classroom and training room. All are available on www.amazon.com, or you can do an Internet search for more information about the books and websites that sell them.

1. One book only? Dave Meier's *The Accelerated Learning Handbook* (2000) is the best. Practical, useful, with just enough of the history of Accelerated Learning, and the brain research behind it, to make you a lifelong believer. Additionally, the book offers a "smorgasbord" of imminently useful ideas, strategies, activities, and suggestions to make you an effective Accelerated Learning practitioner. It also gives you another way of looking at the four-step instructional design and delivery model I call the 4 Cs. I can't say enough good things about this book. Notwithstanding the fact that Dave has been my mentor and friend for decades, his book is a great example of Accelerated Learning in written form—and a very practical resource for anyone who teaches or trains for a living.

2. If you like what you learned from *Training from the BACK of the Room!*, then you'll love its prequel, *The Ten-Minute Trainer: 150 Ways to Teach It Quick and Make It Stick* (Bowman, 2005). Yes, it's my own book. Yes, it's one of my top five. Why? Because I wish a book like this had been available when I began teaching and training for a living. This book gives you a collection of 150 short, quick instructional activities that you can use with any topic and any group of learners. It also offers important brain research that has high impact on how we train. And it includes another way of looking at the 4 Cs instructional design and delivery process. A timely tome, if you don't mind the alliteration.

3. *Informal Learning* (2007) by Jay Cross is a delightfully surprising gem of a book. Rather than writing a how-to book, Jay reintroduces you to a world you are already familiar with—that of informal learning—meaning all the powerful ways you learn, apart from formal classrooms. His book is a fast ride to a very different way of looking at teaching and training, with some great ideas for getting there once you realize how right he is.

4. Harold Stolovitch's *Telling Ain't Training* (2002) makes my top five list as well, perhaps even more for the way it is written: an interactive book

that engages you even as you learn about learning. I don't know whether, in real life, Mr. Stolovitch practices what he preaches when he presents and trains, but he preaches it well in his book. The short, reader-friendly exercises make the concepts both personal and relevant, as well as useful.

5. Because I am an avid reader of books on cognitive neuroscience, it was difficult to choose just one brain research book from the many excellent ones available. So I'm going to cheat and give you three that are all equally good. I'll offer them with a caveat: They are aimed at an audience of educators in schools and colleges. This should not lessen their helpfulness; any corporate trainer should realize that there is no difference (at least as far as how the human brain learns) between "teaching" and "training." The same brain-based principles apply. David Sousa's *How the Brain Learns* (2006) is the most recent and contains a "Practitioner's Corner" of practical application for the concepts in each chapter. Patricia Wolfe's *Brain Matters: Translating Research into Classroom Practice* (2001) is very informative, with a toolkit of brain-compatible strategies. And Eric Jensen's *Brain-Based Learning* (2000) is an excellent synthesis of both brain research and practical application of that research. Ah, I'll add a fourth to this list—just to further confuse the confounded mind! *Learning and Memory: The Brain in Action* (1999) by Marilee Sprenger is a small volume with rich information on neuroscience that she brings up close and personal with her stories about teaching.

Resources Cited in *Training from the BACK of the Room!* (most from the 2000s)

Allen, Michael. (2003). *Michael Allen's guide to e-learning.* Hoboken, NJ: John Wiley & Sons. Allen has some excellent things to say about learning in general, and e-learning specifically. A must if you do any computer-based or e-learning training.

Barkley, Elizabeth; Cross, Patricia; & Major, Howell. (2005). *Collaborative learning techniques.* San Francisco, CA: Jossey-Bass. A research-based book about cooperative and collaborative learning, with a collection of classroom-based strategies that are applicable to corporate training as well.

Bowman, Sharon. (2005). *The ten-minute trainer.* San Francisco CA: Pfeiffer. The perfect complement to *Training from the BACK of the Room!* See Author's Top Five for a complete description.

Brown, Juanita; Isaacs, David; & The World Cafe Community. (2005). *The world cafe.* San Francisco, CA: Berrett-Koehler. A detailed and illuminating book for understanding and applying this process to a variety of learning experiences. You can also access free information from www.theworldcafe.com.

Caine, Renate; Cain, Geoffrey; McClintic, Carol; & Klimek, Karl. (2005). *12 brain/mind learning principles in action.* Thousand Oaks, CA: Corwin Press. This book came in as seventh on my list of useful brain-based research books. A lengthier read, but with some good ideas for putting the research to use.

Cross, Jay. (2007). *Informal learning.* San Francisco, CA: Pfeiffer. Definitely a paradigm-shifting kind of book and a must if you want to understand where education, training, and learning is going in the 21st century. See Author's Top Five for more detail.

El-Shamy, Susan. (2004). *How to design and deliver training for the new and emerging generations.* San Francisco, CA: Pfeiffer. Covers both research and practical application for teaching the generations following the baby boomer generation. Contains a wealth of easy ways to reach younger learners.

Finkel, Donald. (2000). *Teaching with your mouth shut.* Portsmouth, NH: Boynton/ Cook. A little tome with some thought-provoking concepts about orchestrating instruction so that you move from "teacher/trainer" to "guide."

Heath, Chip; & Heath, Dan. (2007). *Made to stick: Why some ideas survive and others die.* New York: Random House. A great resource for really understanding what makes any idea truly memorable. Not a how-to book for training, but its principles should be part of any effective learning experience.

International Alliance for Learning. *The history of accelerated learning.* www.ialearn. org,/ALHistory.php

Jensen, Eric. (2000). *Brain-based learning.* Thousand Oaks, CA: Corwin Press. Easy to read and filled with brain-based research and practical teaching/training strategies. See Author's Top Five.

Margulies, Nancy. (2002). *Mapping inner space.* Chicago, IL: Zephyr Press. Probably the best book about concept mapping and graphic organizers ever written. A "must have" if you want to include this powerful memory tool in your classes and training programs.

Margulies, Nancy; & Valenza, Christine. (2005). *Visual thinking.* Norwalk, CT: Crown House Publishing. A guide for the artistic neophyte, or for anyone beginning the process of converting words into images in order to move information into long-term memory.

Meier, David. (2000). *The accelerated learning handbook.* New York: McGraw-Hill. The most comprehensive book ever written about Accelerated Learning. See Author's Top Five for complete description.

Meier, Thomas. (1999). *The accelerated learning coursebuilder.* Lake Geneva, WI: The Center for Accelerated Learning. A handsomely-boxed kit of six, spiral bound books that cover all aspects of Accelerated Learning and include hundreds of ways to use the AL strategies. Call 262-248-7070 for ordering information.

Owen, Harrison. (1997). *Open-space technology.* San Francisco, CA: Berrett-Koehler. This is the how-to source for this collaborative, innovative process. Access the website at www.openspaceworld.org for more information.

Pierce, Howard. (2000). *The owner's manual for the human brain.* Marietta, GA: Bard Press. Information-packed and research-based, this book is the "everything you wanted to know about the brain but were afraid to ask" resource for readers fascinated with how the human brain functions.

Pike, Robert. (2003). *Creative training techniques handbook* (3rd ed.). Amherst, MA: HRD Press. A trainer's basic how-to book that covers practical information about both training design and delivery.

Quinn, Clark. (2005). *Engaging learning.* San Francisco, CA: Pfeiffer. More for the computer-based and e-learning trainer, this book nevertheless holds some important concepts about learner engagement and motivation.

Sousa, David. (2006). *How the brain learns.* Thousand Oaks, CA: Corwin Press. A good brain primer, covering most of the important cognitive neuroscience research of the past decade. See Author's Top Five.

Sprenger, Marilee. (1999). *Learning and memory: The brain in action.* Alexandria, VA: Association for Supervision and Curriculum Development. Excellent resource for understanding how memory works. See Author's Top Five.

Stolovich, Harold; & Keeps, Erica. (2002). *Telling ain't training.* Alexandria, VA: American Society for Training and Development. An interactive book that uses the thing to teach the thing. See Author's Top Five.

Sylwester, Robert. (1995). *A celebration of neurons: An educator's guide to the human brain.* Alexandria, VA: Association for Supervision and Curriculum and

Development. The educational application of cognitive neuroscience. A fine introduction to the field.

Thiagarajan, Sivasailam. (2003). *Design your own games and activities.* San Francisco, CA: Pfeiffer. A comprehensive collection of Thiagi's best framegames, which are activities that a trainer can use with any training topic. Also includes the research and rationale behind using framegames as an integral part of training.

Weimer, Maryellen. (2002). *Learner-centered teaching.* San Francisco, CA: Jossey/Bass. An in-depth, detailed look at learner-center instruction in college classrooms.

Whittle, Chris. (2005). *Crash course.* New York: Riverhead Books. A businessman's perspective of the educational system in the United States. Contains some intriguing concepts for making it work better, including handing much of the learning back to the learners.

Wolfe, Patricia. (2001). *Brain matters: Translating research into classroom practice.* Alexandria, VA: Association for Supervision and Curriculum Development. Another well-written book combining neuroscience with practical classroom application. See Author's Top Five.

Other Resources (from the 1990s–2000s)

Aldrich, Clark. (2005). *Learning by doing.* San Francisco, CA: Pfeiffer. A useful, albeit highly technical and detailed, resource for computer-based training.

Backer, Lori; & Deck, Michele. (2003). *The presenter's EZ graphics kit.* Sterling, VA: Stylus Publishing. A beginner's step-by-step guide for creating interesting, visually-appealing graphics on charts, handouts, presentation software, and any printed material.

Barbazette, Jean. (2006). *The art of great training delivery.* San Francisco, CA: Pfeiffer. A basic reference book for readers who want a detailed, analytical approach to training.

Biech, Elaine. (2005). *Training for dummies.* Hoboken, NJ: John Wiley & Sons. A reference book that covers traditional information about training design and delivery.

Bowman, Sharon. (1997). *Presenting with pizzazz! Terrific tips for topnotch trainers.* Glenbrook, NV: Bowperson Publishing. A host of easy-to-apply tips and activities for getting learners of all ages more actively involved in their own learning.

Bowman, Sharon. (1998). *How to give it so they get it! A flight plan for teaching anyone anything and making it stick.* Glenbrook, NV: Bowperson Publishing. For readers who want to explore the ways they learn, teach, train, and communicate. Includes detailed descriptions of the four major learning styles and easy-to-follow instructions for forty experiential training activities.

Bowman, Sharon. (2001). *Preventing death by lecture! Terrific tips for turning listeners into learners.* Glenbrook, NV: Bowperson Publishing. A short, easy read with dozens of quick activities—from one to five minutes in length—that you can use with any subject and any size group.

Bowman, Sharon. (2009). *Using the ordinary to make your training extraordinary.* Glenbrook, NV: Bowperson Publishing. Based on a trainer's perspective and application of the research on multiple intelligences, this little book contains over one-hundred ways to use ordinary household and office objects, and memory aids, in extraordinary ways.

Bromley, Karen; Irwin-De Vitis, Linda; & Modlo, Marcia. (1995). *Graphic organizers: Visual strategies for active learning.* New York: Scholastic Professional Books. Contains a variety of visual/spatial ways for learners to take notes and organize information.

Campbell, William; & Smith, Karl. (1997). *New paradigms for college teaching.* Edina, MN: Interaction Book Company. Although written with the college instructor in mind, this collection of thoughtful essays is valuable for anyone who teaches adults.

Charles, C. Leslie; & Clarke-Epstein, Chris. (1998). *The instant trainer: Quick tips on how to teach others what you know.* New York: McGraw-Hill. A delightful "Dear Abby" approach to learning about training, with two dedicated authors answering, in their own unique styles, commonly asked questions trainers (and would-be trainers) ask.

DePorter, Bobbi. (1992). *Quantum learning: Unleashing the genius in you.* New York: Dell Publishing. A reader-friendly, hands-on guide to learning and remembering.

Gibb, Barry. (2007). *The rough guide to the brain.* London, England: Rough Guides. A more medical approach to understanding the human brain.

Hale-Evans, Ron. (2006). *Mind-performance hacks.* Sebastopol, CA: O'Reilly Media. Written for the learner or anyone who wants to improve memory skills and critical thinking, the book contains dozens of tips for better brain performance.

Hannaford, Carla. (1995). *Smart moves: Why learning is not all in your head.* Arlington, VA: Great Ocean Publishers. A compelling argument for the need to include the body in learning and the link between kinesthetic intelligence and long-term memory.

Hunter, Madeline. (2003). *Enhancing teaching.* Englewood Cliffs, NJ: Prentice-Hall. Geared to the educator, this resource compiles a century of educational and related research into practical classroom application.

Maples, Tim. (1996). *Accelerated learning* (2nd ed.). Amherst, MA: HRD Press. An introduction to Accelerated Learning in a simplified, workbook-type format.

Millbower, Lenn. (2000). *Training with a beat.* Sterling, VA: Stylus Publishing. An easy read that offers brain-based reasons for including the power of music in every learning experience.

Pink, Daniel. (2006). *A whole new mind: Why right-brainers will rule the future* (2nd ed.). New York: Riverhead Books. A new and refreshing look on the whole right/left brain continuum, with some implications for the class and training room as well as the world at large.

Ratey, John. (2002). *A user's guide to the human brain.* New York: Random House. Very detailed and psychiatric in its approach, this resource is an intense read and probably more information than most trainers would have the time to learn or the interest to explore.

Robinson, Adam. (1993). *What smart students know.* New York: Three Rivers Press. For students of all ages, this is an excellent resource on how to study, organize and remember information, pass tests, and, oh yes, how to *think.*

Rose, Colin; & Nicholl, Malcolm. (1997). *Accelerated learning for the 21st century.* New York: Dell Publishing. Another detailed look at Accelerated Learning and how to orchestrate instruction for maximum learning and retention.

Silberman, Mel. (2005). *101 ways to make training active* (2nd ed.). San Francisco, CA: Pfeiffer. A practical and useful collection of active-learning techniques and a necessary staple for most trainers' bookshelves. The second edition contains an even bigger collection of strategies, tips, and case examples.

Slan, Joanna. (2001). *One-minute journaling.* St. Louis, MO: EFG Publishing, Inc. Although the focus of this workbook is "Scrapbook Storytelling," it also provides a variety of quick journaling ideas for teachers and trainers.

Slan, Joanna. (1998). *Using stories and humor—grab your audience!* Needham Heights, MA: Allyn and Bacon. A practical, down-to-earth guide for using stories as powerful speaking and training tools. Contains dozens of tips to help readers create their own original stories.

St. Germain, Cliff. (2000). *Study whiz: A guide to better grades.* Chicago, IL: Pivot Point International. A learner-focused resource for both children and adults who wish to be successful in attaining their learning goals. Also another resource for Graphic Organizers (the author calls them "MindFrames"). Call 800-886-4247 for ordering information.

Sugar, Steve. (1998). *Games that teach.* San Francisco, CA: Pfeiffer. A good resource for trainers who want to use competitive games as review activities.

Thompson, Carolyn. (2000). *Creating highly interactive training quickly & effectively.* Frankfort, IL: Training Systems, Inc. A practical, step-by-step approach to designing training that includes checklists for determining training needs and return on investment. Call 800-469-2560 for ordering information.

Wacker, Mary B.; & Silverman, Lori L. (2003). *Stories trainers tell: 55 ready-to-use stories to make training stick.* San Francisco, CA: Pfeiffer. Gives the reader useful tools for crafting memorable stories. Includes fifty-five ready-made stories that cover a variety of general training concepts and that readers have permission to use in their own training.

Westcott, Jean; & Hammond, Landau. (1997). *A picture's worth 1,000 words.* San Francisco, CA: Jossey-Bass/Pfeiffer. An easy, how-to resource that shows you how to add simple yet powerful graphics, images, cartoons, shapes, and doodles to written or printed information (charts, slides, handouts, note-taking tools, and the like).

Extra Resources

Websites

Note: These websites offer free information, downloadable tips, articles, and practical content for trainers and teachers. Some also offer free newsletters. All list products and services as well.

www.accelerated-learning-online.com
   Memletics Accelerated Learning System
   Sean Whitely, Founder and Creator
www.alcenter.com
   The Center for Accelerated Learning
   David Meier, Director

www.activetraining.com
   Mel Silberman, President
www.bobpikegroup.com
   Creative Training Techniques, International
   Bob Pike, President
www.Bowperson.com
   Bowperson Publishing & Training, Inc.
   Sharon Bowman, President
www.co-operation.org
   The Cooperative Learning Center
   David and Roger Johnson, Directors
www.jaycross.com
www.intenettime.com
   Jay Cross and the Internet Time Group
   Jay Cross, CEO
www.guilamuir.com
   Guila Muir and Associates
   Guila Muir, President
www.learnativity.com
   Learnativity Organization
www.mljackson.com
   Training Resources
   Marcia Jackson, President
www.nancymargulies.com
   Nancy Margulies, Artist and Creator
www.newhorizons.org
   News from the Neurosciences
www.offbeattraining.com
   Lenn Millbower, The Learnertainment® Trainer
www.openspaceworld.org
   Open Space Technology (official website)
www.thebrainstore.com
   The Brain Store
   Eric Jensen, President
www.theworldcafe.com

The World Cafe (official website)

www.trainingsys.com
Training Systems, Inc.
Carolyn Thompson, President

www.thiagi.com
The Thiagi Group
Sivalsailam Thiagarajan, President and Mad Scientist

Magazine and Newsletter (Subscription-Based)

Training Treasures
www.trainingtreasures.com
360-883-0610

Creative Training Techniques Newsletter
www.creativetrainingtech.com
800-383-9210

Catalogs

The Brain Store (800-325-4769). Products and services on teaching, learning, and brain research. Also includes some unusual brain-related items.

Creative Training Techniques (800-383-9210). A great assortment of training books and learning aids. Especially for the busy trainer who wants some shortcuts in preparation time.

The Humor Project (800-225-0330). Upbeat items and books to help trainers add fun to their presentations.

Jossey-Bass/Pfeiffer (800-274-4434). An extensive variety of books, tapes, and other useful training resources.

Kipp Brothers (800-428-1153). A huge assortment of wholesale toys for bulk purchasing.

Oriental Trading Company (800-228-2269). Unusual toy and craft items that can be bought in bulk.

The Trainer's Warehouse (800-299-3770). A fun and eclectic collection of products especially selected and developed to make training more hands-on and learner-centered.

A Word of Thanks

It is always difficult to write acknowledgments because, as with other creations, a book is the product of many people, without whom it would not have become a reality. While I studiously put pen to paper (or fingers to keyboard), dozens of others had a hand in the production and, more importantly, cheered me on in the middle of long bouts of writing.

With that said, my heartfelt thanks goes to:

- Marisa Kelley, Kathleen Dolan Davies, Janis Chan, and the wonderful Pfeiffer Company editing and production team, for their helpfulness, patience, kindness, and professionalism.

- Excellent peer reviewers—Lenn Millbower, Paul Plamondon, and Jennifer Bircher—for their insightful suggestions and enthusiastic comments.

- Jay Cross, author of *Informal Learning*, for his thoughtful foreword to the book.

- Juanita Brown, author of *The World Cafe*, for her time and invaluable guidance in revising the chapter on this innovative process.

- Mimi Banta, Amy Perry, and Marcia Jackson, for their excellent contributions.

- All the fine authors who gave their permission to be quoted extensively throughout the book.

- My family and friends—each and every one of them—for their understanding, support, encouragement, energy, and spirit.

What will you find on pfeiffer.com?

• The best in workplace performance solutions for training and HR professionals

• Downloadable training tools, exercises, and content

• Web-exclusive offers

• Training tips, articles, and news

• Seamless on-line ordering

• Author guidelines, information on becoming a Pfeiffer Affiliate, and much more

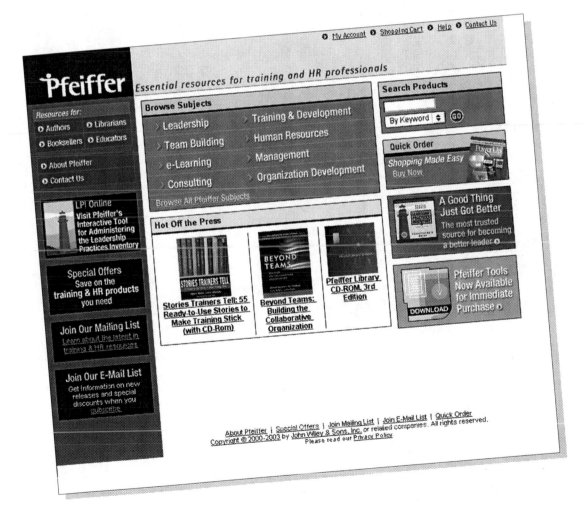

Discover more at www.pfeiffer.com

About the Author

Meet Sharon Bowman

- Professional speaker and corporate trainer
- Staff development consultant and instructor for school districts and colleges
- Author of eight popular training and motivation books
- President, Bowperson Publishing & Training, Inc.
- Director, The Lake Tahoe Trainers Group
- Professional Member, National Speakers Association (NSA)
- Member, American Society for Training and Development (ASTD)

When asked what Sharon does, she replies: "I teach teachers how to teach and trainers how to train." She is a veteran trainer who walks her talk and engages learners from the moment they walk into the room until the moment they leave. She uses a unique, high-energy, informal, hands-on approach to learning. Her classes and seminars are practical, useful, memorable, and fun. Over 70,000 of her first seven popular training and motivation books are now in print. In fact, her previous book *The Ten-Minute Trainer*, is one of Pfeiffer's best-sellers.

If you treat yourself to one of Sharon's training programs or conference sessions, you'll find yourself standing and moving more than sitting and listening. You'll also find yourself teaching others what *you* know and learning what *they* know. All the while, Sharon guides the entire learning process from the *BACK* of the room!

For more information about Sharon Bowman and her books and training services, log onto www.Bowperson.com. While there, you can browse and download over four dozen free articles about effective training and teaching. You can also email Sharon at SBowperson@gmail.com.